TWENTY CASES

The Last Frontier: Memoirs from a
Neurosurgical Career

Thomas Lansen, MD

Barringer Publishing, Naples, Florida
www.barringerpublishing.com

Design and layout by Linda S. Duider

ISBN 978-1-954396-10-4

Library of Congress Cataloging-in-Publication Data

Printed in U.S.A.

Twenty Cases
Thomas Lansen, MD

ACKNOWLEDGEMENTS

I want to thank two families: my own and my neurosurgical family—the dozens of colleagues, teachers, and students with whom I have had the privilege of associating over the past forty years.

I dedicate this book to my mentor and hero—Albert L. Rhoton, Jr., MD.

I want to thank Jeff Schlesinger and the team at Barringer for their promptness, professionalism, and general assistance. And I want to thank my editor, Emily Crawford-Margison, for her wise advice, talented corrections, and encouragement.

I hope you enjoy the bittersweet tales that follow, and if you're left wondering about this one or that, him or her . . . well, just make up an ending that suits you.

CONTENTS

INTRODUCTION

This is a story about medicine. More specifically, it's the story of a very particular branch of medicine. One that I consider the most remarkable, in that everyone who practices it must be both a scientist and a surgeon. I may be a bit biased when it comes to neurosurgery, but you must admit that most people agree it's not a very routine way to spend your life.

This story and its episodes are true to the best of my recollection. The chronology may be a tiny bit twisted, as age seems to affect the memory of time most of all. And there are two conditions that you must be kind enough to keep in mind. First, I have changed some people's names, including all of the patients and some of the doctors to protect their privacy. I've named most of my colleagues truthfully because they are remarkable people who deserve a lot of praise. To paraphrase Will Rogers, in all honesty, I have never met a truly bad person. And I don't think there's anyone in my life that I would consider an enemy. Second, I will only briefly allude to the personal—that is, the non-professional—side of my life. Like most people, I've had my share of pleasures, victories, sins, disappointments, heartbreaks, and intrigues. I don't want to overemphasize my strengths or faults, and I don't want to place blame on any of the fine people with whom I've had the privilege of sharing my life.

1

Thomas Lansen, MD

CHAPTER ONE

Brain Surgery
Isn't Brain Surgery

Many years ago, I was doing the final prep on a patient, anesthetized and positioned for surgery. I had placed the patient in a Mayfield head holder—a large metal clamp with three very sharp pins that penetrate the scalp and push firmly against the skull to make sure that there is absolutely no movement of the head during surgery. You can appreciate that movement could be a big problem during a delicate operation on the brain. A small wheel on the device was turned clockwise to increase the pressure, the clamp holding the patient's skull securely. When the skull was gripped, completely immobile, in exactly the position required and attached by a lever to the base of the operating table, I shaved the patient's scalp with a straight-edged razor like an old-fashioned barber's—still the most efficient way to shave the scalp. This was followed by a vigorous scrub with a plastic brush soaked in betadine soap for about ten minutes, a quick toweling of the scalp, and then another wipe with an antiseptic solution. The patient had also received a dose of intravenous antibiotics. In short, we had done everything we could to prevent a surgical infection.

My assistant and I then went to the scrub sink where we spent ten minutes cleansing our hands and arms. We returned to be gowned and gloved by the young scrub nurse, who seemed visibly nervous. I watched him from the corner of my eye as I surrounded the pertinent area of the scalp with surgical towels and then drapes. Finally, a large, absorbent paper drape with a central sheet of adhesive plastic was applied to what would become the surgical wound. The end of this drape was passed over a large, metal table that stood above the patient and came up to his shoulders. Suction tubing, sterile electrical lines, and special surgical equipment were passed from the surgical "field" over the draped table to the patient's feet and off to myriad outlets, receptacles, and monitors. The anesthesiologist's station was separated from us by a sterile barrier. The circulating nurses had completed their inventories and pre-operative checklists.

The patient was a sixty-something business executive who had suddenly passed out at work and hadn't reawakened. He was rushed to the emergency room, where an emergency CT scan showed a large blood clot in the temporal lobe of the right side of his brain. A breathing tube had been introduced, and he was given a dose of steroids and a diuretic—a medication to empty fluid from his body to try to reduce the swelling in his brain as much as possible. He was then rushed to the operating room.

I had been through this hundreds of times before. For me, doing this operation was nearly as mundane as driving to the office, though a lot more interesting. My assistant had as much experience as I did, and the circulating nurse was also a veteran. But Ed Merritt, the young scrub nurse, wasn't. In fact, the head nurse in the room was tutoring him through his first brain case, his first craniotomy. Ed would later go on to run his own OR and become a successful hospital administrator. But he was a long way from those days just now.

Ed had meticulously arranged all of the instruments that I would need. Everything was organized just as I wanted it. I glanced at Barb Kolba, our neurosurgical operating room leader, and she nodded slightly at the smile behind my mask. She was proud of the effort she had put in to help Ed be ready for this. I looked up at Ed; a tall young man standing at the ready beside the overhead table. He was alert and attentive. His hands were steady, but there was a trace of moisture on his forehead.

"Okay, Ed?" I said, hoping to impart some reassurance in my voice.

"Not really, sir . . . I've never scrubbed on a craniotomy before. I'm going to ask you to be patient with me. But let me know if you think I'm headed in the wrong direction so that Barb can take over." I thought to myself that he was making more of the situation than it deserved.

More than it deserved? This was brain surgery, the inner sanctum, the ultimate in complexity, danger and technical skill. If we lost the patient because of a preventable error, it might be due to the use of the wrong instrument at the wrong time or because the right instrument had been handed too slowly or mis-handed. It is up to the scrub nurse to place the instruments in the surgeon's hand in just the right way. The surgeon has to keep his or her eyes on the operative field, the wound, not look away to take the instrument from the nurse or technician. In other words, a catastrophe could be Ed's fault.

I had been taught as a young resident, some twenty years earlier, that the secret of doing this work right is to do it exactly the same way every single time. Each step carefully following the other, planned, and coordinated. Everything must proceed without hurry, without emotion . . . no matter what happens. This protocol gives us foreknowledge and confidence. Nothing is omitted from the plan.

You see, there isn't a lot of difference between the appearance, size, and setup among skulls and brains. One brain is pretty much like another, and the structures in the brain are in the same place and orientation in each skull, give or take a few millimeters. For this reason, approaching each brain disorder the same way each time makes sense and helps reduce errors.

How could I express this confidence to Ed? How could I explain to him that when you do one thing a thousand times, it enters your comfort zone. Whether it's making a great pizza, pitching a baseball a hundred miles an hour, flying an airliner or removing a brain tumor. It's an understandable, repeatable exercise.

My mind went to the clichés about the complicated exercises of life—rocket science, brain surgery, etc. Ed brought me out of my reverie as I adjusted the last few elements of the surgical field to the perfection that my mind's eye sought.

"Whew! I can't believe I'm about to assist in brain surgery!"

I looked at Ed with a smile in my eyes. "Ed, brain surgery isn't brain surgery."

The surgery went well, and Ed never forgot that phrase. Years later, when he helped run a large hospital, we met at a social function.

"You know, Tom, I still use that story to break the ice whenever I try to help a newbie get over the jitters." We laughed as a companion listened without comprehension. You had to be there.

In his widely acclaimed book, *Outliers*, Malcolm Gladwell made the important point that in order to master a skill, any skill, you've basically got to put in ten thousand hours practicing. My mentor, the great neurosurgeon Albert L. Rhoton, Jr., subscribed to this principle and added his own modification: "Always approach each procedure the same way every single time. Break the operation up into segments and perform each segment sequentially, following your plan."

This accomplishes two things. In an operation requiring perhaps a thousand steps, sequencing prevents missing something important. It also keeps you from "getting lost" following the wrong anatomical landmarks or missing the essential structures that you need to find, which costs time and effort and increases the possibility of error. It seems simplistic; basically, keep your eyes on the ball. But when distractions occur—the spurt of an artery cut before it is completely cauterized or a sudden gush of spinal fluid when drilling through the cranial bone—they can pull your mind away from the plan. That is, unless you do it the same way every single time. That also doesn't seem too complicated until you realize that there are dozens of different approaches to the various parts of the brain, as well as hundreds of possible disease processes that can occur in any given part, from aneurysms to brain tumors to congenital malformations.

CHAPTER TWO

Car Accident

In the very beginning of my career, I had not set my sights on becoming a neurosurgeon. In fact, in college I wanted to be a medieval historian. I loved and still love the study of the past. I find the lives and actions of people who lived a thousand years ago so similar to our own, and I relish the continuity of life and the endless relationships among people and cultures. Unfortunately, making a living as an historian isn't exactly a cinch. Yes, you can get an advanced degree and teach, but I never liked teaching. That meant my options were pretty limited.

The core curriculum at Marquette University required taking a science course or two. I disliked chemistry in high school, so I figured I'd take an introductory course to see why I hadn't liked it. I loved it. I took several more science courses and liked them, too. So, I decided to start thinking about a career in medicine. I was more than a little interested in physiological psychology—how the brain and its cells and chemistry make us behave the way we do. I entered medical school with the goal of becoming a biological psychiatrist. This field, combining biochemistry, neuroanatomy, and psychology, was new and exciting.

Medical school was not what I expected. I had always been a good student, and studying and testing came easily to me. So, I was quite surprised, though I shouldn't have been, to learn that my 107 classmates (100 men and 7 women) had all been at the top of their class, and that I had just entered the world of cutthroat competition. My first morning in medical school started with a biochemistry lecture. The pace was fast, the information confusing. At the end of the hour, the professor gave a short list of journal references that would flesh out the material given in the lecture. At about eleven that morning, I sauntered over to the medical school's library. This was long before the easy availability of most scientific information on the internet. Opening the volume of the first reference cited, I found that the article had been ripped out—stolen. With a bit of trepidation, I approached the second article. Also stolen. All six of the references had been stolen. Clearly, one or a group of my new colleagues not only wanted the convenience of having the articles; they wanted a competitive advantage by denying the rest of us. Well, that was pretty much the story of my medical school education. Of course, most of the class wasn't like this, and there were many good, dedicated young men and women there. But it *was* very competitive. Maybe it was the cultural difference between the type A students from New York and New Jersey who came west for medical school and us more laid-back Midwesterners. Maybe not. Whatever the case, it was an atmosphere where I learned to keep my head in the game.

In the first two years of medical school, the pre-clinical years, I found that I really liked anatomy, particularly (and predictably) neuroanatomy. I also enjoyed microbiology. I found physiology and pharmacology tedious, and I despised biochemistry. But that was okay. After all, how much biochemistry would I use as a psychiatrist? But I was amused at finding myself absolutely loving gross anatomy, with its hours of memorizing the body's parts: the muscles, the organs (lungs, liver, kidneys), the brain and its nerves, the bones and joints. The truth was, I enjoyed anatomy much more shamelessly than any budding psychiatrist should. As a matter of fact, my "dissection partner" (a triple type A who would go on to become a heart surgeon) and I requested a second cadaver after we had exhausted every piece of information from the first. Our cadavers were treated with dignity, and the anatomy laboratory was a silent, almost church-like place, even when filled with medical students.

During my first year of medical school, I also found a lifelong friend in Al Krug. Al, a very bright graduate of the University of Wisconsin, had grown up in the Milwaukee area. He had a gentle, self-effacing sense of humor but an intellectual intensity that was admirable. Al would go on to become an esteemed Orthopedic surgeon and businessman in Wisconsin.

Then came the third and fourth years, the clinical years. Now almost everything was interesting. We learned to examine patients, record our findings, and present them to our teachers in an organized way, coming to conclusions about diagnosis and therapy. I liked obstetrics and gynecology, neurology, and pediatrics. I found the medical specialties, with the exception of endocrinology, boring. I couldn't get excited about heart sounds or the cascade of blood coagulation. And I was chagrined to find that my psychiatry tutorials were more BS sessions than an exposition of the diagnosis and treatment of brain disease. But more disconcerting was my enjoyment of every surgical rotation, from urology to otolaryngology. And then I met Dave Hemmy.

David Hemmy was one of the most interesting and intelligent people I had ever encountered. He varied between absolute calm and a hair-trigger temper. I was a fourth-year medical student and had committed to a residency in psychiatry at New York University after medical school to pursue my interest in research in the biological basis of behavior. I decided to use some of my elective time in neurosurgery, as it seemed like a logical segue, and it built on my interest in neuroanatomy.

Following David around was like watching a tornado—fascinating and a little scary. Dr. Hemmy had been a MASH surgeon in Vietnam. Although he hadn't completed his residency before going to war, he was the closest thing they had to a neurosurgeon in the field, and so he had more neurosurgical experience by the time he returned to the States to finish his residency than most neurosurgeons did in their first five or six years in practice. He was quiet, deep, and now he was the chief neurosurgical resident at the Medical College of Wisconsin, and I was lucky enough to land on his service.

I quickly became more than a medical student who followed the chief around. I became a groupie. Making rounds, doing the "scut" work (starting IVs, changing dressings, gathering lab and x-ray information), stealing into surgery to watch the action, and, occasionally, when the surgeons were shorthanded, scrubbing in. It was magic—serene and beguiling one minute, frantic and life-threatening the next. Unlike general surgery or orthopedics, with lots of blood and noise, neurosurgery was quiet, almost religiously so; the strong overhead lights concentrated on the small field of interest—the brain, pulsing steadily, a beautiful pink-white in hue, with tiny arteries on its surface spreading like coral fronds. It was mesmerizing. I was clearly witnessing the center of human life. I could almost see the brain working, functioning, thinking.

At night, I would follow Dave to the ER to consult on trauma cases. His experience made him calm and decisive there. He walked quickly, and, as he entered the trauma room, there were always the quiet voices of the staff: "Neurosurgery," "Neurosurgery's here." Dave wouldn't say much, he'd just walk over to the x-ray panel and start to study the films; a skull x-ray, a cervical spine. As he pondered, another resident, usually a general surgeon or an ER doc, would start presenting the case. "Forty-two-year-old guy, going at a pretty good clip on the expressway, ETOH positive (read drunk), flipped the car, unconscious at the scene, neck immobilized. BP 80/60. Belly distended, probable ruptured spleen. Big temporal scalp laceration, oozing steadily."

I looked at the man. He was obese, most of his clothes removed by the ER staff, caked blood on his arms, legs, and chest. His hair matted around the jagged cut on his left temple, he reeked of blood and alcohol. A nurse was squeezing rhythmically on a large, green, rubber bag connected to the breathing tube inserted into his trachea and taped to his cheeks and chin. A resident was trying to start an IV in a small vein on the man's right arm. Dave was suddenly multi-tasking. "Don't bother with that," he gestured at the resident. "If you're right about the spleen, you'll need better access. Start a central line." He turned to another nurse, who was drawing medication into a syringe to raise the patient's faltering blood pressure. "Kathy, call the OR. Tell them we're bringing this guy . . . what's his name? Murray, to the OR STAT. Type and cross six units of whole blood, get the family gathered outside." Turning to the junior resident who clearly was over his head about the central line, Dave rolled up his shirt sleeves, tossed his loosened tie over his shoulder, and put on a pair of sterile gloves. Gently nudging the resident out of the way, he sponged some betadine onto the patient's chest over an area just below his right clavicle. He then chose a spot three finger breadths to the right of the sternum and stuck a large-gauge needle into the chest at a very low angle, just below the clavicle and in the general direction of the heart. About a third of the way in, the needle hit pay dirt, or, in this case, the subclavian vein, one of the large veins leading directly to the heart. Dark blue blood jetted from the hub of the needle. Passing a catheter into the vein, he withdrew the needle over it then attached a device to the catheter tip, which a nurse quickly attached to a large bag of fluid. The fluid challenge quickly elevated the man's blood pressure into a less dangerous range. Dave sewed the catheter to the man's skin, and another nurse stepped in to place a dressing.

Dave stood back and assessed the patient. He called the man's name—no response. This was partly understandable due to the sedation he'd been given to allow the team to place the endotracheal tube down his throat. Dave then pinched the skin of the patient's chest. The man sharply drew his left arm toward his chest and kicked his left leg into the air. His right side barely moved. Taking out a pocket flashlight, Hemmy shone it into each eye. The right pupil reacted quickly, the left was wide and sluggish. He then stroked the bottom of the man's right foot. "Babinski," he stated, noting the abnormal elevation of the great toe, suggestive of emerging paralysis. To no one in particular, Dave instructed, "Give him fifty grams of mannitol." The diuretic would empty fluid from the man's body, perhaps reducing the swelling in his brain enough to buy Hemmy a little time. He turned to the chief resident of general surgery, who had just arrived. "Going to get that spleen out, Peter?" The resident nodded. "Good, I'll take the clot out at the same time." The rest of the staff looked at each other. Had they missed something? Indeed, they had.

Now the chief turned to me. "Put it together for me, Tom." I thought as quickly as I could. Dave couldn't waste a lot of his patient's time teaching me, but he knew that I was his responsibility as well. I knew the dilated pupil on the left and the right-sided weakness and Babinski sign indicated a problem on the left side of the brain. Adding this to the location of the laceration, I blurted, "Left-sided hematoma," (blood clot on the brain).

"Good. What kind?" I was clueless. There were three possibilities: an intracerebral hemorrhage, within the brain itself; a subdural hematoma, between the brain and the dura, the membrane covering it; and an epidural hematoma, a more rapidly accumulating clot outside the dura, usually related to a torn artery. Dave motioned me toward the x-ray view box. He pointed at the lateral view of the patient's skull, at the unmistakable sign my neophyte's eye had missed. Superimposed over the dark grey shadow of the patient's skull was a white circle, about the size of a half dollar. Through the center of the circle was a dark jagged line. "Depressed skull fracture, epidural hematoma," Dave said quietly. The patient's laceration was clearly the result of his head striking a sharp object in the car. That blow had pushed an oval portion of his skull inward, buckling into a sharp, serrated central fracture. The fracture had torn a major artery in the patient's dura, and the

14

rapidly enlarging clot was now pushing the left side of his brain into the brainstem, the center for all vital signs. He would be dead in minutes without urgent action. I turned to Dave, but he was already pulling the corner of the stretcher out the door. "Let's roll," he said, trailing a team of doctors and nurses in his wake. Half-jogging down the hall towards the OR elevator, I caught up with the relentless chief resident. "I can't believe I missed that fracture."

"The cranial fracture or the cervical one?"

I was mortified. Dave said, "If you look closely at the C-spine x-ray, you'll see a slight compression of the C5 vertebra." I looked at the patient's neck and now noticed that Dave had replaced the soft cervical collar with a firmer, latex one. I shook my head at the depth of my own ignorance. Dave turned to me and smiled. "It'll come."

I felt somehow reassured that I could learn this complex world of knowledge. Medical school to this point had been tedious for me. But now, I could see the science and the art coming together, working to save a man's life.

Mr. Murray's family was gathered at the entrance to the operating suite. Hemmy was gentle but candid, and not reassuring. "I'm sorry, but Mr. Murray has some very serious injuries, the most life-threatening of which is a blood clot pressing on his brain. I need to operate to save his life, but I can't promise that he will live or recover. Do you understand?" The patient's wife nodded through her sobs. Dave squeezed her hand for a moment. "I'll do my best." Dave put a call in to the attending neurosurgeon on call, advising that there wasn't time to wait for him to come in. He understood, and permission to go ahead was given. The attending would get there as soon as he could.

Mr. Murray was quickly lifted onto the operating table, and, as the general surgeons prepared his belly, Dave gently elevated the left shoulder on a pillow, which had the effect of turning the head to the right without rotating the injured neck. He positioned the head on a doughnut-shaped pillow and splashed some betadine antiseptic on the laceration. There wasn't time for a full prep, but antibiotics were already on board via the IV. We quickly scrubbed and gowned, then covered the area around the wound with sterile towels and drapes. Dave took a scalpel and deftly extended both ends of the laceration, then opened a large Weitleiner retractor in the wound, the sharp vertical teeth on each limb of the scissor-like retractor pulling the edges of the wound apart. He then touched a cautery wand, the Bovie, to small bleeding points along the wound. Using the Bovie to cut the thick temporal muscle over the skull, he scraped back the edges of the muscle, including its cut margins in the retractor. Now, I could see the fracture clearly—the oval shape, the central v-shaped depression, with the long, jagged line through its center, pulsating blood that oozed ominously from beneath the fractured bone. I held a plastic suction tube with a metal attachment at the working end to keep the wound clean of blood. Dave took a large rotating manual drill, applied it to an area of skull just outside the depression, and turned it rapidly, creating a hole through the skull. Then, using a large rongeur, a biting device with a cup-like mouth, he bit across the isthmus between the burr hole and the fracture, quickly loosening the depression until he could slide a probe beneath the oval fracture and elevate it. Levering the fractured bone, he removed the entire piece as a single unit. Beneath it lay a large purple, gelatinous blood clot. Like an alien beast, it first oozed then shot out of the wound, spilling from the field onto the adjacent drapes. The compressed brain beneath was literally pushing the clot out. The chief took the suction from my hand and gently removed the remaining clot, the movements of his hand like an artist gently painting a canvas. Suddenly, an artery spurted bright red blood about a foot above the wound. As I pulled my head back, Dave murmured, "there she is." It was the torn artery that had caused the clot. With his left hand suctioning the area over the tear, Dave placed the bipolar cautery (a long, delicate forceps that allows an electric current to flow only between its tips) over the torn vessel. He stepped on a pedal that sent current to the bipolar, and, within seconds, the arterial fountain stopped, replaced by a small patch of blackened dura. He then closed the wound, leaving the fractured portion out so that the injured brain beneath could have room to swell post-operatively without being compressed against the bony surface of the skull. Of course, this would mean that Mr. Murray, if he survived, would have to undergo another operation in a month or two to replace the piece of bone we had removed. But he was alive.

After swathing the patient's head in a soft, winding, turban bandage, we left the general surgeons to finish removing Mr. Murray's spleen. It was now 2 a.m., and I sat with Dave in the cafeteria talking about the next morning's plans for the sixteen patients on the neurosurgery service over coffee and a cigarette. I glanced at my watch and realized that I was so wired by the evening's activity that I would never be able to sleep. From the corner of my eye, I saw a group of nurses and residents at another table. Dave's eyes followed mine to the other table. "Nice job, Dave," one of the residents shouted. Mr. Murray was in the recovery room moving all of his limbs and beginning to open his eyes. I basked in the reflected glory of the remarkable Dr. Hemmy, not realizing that my personal addiction to neurosurgery had begun.

However, I had been drawn to medicine initially because of my fascination with physiological psychology, and I decided to stick with this goal. I had applied to New York University-Bellevue's Psychiatry residency program because it had a cutting-edge biological psychiatry program. I planned to combine clinical psychiatry with biopsychological research. I was off to New York to study the workings of the mind.

CHAPTER THREE

Bellevue

It was a steamy, New York, July day when I first walked up the stone staircase of the "Old Bellevue." Founded in 1736 (George Washington was four years old) as an almshouse and penitentiary, Bellevue gradually evolved into New York's, and one of the nation's, first great public hospitals. By the mid-1800s, the building was devoted exclusively to healthcare. Its "firsts" are legendary—the first ambulance service, residency teaching program, nursing school, and the "Iron Lung." It had been home at one time or another to some of the giants of American medicine: Edward Dalton, New York's Sanitary Commissioner and Chief Medical Officer of the Army of the Potomac during the Civil War; William Halsted, the father of American surgery; Andre Cournand, Nobel Prize winner and founder of the world's first cardiopulmonary unit. New York University's medical school began teaching at Bellevue in 1847. By the time of my arrival, the elegant building, designed by the famous architectural firm McKim, Mead, and White (the same firm that designed Pennsylvania Station, Columbia University, and Washington's Natural History Museum between 1908 and 1939), had declined to institutional drab. By 1984, it would stop treating patients and become a homeless shelter. But the building, which would be supplanted by the "New Bellevue," a glass and brick tower on the East River two blocks south and east of the old building, held many secrets. Its inmates had included Norman Mailer, Charles Mingus, Charlie Parker, and George Corso. Its subterranean crypts were rumored to hold ancient equipment, stretchers, and more. The walls of the entrance atrium were now an antiseptic, pale green, and it was stripped of all furnishings, including most of the beautiful WPA (Franklin Roosevelt's Work Projects Administration, which provided work for laborers and artists during the Great Depression) murals and sculpture. A food stand had been built into the front wall, small but efficient. For the next several months, I would order the same lunch nearly every day: turkey on a roll, mayo and pepper, with a "regular'" coffee— New York for coffee with plenty of milk and sugar.

I made my way to the office of the director of the psychiatry residency program. A dour, humorless man, the director seemed to have seen all of the troubles of the world and bore their scars. He was gentle and soft-spoken, his voice just audible. He welcomed me to the New York University Psychiatry program. I was to commence my duties as a first-year resident (what used to be called an intern) on the adult inpatient service at Bellevue. I glanced around his office. It was a jumble. Books of all kinds spilling from bookcases onto a large desk, papers on the books cascading in all directions. There was the mandatory psychiatric fixture, an oriental rug in the center of the office (a dynastic reference to Sigmund Freud's Vienna office); a leather couch covered with journal articles; piles of psychiatric journals on the floor; and the suggestion of a multi-paned window, painted over and now almost covered by a mound of books.

I tried to listen. I was to meet with the chief resident daily to discuss my patients. I was to read a chapter of the large standard psychiatry text each week for discussion with the other residents and an assigned attending psychiatrist at Wednesday conference.

The next morning, I reported to 3 West, the enormous locked ward that housed Bellevue's inpatient male population. I was admitted by an attendant who led me to the nurses' station. An attractive, raven-haired nurse was efficiently handing out medications in paper cups to a line of disheveled and confused men of various ages, races, and sizes. Each man dutifully swallowed his pills, washed down with a slug of orange juice. Despite their physical differences, there was a kind of uniformity to their glazed stares—the slightly open mouths, the shuffling feet. The nurse's eyes barely met mine, but I could see that she was sizing me up. The new blood. He'll soon find out what this is all about. "Dirk's not here yet." Dirk Berger was the chief resident. He was in charge of everything and everyone. Everyone called Dr. Berger by his first name, but her statement implied a special relationship—I'm in, you're not. Linda Clark handed me a key to the ward. Just what you'd imagine: a large, clunky, metal turnkey.

I sat down in one of the metal office chairs in the glass-walled station and opened a chart, beginning to synthesize the way information was recorded on each patient: vital signs, nurses' notes, resident progress notes, medication records, orders. This also served to avoid small talk with Miss Clark—I somehow felt that anything I said to her would be misinterpreted.

Paul Gonzalez introduced himself. He was also a first-year resident and had started a day or two early. He had an easy, friendly manner. A native New Yorker, he had grown up in Spanish Harlem, attended the City College of New York and Mt. Sinai Medical School. He was clearly very bright and self-confident. The gothic nature of my surroundings seemed to fade a bit.

"Hi Dirk." Paul was smiling at the chief, who greeted both Gonzalez and Linda with a warm smile. He turned to me. "Hi, Dirk Berger. You must be Tom Lansen." He wasn't what I had expected. Young and handsome, with thick, wavy, blond hair and bright blue eyes, he wore jeans and a white shirt, sleeves rolled up, tie loosened. I returned his firm handshake. "You've met Linda and Paul, I see. Good. Let's make chart rounds." Dirk got down to business. The patients' problems were summarized, current medications reviewed, changes made, and prognoses discussed. I was impressed with Linda's knowledge of the patients, and with one other thing. In this big, heartless, caged snake pit, this young woman talked about each patient as if he were her brother or father. It was clear that she cared deeply about these patients. She looked at me, and I stared down at a chart, hoping my face hadn't reddened a bit. Dirk was out of his chair and walking through the ward, the three of us trailing. Some of the patients didn't say a word, just rocking silently in a world of their own; others were hostile, paranoid at any human approach; still others were anxious to talk, needing Dirk's interaction, hoping that some magic word from him would erase the reality, quiet the dreams and the voices, or open the locked door.

Dirk Berger was a strong leader and was already attracting local press in New York. He was personally offended by the lack of social services in the city. He argued ferociously that we were stabilizing really sick patients, then were being forced to release them to their own devices as soon as their medications quieted them. Outside, they dealt with violence and loneliness. Dirk had begun a halfway house, raising money to allow patients to occupy a large, neglected hotel where he lived along with volunteers who could monitor the progress or regression of these sad souls who had found their way to Gotham, whose families could no longer deal with the breakdowns, whose resources were exhausted and whose hope was extinguished.

I quickly settled into the routine of Bellevue's locked ward. I learned the unwritten rules: not too close to the patients, stay non-threatening, no touching, and no drastic medication changes without discussion with the chief. Morning chart rounds, therapeutic sessions with each of my six patients (I didn't know much, but I was clearly better than nothing and I had experienced people with whom to discuss the issues), lunch, discussions about my patients with Dirk, Linda, and the other nurses and residents, then a one-mile walk to Grand Central for the commute home to my Scarsdale apartment in the Westchester suburbs.

Danny Sullivan was from Queens. In his early twenties, he was no stranger to Bellevue. A small, thin, young man, friendly and glib, Danny was a very disturbed, paranoid schizophrenic. During our first few sessions, he would divert each of my questions with a snide remark or a joke. I was amazed that he was so alert when I saw that he was taking 2,000 milligrams of Thorazine and a similarly whopping dose of Haldol, another major tranquilizer, every day. Fifty milligrams of Thorazine would have knocked me unconscious for two days. The only clues were a slight thickness of his speech, a bit of caking on his lips, and a stiff gait, with his arms held rigidly at his sides. After a week or two of our daily meetings, he began to confide in me. His delusion was convoluted, but the gist of it was religious—the Virgin Mary used to appear on the back of his bedroom window shade at night, awakening him. She gave him no initial message but ultimately revealed that he was to share a special sacrament. This, Danny finally revealed to me, confiding his most precious secret. I had been initiated into his world. He was to go to the neighbor's back yard and eat the feces of their dog. That's what got Danny hospitalized this time.

"Do you believe me? About the Blessed Virgin?"

"I believe that you believe it, Danny. That's what counts." I knew I had lost him. Dirk said he was maxed out on meds; the next step would be ECT (electro-convulsive therapy). The attending psychiatrist agreed. I dreaded this for Danny, somehow hoping that, in the nick of time, I would break through his delusion and get him back into contact with reality.

The next week, we were all brought to instant attention when Danny jumped onto the shoulders of a large, silent, black man, riding him around and screaming, "It's him! It's Satan! Can't you see him?" The attendants had trouble dislodging Danny from his victim. Fortunately for Danny, his victim was as catatonic as a zombie and barely noticed the entire episode. Danny was given an extra injection, sucking all emotions out of him. That was the last time I saw him. He was transferred to the less acutely therapeutic Wingdale Sanitarium in upstate New York. That sight disturbs me to this day. On a practical level, I thought to myself, *Well, Toto, we're not in Wisconsin anymore.*

The days were getting darker and colder, and the commute was taking on a familiar, enjoyable routine; but the job wasn't. I liked the crowded train to Scarsdale, its occupants like sardines in a tin. Sometimes it would be SRO, holding onto one of the steel posts near the sliding doorway of the car. The commuters were all sizes and shapes, mostly white and well-dressed. In the morning, they were all attentive and serious, reading the *Times* or *The Wall Street Journal*, getting the jump on the rest of the pack, nearly sprinting out of the train as it eased and sighed and steamed into the Grand Central terminal. At night, they slumped into the seats, falling asleep on the cradle ride home or nursing a beer grabbed from the train-side vendors. I noticed the smells. I had rarely been cramped into a closed space with so many people. So, it surprised me that, aside from the gritty, steamy smell of the terminal's tunnels and a bit of indefinable "peopleness," the train cars smelled good. All sorts of perfumes and aftershaves, soaps, dry-cleaned clothes, newspaper print, and briefcase leather. The train was full of strivers, ". . . with the slam, bang, tang reminiscent of gin and vermouth," in the Frank Loesser verse for "I Believe in You." I began to recognize some of the same faces, an occasional nod, and a rarer smile.

The walk to and from NYU Medical Center, the larger context of Bellevue, was also interesting. The seasonal changes in the small, hardy trees along the avenues and streets; the rush of warm steam from the subways through the sidewalk gratings; the quick stops at familiar delis for cigarettes, coffee, gum, the *Times*; the rows of red brick walk-ups topping Chinese take-outs, delis, dry cleaners; the scurrying businessmen; the hustling Latin laborers; the homeless. But while I was getting used to New York, beginning to like the sights and sounds and smells of Gotham, I was surprised to find that, for me, psychiatry was boring and unscientific.

After three months on the ward at Bellevue, I began my rotation at New York University Hospital. The contrast was fairly striking. The Psychiatric Unit at University Hospital was attractive, immaculate, and not noticeably different from the medical and surgical floors of the hospital. The patients were generally upscale, admitted by their private psychiatrists. They suffered from depression, eating disorders, anxiety. I was sure that my change in rotation to University Hospital would turn the tide, catch my interest, and energize me. I was wrong. Most of the residents were excited about the correlations between the behaviors their patients were showing and the reading they were doing. At the resident conferences, they were beginning to demonstrate their understanding of the mental disease processes. But I wasn't getting it. It all just seemed to lack scientific validation to me. At the end of the day, my explanation (or anyone else's) for a behavior was just as well proven as the authors of the textbooks. It was disappointing.

CHAPTER FOUR

Agoraphobia

One morning, after I had finished my University Hospital rotation and was back at Bellevue, I watched as a middle-aged man walked down the hall of 3 East. He would not stand up straight but would lean against the wall, as if he would fall if he pushed away from it. I discussed the symptom with my team. Nothing else neurologically abnormal about him? Headaches? One of the other residents explained that he was crippled by agoraphobia, a fear of crowds and public spaces, to the extent that he had finally simply stopped going to work, avoiding his friends and family. Symbolically, he was avoiding the center of life, marginalizing himself. The answer always seemed the same to me—major tranquilizers and psychotherapy. I piped up, "What if this is a balance problem? Why don't we order a CAT scan?" The new machine could show the neuroanatomy and its abnormalities that we had all studied as medical students. "I suppose. Why not?" The resident in charge of the patient consented. Three days later, the neurosurgeons were removing a tuberculous abscess from the man's cerebellum, the organ of coordination, the destruction of which had caused the man to stagger down the halls of Bellevue. He might still be agoraphobic, but at least he wouldn't die from a curable abscess pressing on his brainstem.

What had brought me to psychiatry in the first place was being back-benched by the lack of interest I had in the clinical work. I had chosen New York University to fulfill my interest in the biological basis of behavior, an interest that had started as an undergraduate fascination. I had planned to combine clinical psychiatry with biopsychological research at the renowned Millhauser Laboratory, hoping to attract the attention of Arnold Friedhoff, professor of psychiatry and director of the laboratory. His pioneering work on anti-psychotic medication based on the neurotransmitter dopamine was already on the therapeutic radar. Friedhoff was brilliant, straightforward, and encouraging, but he wanted me to demonstrate my interest by developing a plan for the integration of my training into a research career. Of course, he was absolutely on target, but somehow this wasn't going at all as I had planned. In addition, I was experiencing an intellectual and emotional itch. I remembered with relish the joy of my surgical experience in medical school, particularly neurosurgery. I dismissed this as a typical manifestation of "the grass is always greener" disease and dug in to try to master conventional psychiatry as a steppingstone to a career in biological psychiatry.

The city was cold now, the winter wind tearing through the concrete canyons, each storefront door beckoning with light and warmth. The on-call room for the psychiatry residents at the Old Bellevue was spare—a bed, chair, bathroom, a bare bulb hanging over the bed, and a hissing green radiator underneath the single, towering window opposite the door. It was eleven p.m., and I was beat. The ER had been busy, and I had consulted on six really ill patients. I threw my white coat on the chair, pulled off my shirt and pants, switched off the light bulb, and lay down under the sheet. I was asleep in about ten seconds. What seemed like a moment later, I was awakened by a kind of whooshing sound over my head. In the purple darkness, a dull backlight shining through the window, I thought I saw something whipping around the still warm light bulb. It was too fast to be a bird, too big for a fly, it must be a . . . a *bat*!

I pulled the sheet over my head and dove under the pillow. Jesus Christ, a bat! I couldn't lie here all night with a bat circling six inches above my head. Sooner or later it would land, and I knew where it would land because my mother told me—in my *hair*. Gripped by fear, I leapt from the bed toward the light switch. I flipped it on. Nothing. Not a sound. No more sounds of paper-crumpling wing motions. Nothing. I picked up the bedside phone and dialed the operator, all the while glancing around the room, but still as a deer in headlights. After thirty or so rings, the operator answered. No, she didn't think housekeeping would be interested in getting a bat out of the on-call room. She connected me to the local precinct.

"Sgt. Monahan."

"Yes, this is Doctor Lansen, the psychiatry resident on call at Bellevue. There is a bat in my room, and I wonder if someone could come and dispose of it."

"So this is the shrink at Bellevue, and you have a bat . . . where? In your belfry? Who the hell is this? Is that you, Devlin?"

"No, honestly . . ."

"Look, wise guy, even if you're for real, the NYPD doesn't make house calls or bat calls to Bellevue. Call ASPCA."

I hung up and looked around for the bat. I was beginning to resent the fact that it wasn't whizzing around; it was turning into a non-threatening menace. The Bellevue operator helped me contact ASPCA. Yes, they did have a pest disposal unit and they would come over, although the fact that it was the middle of the night did not endear me to them.

The two men entered the on-call room in what looked like HAZMAT uniforms, one carrying a trap about the size of a shoebox. "Where's the bat?"

"Well, it disappeared as soon as I switched on the light. I actually more heard it than saw it." The men looked at each other meaningfully. "You guys must have to work long hours," one said. Where was the little son of a bitch? Was he playing a little Bellevue game? Had other residents fallen for this? I would be the laughingstock of the hospital. Or worse, what if it was a hallucination? I could wind up on the inside without the key.

The men searched the small room pretty thoroughly, and one of them was sidling toward the door. The other ran a small whiskbroom underneath the radiator. "Whoa, here's our little guy." The bat was curled up, about the size of a golf ball, as the broom propelled him from his hiding place. A gloved hand grabbed him and popped him into the trap, paper wings flapping. The men began to leave, one with the box tucked under his arm. I was effusive with gratitude on many levels. "Thanks so much, guys! Can I give you anything . . . ?"

"Nah, don't worry about it, doc. Get some sleep." I did not close a lid until dawn.

Spring was beginning to show small leaf buds on the little trees along my daily trek. But it was still cold enough to make spending the night in a cardboard box under an overpass unappealing. It was the pre-Giuliani era, the seventies, and the city was continuing its descent into a hell of civil unrest and decrepitude. The streets were starting to fill with the homeless. The homeless emotionally and mentally ill, the homeless unemployed, the homeless orphans of smaller cities where they would stand out, be noticed, be persecuted. New York was their haven, their anonymous refuge and personal hell.

It was about one in the morning, and I was tired from a busy night on call. The bizarre underbelly of Manhattan was beginning to become routine for me. It was no longer exciting, not even interesting, just numbingly bureaucratic. "Ms. Dolan, bring in the next patient, please," I shouted to the nurse I knew was doing her paperwork in the hallway. The examining room was small and windowless, with a filing cabinet, a desk, chair, and examining table. A muscular, young, black man was escorted into the room. I was too tired to take the standard unwritten precaution of placing myself between the patient and the door. He sat down next to the desk. I sat with my legs under the desk and looked up. He seemed tired—no, weary, and somehow angry, or surly. He was scruffy and dirty.

"How are you feeling?"

"Bad."

I decided to cut to the chase. "Look, I know it's still pretty cold out. But we can't admit you like a shelter. We're full up, and we can only admit people who are homicidal or suicidal. Do you feel like killing yourself?"

"No."

He was not a conversationalist. "Do you feel like killing someone else?"

"Yes."

"Who?"

"You." He was out of the chair and behind me in a heartbeat, my legs stuck under the desk, and he was pummeling the living daylights out of my head and neck with his powerful fists. It didn't really hurt, and I knew that was a bad sign. I finally managed to push the chair against him, throwing him into the wall. I staggered into the hallway, where I saw the horrified look on Ms. Dolan's face. There were always armed cops in Bellevue's ER, and in a moment, two of New York's finest were engaged in a rather intense discussion with the patient behind the now closed door of the small cubicle. "It's not nice to beat up our doctors." I could hear a few dull thuds.

The next morning, I passed my assailant in the locked ward, 3 West. He barely made eye contact and showed no emotion. Maybe he really did beat me up just to get a warm bed to sleep in.

Aside from a few bumps and bruises, no real harm done. X-rays of my skull and cervical spine were normal. But the experience was just one more nail in the coffin of my career as a psychiatrist. How could I develop protocols for the care of my patients if I couldn't even be sure if they were ill? I found the field to be amoeboid, without a firm scientific basis. The papers that I read were invariably anecdotal, based on the subjective observations of the researchers. There were few, if any, prospective studies on medication treatments, or even large retrospective studies of the various treatments (psychotherapy, medication, electro-convulsive therapy) being applied. When therapies were rejected, such as psychosurgery, it was usually on the basis of moral, sociological, or even religious conviction rather than scientific evidence. I was becoming increasingly sure that this field was not for me. This decision did not alienate me from my fellow residents, and I remained friendly with Paul, Melanie Bacall Korn (she and I would often share our walk home discussing our patient care experiences until she veered uptown and I down to Grand Central) and one or two others. But their enthusiasm for the field and my ennui kept us apart. By mid-year, I had begun to look around for a broad-based, surgical program that would expose me to different surgical specialties.

Lenox Hill Hospital in New York City seemed to fit the bill— an excellent hospital with a Columbia University affiliation. It was home to many of the most prominent private surgeons in the city, and it was a kind of anti-Bellevue, upscale and private, located on Park Avenue on the Upper East Side of Manhattan. The change would do me good. I had also thought about applying for a surgical spot with a track to neurosurgery at NYU.

I made an appointment to interview with the world-renowned chairman of the Department of Neurosurgery at NYU, Joseph Ransohoff. Ransohoff was legendary. Short, trim, and muscular, he ran an incredibly tight ship. He had served as a surgeon during World War II in Normandy and at the Battle of the Bulge. He was one of the young men in George Patton's circle. He had developed the neurosurgical training program at NYU into one of the best in the country. He had been the consultant (and some say the model for the protagonist) for the successful 1960s television show about a brain surgeon, *Ben Casey*. The neurosurgery residents were reportedly simultaneously worshipful and terrified of him. He was a chain smoker with indefatigable energy. He would operate and teach all day, then see patients and meet with the families of his surgical patients at night. He had no patience for inadequately prepared residents but would listen to patients and their families sympathetically for as long as they felt they needed to talk to him.

As a teacher, he was an amazing performer. During the course of my year at NYU, I attended a couple of his grand rounds teaching conferences. The conference was always well attended. Mandatory, of course, for the neurosurgical residents, it was also a hit with faculty from other departments, neurology and psychiatry residents, and medical students. Ransohoff would stand at the blackboard of the amphitheater lecturing on malignant brain tumors, drawing the tumor and its relationship to adjacent normal brain structures with his left hand while simultaneously writing notes relevant to the subject with his right hand. He would ask a question and call out a name for the answer. The respondent had better be quick with the correct answer, or he would be in for a withering diatribe. I always left the room grateful that I hadn't been one of the victims and jealous that I wasn't one of his protégés.

My appointment with Dr. Ransohoff was scheduled for one p.m. I was there on the nose. As I walked into the anteroom, I could see that his secretary was typing away to verbal dictation obliviously as her boss shouted his thoughts from the other room. After a few minutes, she noticed me standing in front of her desk.

"Thomas Lansen?" I asked quietly.

She turned her right ear slightly in my direction, the typing and the shouting had continued. I cleared my throat.

"Thomas Lansen," I stated more assertively.

"Oh yes, go in."

I rounded the corner to confront the vision of Dr. Ransohoff, naked from the waist up, doing jumping jacks as he dictated his letter to a referring physician. "Be with you in a minute," he wheezed. This was beyond my pay grade.

"I'll come back another time, Dr. Ransohoff."

"No problem."

The second anecdote I had heard about Dr. Ransohoff also gave me pause. It appears that one morning, a gifted first-year general surgery resident presented the case of a woman with an acute gallbladder attack to his chief resident. At the completion of the presentation, Nick DePalma reasoned that the lady should go to surgery that morning. The chief resident agreed and told Nick to get her ready and that he, the chief, would come in and do the case. "But I've been up all night working this patient up, I'm confident that I can do the case. Will you help me do it?" The chief was adamant: Nick was to go upstairs and get started with the morning's ward work. He would not do the gallbladder. The argument escalated and tempers flared. Nick punched the chief resident.

Later that afternoon, Nick presented himself to NYU's chairman of surgery—the courtly Texan, Frank Spencer. "Now Nick, you're a very talented young man and a fine surgeon; but you know, of course, that I have no choice but to let you go."

"I understand, Dr. Spencer." As a dejected Nick DePalma walked down 1st Avenue regretting his rashness, he nearly bumped into Joe Ransohoff walking in the opposite direction. "You the kid who cold-cocked your chief resident?" Nick nodded, speechless. Bad news travels fast, he thought. "You sound like my kind of man. How'd you like to be a neurosurgeon?"

Years later, I shared a dinner with both men. Dr. Ransohoff was in the twilight of his remarkable career and Dr. DePalma was a long-established and respected New York neurosurgeon. Both confirmed the story. Nick became a dear friend and colleague. Initially friendly competitors, I would never forget that when I first moved back to New York after completing my residency, my older son Tom was born. Nick, my competitor, sent me a magnum of Dom Perignon. We would go on to operate together and to share many wonderful Italian dinners.

I decided that a neurosurgery residency at NYU required just a bit more testosterone than I had.

CHAPTER FIVE

Lenox Hill

I met with the chairman of psychiatry late one afternoon to inform him that I was changing career paths. Although I had had little contact with him, he was surprisingly disappointed that I had decided to leave. Would it make a difference to me to know that the faculty had been watching me, found my scientific approach to the field laudable, and had decided that I would be the chief resident during my third year? It would not. I thanked him for the honor and for a very interesting year, but psychiatry and I were clearly a bad fit.

In June, I began to gear up for the sea change that would occur on July 1st. I was having trouble staying focused on my responsibilities at the hospital, but things always have a way of drawing your attention. One warm morning, as I sat in the main ER hallway of the ancient building writing up an admission, I heard the voice of one of the cops with whom I had become friendly during the course of the year.

"Hey doc," announced the Brooklyn basso.

"Just a minute, officer."

"*Doc*," he repeated with uncharacteristic insistence.

"Let me finish this workup, Vito. I'll be with you in two seconds."

"Doc, I think you better make time for this one." Petulantly, I glanced up from the page. Before me stood a very attractive young woman, probably in her mid-thirties. Her face was proud, almost arrogant, as she peered down her nose at me. There was just one small issue—except for a lovely strand of pearls and high-heeled, black, patent leather pumps, she was stark naked. I shot icy glares at the two cops flanking her, their eyebrows raised, and just a trace of an upward curl at the corners of their lips. "Very amusing, Vito." She had been standing on the median parkway at the corner of 52nd Street and Park Avenue calmly watching rush hour traffic, which had been getting pretty jammed up by the time the officers arrived. She had not said a word to them, not even given her name. Obviously, she carried no identification. With some difficulty, the nurses and I managed to get her to sit down in a wooden wheelchair. We placed a sheet over her, up to the neck, and I began to ask her a few questions: her name, where she was from, had someone taken her clothes or had she "forgot" to put them on. Nothing. Not a word. She stared at me quietly, almost sympathetically, but would not say a word. The staff tried various languages; no luck. We finally gave up, and I turned to write admitting orders.

"Doc." It was Vito again. I looked up to find that Lady Godiva had pulled the sheet off and thrown it over her shoulder and down the hall. "Look, Miss," I started, but one of our no-nonsense nurses had brought out wrist and ankle straps. She quickly secured her arms and legs to the wheelchair and placed a fresh sheet over her.

Ah, but never underestimate the power of a determined woman. As we watched in disbelief, our patient leaned forward, grabbed the edge of the sheet with her teeth, and removed a fair amount of it. Defeated, the nurses transferred her to a stretcher, secured her there, and gave her a sedative. A few days later, I saw her in the locked ward clothed in a hospital gown, sitting and staring with the glazed look to which I had become uncomfortably accustomed. Another victim of a society that proved just too difficult for its most vulnerable.

At the end of the day, I left Bellevue with bittersweet feelings. I had found that psychiatry just didn't do it for me, but I had met some great doctors and nurses, dedicated to the uphill battle of treating horrific mental disorders without the benefit of a real commitment to the effort by society. No one really wanted to deal with the issues of these patients. They just wanted them to disappear. I marveled at the Dirk Bergers and the Linda Clarks of the world who kept positive attitudes despite everything, who did their best to make their patients better when possible and to create a safe environment for them when it wasn't.

On the lighter side, I would miss the great, old federalist cathedral of a building and the New York friends I had made, so different from the more superficially friendly but less self-revealing friends of my Wisconsin youth. I would miss the ethnic sweep of the place, the ritual of my walk to and from Grand Central, my Metro-North commute and my other daily rituals—especially reading the *Times* over my cup of regular coffee.

At the beginning of July 1974, I walked into the impeccable edifice at the corner of 77th and Park. What a contrast to the venerable but dilapidated Bellevue. I planned to commute by car now and had acquired a small Ford, which I parked in a garage on 77th Street at the exorbitant, though subsidized, monthly fee of $75. It was seven in the morning, and I found the team of surgical residents attached to Dr. John O. Vieta, the hospital's chief of surgery. A renowned cancer surgeon, Dr. Vieta would allow me to start my rotation on his general surgery service. The rest of the team was a largely standard group of young resident doctors educated at American medical schools with a few colorful exceptions: a son of British diplomats who had decided to stay in the States for his post-graduate education when his parents' tour was over; a talented Nicaraguan who had completed a full residency in Central America and now was repeating the entire process in the United States to obtain the requisite credentials; and an Egyptian, quiet and gaunt, with a facial resemblance to the mummies I had seen as a child at Chicago's Natural History Museum and a prayer mark in the center of his forehead.

I immediately learned that the pace of the surgical service was not psychiatric. The chief resident, a young African-American whose size and muscularity indicated that he must have been a college linebacker, turned to me as he plucked a metal chart from the rack where we had gathered.

"Lansen, what's Mrs. Peters' sodium level this morning?" Of course, I had never set foot on the ward before and I had no clue as to the existence of Mrs. Peters, much less the state of her metabolism. Weighing that as an answer, I rejected it out of hand and pled ignorance.

"Don't give me that answer tomorrow."

My face reddened as I was singled out for criticism before I'd even had a chance to step up to the plate. What I didn't realize until much later was that the surgeon's world is one of preparation and diligence, that a really good neophyte surgical resident would have arrived two hours earlier on that first day to make sure that he had all the data available. I would learn that painful lesson thoroughly over the next six years.

Herman Watson was a real chief resident. A naturally gifted surgeon, he was straightforward yet deferential to the attending surgeons and a calm leader to the junior residents. He always knew all the answers, and I never knew him to lie. Not one to gab about his personal life, I knew very little about him other than that he was from Kansas, that he actually had been a college football player and that he loved to operate.

Immediately after morning rounds, Herman was off to the operating room. I spent the morning scrambling to change the post-operative dressings, check the labs and x-ray reports, evaluate the patients for fever, discomfort, and new symptoms and make rounds with any of the surgical attending physicians who happened to be in the building. I reported anything of significance to the senior assistant resident or the assistant resident, whoever wasn't in the OR.

Let me pause here for a word about the pyramid, the five-year general surgery training program. The first-year resident is basically the person formerly referred to as an intern, aptly named for someone who lives in the hospital. You're there all the time, picking up sticks, running errands, doing the "scut" work. The second, third and fourth-year residents are usually referred to by their year—"the Two," "the Three," "the Fourth year." Technically, the second-year resident is the assistant resident, the third-year is the senior assistant resident, and the fourth-year the resident, with the fifth-year being the chief. Every year, each resident spends progressively more time in surgery, first rotating through several specialties, then focusing on one. There are geographical and institutional variations on this theme. The important issue regarding this arcane nomenclature is *The Pyramid*. As the name implies, a fairly large number of first-year residents is gradually culled to one (or two, or three, depending on the number of major teaching hospitals covered by the medical school or training program) chief residents. This attrition is partially natural, with residents leaving general surgery as the years progress to fill the ranks of the surgical specialties, and partly by selection, with eliminated residents moving on to smaller or less important programs. By definition, it is a competitive model, like most of medicine, bringing out the best and worst in the men and women who have committed years of their lives to succeeding in the field.

I immediately found the combination of "floor work" (running down laboratory and x-ray data, carefully performing and recording history and physical exams, reporting my findings to senior residents and attending physicians and updating patients' hospital courses in daily progress notes) an oddly reassuring routine that reinforced my medical knowledge while I actually helped sick people. I enjoyed my interaction with the nurses and the patients. I loved being part of the team, and I was overwhelmed when a patient would actually thank me for my help.

I also found that my educational foundation in medical school was not so sparse after all, and I continued to dip into that reservoir (as I do today, forty years later) for corroboration. The internet is a fabulous tool that I wouldn't do without for my daily medical practice; and yet, there is something about learning by repetition, by immersion, by osmosis, that I consider priceless.

Lenox Hill, now a part of the Northwell system, is an unusual hospital. At the same time, a community hospital for the mostly affluent neighborhood of New York's Upper East Side, staffed by society doctors, and a private hospital for some of the patients of Manhattan's academic physicians, creating both an academic and private practice atmosphere. It also has a reasonably busy emergency room.

Originally founded in 1868, as the German Hospital serving the large immigrant community in the neighborhood, Lenox Hill was renamed for the adjacent neighborhood, once a thirty-acre tenant farm belonging to a 19th century, Scottish merchant named Robert Lenox. After World War I, anti-German sentiment rose sharply against America's enemy. This change occurred despite the fact that the overwhelming majority of doctors, nurses, and staff at the time spoke German.

While always priding itself as a strong teaching hospital with major academic affiliations, Lenox Hill never submitted to becoming a subservient affiliate of a medical school. It is noted for being the first hospital to have a tuberculosis pavilion, the first Hemophilia center, and the site of the first coronary angioplasty. Its medical staff have been important leaders in many fields; perhaps its most famous doctor being Abraham Jacobi, the father of American Pediatrics.

The patients taken care of at Lenox Hill read like a Who's Who of high society at the time: Winston Churchill, Elizabeth Taylor, Ed Sullivan, Joan Rivers, Joe Namath, Douglas MacArthur, Alger Hiss, Brooke Astor, James Cagney, Myrna Loy, James Levine, Mike Wallace, and too many others to mention. So, imagine a twenty-five-year-old Midwestern boy suddenly interviewing and examining such people. In addition to a Greek shipping magnate (who occupied his own luxurious suite at the hospital overlooking Park Avenue, of course), and the wife of the French consul, I participated in the care of the elegant Dorothy Rodgers, wife of composer Richard Rodgers, and several other celebrities. My father always told me that "the bigger they are, the nicer they are." I found the maxim absolutely true. Not once did any of these people treat me with anything but respect and kindness. Despite my youth and inexperience, they understood that I was part of their team and that I was being trained for the future. Never did I hear a cross word from anyone, nor did anyone ask that I not interview or examine them because of my low position on the totem pole.

After a long day of surgery and meticulous post-operative rounds punctuated by visits to the emergency room, my co-residents and I would often repair to one of the wonderful little bistros in the neighborhood for a beer or a glass of wine and a lot of camaraderie and commiseration. These were never late evenings, as seven the next morning always loomed large in our minds. The hospital also provided great resident accommodations so that if we couldn't get home, we would be comfortable as "interns."

Then there were the doctors. In addition to our stalwart chief resident, three physicians especially stood out, all for different reasons. James Donaldson was a gentleman's gentleman. A member of the Columbia College of Physicians and Surgeons class of 1936, he served as a Navy surgeon, landing on Omaha Beach on D-Day. Throughout his career, he quietly gave his services to the police and fire departments of the city. In his practice, his dignified approach to his patients was the same whether the patient was one of the many society notables he took care of or an emergency patient without connections. This simple decency and respect, almost a reverence he offered to the people who trusted him with their lives, has always remained the gold standard of patient care for me. I only assisted him in a handful of surgeries, but he displayed great expertise and kindness—the best model of a physician and a man.

Paula Moynihan was a plastic surgery fellow during my year at Lenox Hill. She had completed her five years of general surgery residency at a time when females were rare in the field, so she had either learned or been born with a delightful combination of femininity and forcefulness. She was firm with the more junior residents in getting the job done, but she was attractive and charming in social settings. Technically, she was one of the most gifted surgeons I have ever seen in action, and I almost followed her into cosmetic surgery purely on the basis of her inspiring technique. At this mecca of beautification, in New York's most upscale neighborhood, celebrities were already seeking her out for their facelifts, rhinoplasties (nose jobs), and eyelids even though she was a plastic surgery fellow and not an attending physician. My best recollection of Paula was calling her from the emergency room for the repair of a particularly nasty and disfiguring set of facial lacerations suffered by a young man who had experienced a bad combination of alcohol and motorcycle. Paula arrived, without protest, a few minutes after my call to her. She was dressed in a beautiful evening gown, having left a formal affair of the Knights of Malta (despite her youth, she was a Dame of Malta). Smiling merrily, she sat at the emergency room's operating table, pulled the gown up to her knees, scrubbed, donned a mask and gloves, and proceeded to restore the young man's face to near perfection. I could only stand by, cutting the sutures as she tied them, mouth agape, listening to her chat happily about the evening's festivities. The job completed, she headed back to the ball. What a woman! At the end of the rotation in which I was obviously devoted to her, she presented me with a Tiffany Caduceus key ring. This lovely gift, recognition of how hard I had worked on her service, was unprecedented to me, and a gesture that I obviously have not forgotten for more than forty years.

September of 1974 was an especially happy month for me. In addition to loving my experience in surgery at Lenox Hill, my first child, my daughter Nora, was born at the hospital. She was feisty, bright, and adorable from the start; and has remained so. She, too, became enticed by the medical profession and is now a family physician and executive.

But back to physician influence number three. Fate delivered me to James McMurtry. Jim was the director of neurosurgical residency teaching at Columbia University. The scion of a prominent Texas family, his first cousin is novelist Larry McMurtry of *Hud*, *The Last Picture Show*, *Texasville*, and *Terms of Endearment* fame. Independently wealthy, with a beautiful multi-story townhouse just blocks up Park Avenue from the hospital, Dr. McMurtry was brilliant and self-effacing. He treated everyone with deference and respect despite his extraordinary gifts and accomplishments. And that included me. By this time, I was enjoying all of my surgical rotations, happy that I had left psychiatry, happy with being busy to the point of exhaustion, and happy with learning the medicine and the technical skills. I was enchanted by cosmetic surgery, really enjoying the art of making people beautiful. I enjoyed urology, radiology, and ENT. But the first time I scrubbed with Jim McMurtry, on an operation to relieve spinal stenosis, I was right

46

back with Dave Hemmy in the world of neurosurgery.

I quickly realized that they were kindred spirits: scientists, diagnosticians, technical experts. And, strangely, I found a sense of serenity in a neurosurgical case that I'd found nowhere else, not even in my life outside the hospital. I felt a remarkable sense of coming home, and I must have conveyed this feeling of comfort and familiarity to Dr. McMurtry, for at some point in my rotation he suggested that neurosurgery was the specialty I should concentrate on and make my career. I was thunderstruck and flattered. He suggested that I apply to the Columbia program but acknowledged that, even if I were accepted, I would have to complete an additional year of general surgery, as was the custom of the residency there. Another entire year of general surgery before even beginning the long neurosurgery residency? Were there other programs that didn't require two years of general surgery? He gave this serious thought and suggested several other programs, which I dutifully visited. He especially recommended my applying to the program of a rising young star among neurosurgery professors, Dr. Albert L. Rhoton, Jr., the chairman at the University of Florida who had just moved from the Mayo Clinic to build the UF program. I had never heard of Dr. Rhoton and knew little of the University of Florida, other than that it was a large university and therefore probably had a pretty good medical school. But I did some research and found that, even though he had been chairman for only three years, the journal *Surgical Neurology* had surveyed residency program directors from across America and his program was now ranked sixth in the nation, in their opinions.

I immediately applied to Dr. Rhoton's program and was surprised to receive an early reply inviting me to Gainesville for an interview. *Great,* I thought, *but this is an outside shot.*

The next week, I was driving north to Gainesville from my parent's home in Cape Coral, Florida. I walked into the anteroom of neurosurgery's departmental headquarters at UF Health Shands Hospital, the main teaching hospital of the university; Dr. Rhoton ambled out to greet me. I had been impressed by how beautiful the city and the university were; floral, green, warm. But I wasn't ready for Dr. Rhoton. Well over six feet tall, bald, with a pink complexion that gave him an almost baby-like appearance, his voice was crystalline and preternaturally high, with a southern drawl that somehow tossed the words out like tennis balls.

"Well, hey, come on in to my office." I followed dutifully. Dr. Rhoton was one of those men whose age is indeterminate but whose energy and intelligence were unmistakable. He asked about my education (he had all the information, but he wanted my slant), my interest in neuroscience, and my willingness to relocate from New York to north central Florida. He further probed my work ethic, my commitment, why I had decided that neurosurgery was for me. Not a single quiz about my knowledge of neuroanatomy or neurophysiology. What a very strange and interesting man. I didn't realize at the time that he didn't need me to know much, that if I had the capacity to learn based on my credentials and the desire to take this path, he could do the rest. He could mold the clay.

I returned to New York deeply impressed with the university and with Dr. Rhoton, but I harbored little hope that I would be chosen. Two days later, the now familiar high-pitched voice was on the phone as I was paged during rounds. "Tom, this is Al Rhoton. If you'd like to join the team, I'd like to offer you a residency spot with us." Would I like to join the team? You damn bet I would.

Nothing could stop me. "I'd be honored, Dr. Rhoton." Funny how I always referred to him as Dr. Rhoton. Forty years later, as neurosurgeons all over the world bragged about their acquaintance with the great Al Rhoton, possibly the greatest neuroscientist of the late twentieth century, I could never bring myself to reduce the honor and respect I felt for him by calling him anything but Dr. Rhoton, whether to his face or behind his back.

Now there was the not-so-slight problem of extricating myself from the Lenox Hill program. Not realizing that I would follow the neurosurgical pathway, I had committed myself to the second year of the pyramid at the hospital. Dr. Vieta had been kind enough to commit to me. Now I told him that I had been accepted at Florida for a neurosurgical residency, and that I would like to resign. He went ballistic. Of course, I couldn't resign. A commitment is a commitment. It was out of the question. Once again, Jim McMurtry to the rescue. He explained to the chief that I had been accepted into a newly prestigious residency program, that I certainly wouldn't be happy if forced to remain, and that slavery had been abolished more than a century ago. Dr. Vieta was not happy. In fact, he largely ignored me for the rest of the academic year. But he tore up my contract. Lenox Hill had been an enormously happy year for me—the camaraderie, the sophistication of the neighborhood and the people, the romance of New York.

And so, in 1975, after two fascinating years learning New York, with its sounds, sights, and smells, fast-paced and exciting, I would now go South and spend the next four and a half years in a bucolic setting, but living and learning at a pace that made my New York experience seems like, well, a walk in Central Park.

CHAPTER SIX

Gainesville

On the day I arrived in Gainesville, Florida, I met two young men who would have a profound influence on me—Henry Shuey and David Bruce Woodham. Both sons of the South, they were my co-residents. They were on the same path and ready to spend the next four or five years learning the basics of our amazing craft. "Hank" Shuey was a southern aristocrat, tracing his Huguenot roots to well before the Civil War. His undergraduate years had been spent at the Citadel, a military college steeped in the traditions of the South. As I walked into his call room at the VA Hospital, just across the street from Shands Teaching Hospital, he stood to greet me. Dark and handsome in his crisp white coat, I noticed that his green tie was decorated with a regular pattern of tiny Confederate flags. As he rose, he put down the *Merritt's Neurology* he had been reading. I realized I was in the big leagues now.

"Well, Dr. Lansen, you must be pretty special. I do believe that you're the first Yankee that Al has chosen for the residency." His Southern drawl was sophisticated and suggested dances with ladies in white gowns, mint juleps, and Cuban cigars. Al? Wow! They must be close. And I hadn't even begun to think that I would face other challenges here at UF. Later, I would discover that it had been less than twenty-five years since a Catholic priest had been lynched in Gainesville. I suddenly imagined a conical white hood covering Hank's head.

"Al and I have pretty much decided that you'll start your rotations here at the VA." So, Dr. Rhoton was also consulting Hank on how to manage the residency. This must be a pretty special guy. He dismissed me and returned his rapt attention to Merritt. Hank had the advantage of having done his internship at Florida, so he was familiar with the place and had a real leg up. When Hank spoke to me, he always seemed to be wearing a wry half-smile. It took me years to dig through the veneer of tongue-in-cheek conversation and to understand the real Hank Shuey, the decent and honorable man that he was. But that first day, he was clearly giving my leg a good yank.

David Bruce Woodham and I became best friends in our first year of neurosurgical residency and have remained so for the last forty-five years. Bruce is one of those larger-than-life figures who tend to inhabit our field. Six-foot-two and wiry, with slow movements and a quick wit, his story is all Horatio Alger. Born in Alabama to poor parents, with two brothers and an extended family living in rural poverty, life was hardscrabble. Bruce told me about going to school in overalls, sharing two pairs of shoes among the three brothers, carrying the pail to privy (no indoor plumbing), and experiencing the trials of growing up in the 1950s. With emerging prosperity all around him, he was always looking through the store window from the outside. But Bruce had two things going for him.

He was very, very smart, and he had incredible energy and drive. He was accepted at the University of Florida. Unfortunately, the heady experience of college life, with its fraternities and a kind of social life he'd never known, took its toll. His studies took second place for a short time. Bruce had always dreamed of being a doctor but that bit of inattention the first year would cost him dearly and teach him a lesson he would never forget. From that moment onward, he would work harder than anyone else. He pulled his grades up to A's for the rest of his undergraduate career, but the competitive medical school class of his graduating year meant that he would have to study abroad.

And study he did. Matriculating at the Université de Bruxelles, Institute Jules Bordet, Bruce learned French during the summer after his graduation from Florida. He loved the university, steeped in the academic tradition but he had little time to loiter there. Studying constantly, Bruce bought a lectern for his room so that he could stand and study, thereby avoiding the temptation to fall asleep. Never requiring much sleep, he became a study machine, and, at the end of his second year, he achieved academic first place, an honor never before awarded to a non-native speaker of French.

Bruce never looked back. After two years at Bruxelles, he was able to transfer back to the States, joining the third-year class at the University of Iowa. Finding his interest riveted to neuroscience, he knew he would become a neurosurgeon. Iowa's program was nationally renowned, and Bruce, now a very able medical student, entertained a residency there. But when he heard that an opening might be available at his alma mater, he jumped at the chance.

I met Bruce that first day in Gainesville, just after my introduction to Hank Shuey. We were all to be "first years" together. Bruce seemed like a friendly guy. I confided that Hank had told me that "we" (presumably he and Dr. Rhoton) had decided on the rotations that would take place among us. Bruce flashed his trademark grin. "Aw, he's just fooling with you. Hank doesn't have any more influence with the boss than you or I." We walked to the cafeteria to share the first of thousands of cups of coffee together.

Dr. Rhoton, perhaps partly reflecting his own challenging early life, later told Bruce that he was one of the finest neurosurgeons he had trained.

My first rotation was in fact at the Veterans' Administration hospital. Essentially, all of the surgery at the VA is elective. White, with huge, reflecting, smoky windows, the VA stands on a large plot of flat land, perfectly manicured, across the street (now highway) from Shands. A strong partner in the university's health care system, the VA is a center for the public care of veterans and a teaching hospital for the training of young physicians and surgeons. There is absolutely no question that these veterans received the respect and honor of all the medical staff. However, there was also a sense that these men were receiving a public beneficence, and that they could not be "picky" about their choice of surgeon or treatment. In all honesty, this was a clear understanding between subject and object. Long before the concept of post-traumatic stress disorder had been elucidated, we understood that some veterans were overwhelmed by their return to society and needed a respite in our institution to pull themselves together or to get ready for another round of self-destruction. We weren't so stupid or bureaucratically correct as to deny them. We would admit them for sciatica, neuralgia, hepatomegaly, neuritis, lumbago and a myriad inventory of real and invented maladies. It wasn't too hard for us to figure out that these guys didn't need a bureaucratic barrage of government solutions. They just needed a helping hand.

I guess the 1970s version of VA health care was a little like European national health insurance. The doctors were part of a university system in which the direct delivery of services was given by doctors in training, supervised by professors. It worked pretty well.

Having learned a lesson the year before, my first day at the VA Hospital (Hank Shuey was right about my rotation assignment) began more auspiciously than my first day at Lenox Hill. I was there at six devouring the twenty-five charts of the patients on the neurosurgical service. At six-thirty, Arthur Day appeared. He was the chief resident. Handsome and self-confident, Art was only a year older than me but had thundered through school at a ridiculous pace. I believe that every nurse in the hospital had a secret crush on Art. The son of a service station man in rural Louisiana, he had worked his way through Louisiana Technical University. Dr. Rhoton had seen the spark in this brilliant and serenely calm young man. As someone who had come from behind, he understood my terror, took me under his wing, and tutored me like a big brother. Our senior resident, Art's assistant, was Warren Wilson, a can-do guy from Rome, Georgia who later had a distinguished career in Fort Worth, becoming president of the Texas Neurosurgical Society. He was a wonderful character. His prematurely bald, bespectacled face was glorified by a big walrus moustache. Warren had a deep drawl and had spent his undergraduate career at Rutgers University in New Jersey, which he eschewed as his first educational experience in the North . . . and his last. Warren immediately christened me Snooky, after Snooky Lanson, a star of *Your Hit Parade*, a 1950s musical television show. The name stuck. At first, I thought it was another jab at a Yankee. But in time, it came to be a precious nickname that would become a symbol of affection and acceptance as "the Team," so carefully assembled by Dr. Rhoton, grew tighter and tighter.

Albert Loren Rhoton, Jr. was born in a log cabin in Parvin, Kentucky, in 1932. Schooled in a two-room schoolhouse, he planned to become a social worker but became interested in biological psychology after an undergraduate course and went to medical school (and I flatter myself to think that our discussion about my story affected his decision to accept me). Brilliant and driven, he graduated Washington University in St. Louis, one of America's most prestigious medical schools, with honors. After the two-year preparatory residency at Columbia University, he returned to complete his neurosurgery residency at Barnes Hospital at "Wash U," under the firm hand of "Black Henry" Schwartz, who was the antithesis of Rhoton. An undergraduate at Princeton, medical school at Johns Hopkins, postgraduate training at Harvard, Schwartz moved west to Barnes in 1946 and educated a generation of neurosurgeons there until 1974. He must have appreciated Rhoton's genius and energy, but the two were hardly *sympatico*.

With or without Black Henry's approval, Rhoton's excellence was apparent. After his residency and a National Institutes of Health fellowship in neuroanatomy, he joined the faculty of the Mayo Clinic in 1966. He began his seminal work in microneuroanatomy and microneurosurgery there, the work that would bring him world renown as the "father of microneurosurgery." It was where he developed his mantra: We neurosurgeons are privileged to be allowed to explore the last and greatest mystery of human intellectual endeavor—the human brain. Six years later, he accepted the chair of the Department of Neurosurgery at the University of Florida at the remarkable age of forty. He would train over fifty neurosurgeons directly and more than a thousand neurosurgical fellows from around the world over the next twenty-five years. In a career that spanned fifty years, he rose to the presidency of the most prestigious neurosurgical organizations in the world: the Congress of Neurological Surgeons, the Society of Neurological Surgeons, the American Association of Neurological Surgeons, as well as the North American Skull Base Society, the International Interdisciplinary Congress on Craniofacial and Skull Base Surgery, and the International Society for Neurosurgical Technology and Instrument Invention. He served as the honored guest or received honorary membership in more than twenty neurosurgical societies in every continent except Antarctica (no neurosurgery there, yet).

I arrived in the third year of his remarkable tenure. Throughout my long journey in neurosurgery, I have always said that not a single day of my life passed without making use of something, personal or professional, that Dr. Rhoton taught me.

My three months at the VA passed quickly. In addition to making rounds and performing the scut work, I now regularly assisted at surgery, generally serving as second assistant to the attending surgeon and the senior or chief resident. The work would finish late in the evening, and, even though we had rented an apartment just a few blocks from the hospital, it took me a while to do anything but drag myself home, read a page or two of Youmans's textbook of neurosurgery, and fall into bed.

In those days, we worked every day except Sunday (assuming we weren't on call that day). On Saturday mornings, Dr. Rhoton conducted our grand rounds, a combination of teaching and execution by flaying. Later, Dr. Rhoton would reluctantly acquiesce to the faculty's request that off-call residents should be allowed to enjoy Saturday and Sunday with their families and move grand rounds to Friday.

That first Saturday, the two chief residents, Robert Mozingo and Art Day, had a series of patients to present, along with their imaging studies. Mozingo, later a distinguished practitioner in Tampa, presented first. Bob was a big, lanky guy. Sort of a young LBJ. He was no nonsense and required all junior residents to be prepared and prompt. He presented his first case of the day. A vascular case. An aneurysm of the brain. A sudden headache, complaint of rigidity of the neck, then loss of consciousness. A quick ambulance ride to the ER at Shands, the presumptive diagnosis of a subarachnoid hemorrhage (blood spilled from an artery into the spinal fluid compartment of the brain), an angiogram (x-ray study in which the blood vessels of the brain are injected with dye) performed.

"Tom. Why don't you come up and review the angiogram for us?"

Absolute silence in the room. I am terrified. I had never seen an angiogram. Not that it would have mattered. I couldn't even remember my name at this point. "Tom, what do you see there?" Dr. Rhoton. Is he now my nemesis?

I search the x-ray for some miraculous sign. Nothing. "Alright, where is the internal carotid artery (the largest and most obvious artery entering the brain)?" I point to the correct squiggle. "And where is the anterior cerebral artery?" I haven't a clue and admit it. All twenty residents and faculty roar with laughter. What a wonderful barbeque. Rhoton is not amused. "Alright, Tom." I sit in misery, knowing that I have failed the challenge that he set in accepting me for the residency. I'm prepared to pack my bags for the trip to New York on Monday.

"Let's see"—an eternity passes—"Hank, show me the anterior cerebral artery." Hank is dismissive, pointing to the correct shadow immediately. He starts to sit. "Hank, while you're up there, show me the anterior choroidal artery." For some reason, Hank can't find it. He sits down, humiliated. "Frank, you can show Hank that, can't you?" Frank Harris, a gifted and intense senior resident, strides to the x-ray panel and points to the correct artery. "Frank, while you're up there, show us the thalamostriate artery." Frank fumbles. Points to the wrong artery. "Frank, let's make sure you know that artery next week." Frank's masseter muscles grind. "Bob (Mozingo, the chief resident), why don't you show Frank where that artery is." Mozingo walks up and points to the correct artery. After all, he and Rhoton are almost colleagues now. Mozingo turns to take a seat . . . prematurely. "Well, Bob, just one more thing. While you're in that neck of the woods, could you point to the artery of Bernasconi-Cassinari?" Mozingo folds his hand. The poker game is over. Rhoton wins, full house. He glances at me, then addresses the room. "Well, I guess we all have a lot to learn. Maybe next time we won't be so quick to laugh at the people who are just starting to train."

My first rotation at Shands increased the pace from the VA. My first day presented ten new patients to be worked up. The inpatient neurosurgery service roster was now at sixty. There were seven residents, and two of them were always in the operating room. The attending surgeons came in to supervise and see their patients, but they had administrative, teaching, and research responsibilities. Dr. Rhoton would not tolerate a lack of activity in any of these areas. It all had to be done, and it had to be done superlatively. That's the only way he knew how to behave.

I got the message quickly. There were no excuses—I couldn't be too tired or sick, I couldn't have too many patients to take care of or have a hole in my racket, and the dog cannot have eaten my homework. You were either in or out. I quickly learned the Rhoton method. No bravado. No prima donna neurosurgeons. Get the job done properly, efficiently, quickly, without complaint and without flag-waving. Get it done and move on to the next case. And meanwhile, figure out what research you want to do— something meaningful, something that contributes to yourself, to the profession, and to mankind. Over many years, I would learn to recognize a Rhoton trainee—more self-effacing and circumspect. Less swagger.

It was amazing how quickly I became used to the routine. Up at six, resident rounds at six-thirty. Then rounding with whatever attending surgeon was ready to go. Then, either to work on the wards or into the OR as an assistant, hoping to get a little surgical experience. There were procedures that I could never have imagined doing a year ago. "Tom, let me show you how to tap this premie's fontanelle." A baby delivered three months before she was ready to come into our world, tiny as a mouse, with her head distended by a large liquid blood clot that kept re-accumulating. We had to put a very small needle into the side of what my mother used to call the "soft spot" at the top her head every day or two and drain the syrupy purple fluid that wanted to keep her brain from growing. At first, I saw the little girl moving slowly in the incubator and thought about the tragic challenges that this little person faced. I wanted to cry. Then I realized that my sympathy was not what she needed. She needed me to perform a skillful procedure without emotion and without mistake. The first time I tapped her fontanelle, I was terrified. Warren Wilson talked me through it. The second time, he saw that I was competent. By the third time, I had become a resolute, emotionless, healing machine. I was more concerned about making sure that the field was sterile and my technique flawless than about the child. Multiply that little girl times twenty that first year. The learning experience was astounding. The effect on the children was curative. Everyone on the team was collegial and helpful. I was completely addicted to my new profession.

There was no such thing as lunch. I might shove down a sandwich from the cafeteria at the nurses' station. Or not. The nurses all seemed young and beautiful. Many had been attracted to the University of Florida for the obvious reasons that attracted medical students, residents, and faculty. A beautiful location, a prestigious university, and association with like-minded people. They were professional and dedicated. Of course. Socially, it was a very different time. But I have never seen brighter or more devoted young women in my life (in my time, there were very few male nurses). Of course, there were outliers.

During my residency, two excellent and beautiful young nurses in their mid-twenties worked in the emergency room at Shands. They were experienced and respected. One evening, federal DEA agents showed up in the ER and put the two ladies in handcuffs. They had fallen in with drug lords and become dependent on them—the money, the drugs, the culture. They were supplying the bad guys with all the cocaine they could steal from the ER's pharmacy. What a terrible waste. Florida in some ways was a vortex swirling around the wild west of the Central American drug world and mainstream America. The university jumped all over this kind of behavior, but the world is not a perfect place.

The afternoon was about new patients. The first-year residents, when not required as assistants in the OR, admitted all neurosurgical patients. This required a history and physical examination, thorough and documented, with all relevant laboratory and imaging (x-ray and CT scan) findings entered and evaluated. Then, a cogent impression of the patient's diagnosis had to be written, along with our plan as to what should be done to help. Every one of these patients, of course, was either admitted by or assigned to one of our attending, faculty neurosurgeons. At the end of the day, we would call each "attending" to present the case and discuss the diagnosis and plan. Often, he would give further details that clarified the case and would refine the plan. Sometimes, it wouldn't be quite so easy.

Ten p.m., the night before Mrs. Stafford's surgery. She had a brain tumor, a metastasis. It was a tumor that was spread to her brain from an aggressive breast cancer. The oncology staff was working on controlling the primary cancer, but the main problem was to remove the secondary tumor that was in her brain, threatening her life in a very real and imminent way. Dr. Rhoton had finished his surgeries and was sitting in his office, reviewing slides for a research project that was evolving.

"Tom, you've got Mrs. Stafford's workup done?"

"Yes, sir."

"I've seen her CT scan and I examined her in the clinic. She has a right hemiparesis (weakness) and a mild expressive aphasia (difficulty expressing her speech), right?"

"That's right, Dr. Rhoton. These have reportedly improved with steroids."

"Her labs okay for surgery tomorrow?"

"Yes, sir."

"Her calcium?" Her calcium, her calcium. There were so many things to think about. Her examination, her imaging studies. But, of course, her calcium. I had thought about her blood count, her platelets, her sodium, potassium, chloride, her chest x-ray, her EKG, all of the routine labs that I should think about in a healthy young woman. But I hadn't thought about this one stupid element—calcium. Of course, elevated calcium was a hallmark of breast cancer because of its spread and its destruction of bones; and it could be life-threatening during her surgery. But I hadn't put two and two together—there was so much deductive knowledge to add to all of the basic information required.

"I don't know, Dr. Rhoton." A brief silence.

"Call me back with it, Tom." I ran to the patient, quickly prepared her arm, and drew a sample of blood. Forty-five minutes later, "Dr. Rhoton, it's 14.5."

"Cancel the surgery, Tom. Get the calcium down. Let's not let this happen again." Crestfallen, I crawled to the nurses' station, our headquarters, and sank down next to my trusted comrade, Bruce Woodham, who was sitting quietly, reading Youmans's *Neurological Surgery*, his long spindly legs perched on the bench that served as a workstation for nurses and residents.

"I screwed the pooch, Bruce. Help me find the best way to get Mrs. Stafford's calcium down." Bruce puts his book down (he could concentrate on a neurosurgical text without distraction in the middle of a tsunami), turned to me, and quickly outlined what needed to be done to pull Mrs. Stafford's calcium into a normal range. I was eternally grateful. He gave his winning smile. Mrs. Stafford was squared away in twenty-four hours, and her surgery went without a hitch. After surgery, Woodham and I headed to the Purple Porpoise where I bought him a beer. The Purple Porpoise, the favored pub of all the house staff at Shands and the VA, happened to be owned by a professor of neurology at Florida. What a school! It may fly in the face of professional and political correctness, but what a school! I love this place!

By ten or eleven p.m., we started to leave for home unless you were on call. In that case, you had to dig in and do whatever "workups" (history and physical examinations, as well as whatever action needed to be taken emergently) had been admitted. Any emergency surgeries were also your responsibility to present and get ready for the chief resident and the attending surgeon on call. I ran on pure adrenaline. I quickly learned about my comrades in arms. Hank Shuey always appeared impeccable, as if he had never missed eight hours of sleep. Intellectually, he was sharp as a tack. Bruce Woodham felt a little sleep-deprived if he got two hours a night, but four hours was all he ever needed for REM-gratified sleep. I thought, *I'll never make it.*

CHAPTER SEVEN

Zulu

A slender, black teenager stood trembling in the waiting room of the Emergency Department at the university hospital. His eyes were brimming over with tears. "We were playin' Zulu. I didn't mean to hurt him. I threw the spear, but I didn't think it would hit him." He shook his head and sank onto the faux-leather orange couch behind him. His mother took his head and cradled it in her arms. Everyone knew it wasn't his fault . . . except him.

A few yards away, under the bright, movable spotlight in the emergency carrel, relatively secluded by a white curtain pulled closed on metal rings, another young, black teenager, thirteen years old, lay quietly on his side. His sleepiness was induced by a combination of intravenous sedatives and the effect of trauma. His father sat next to the gurney, holding the boy's hand, his bent head a study in pent-up anxiety.

The scene wasn't particularly bloody or alarming . . . except for one, incongruous, bizarre feature. Protruding from the back of the upper neck of the youngster lying on his side was a three-foot-long broom handle, the dirty shaft of wood emerging just below the base of the boy's skull, straight outward and secure. The child couldn't know how incredibly strange he looked as he yawned from boredom and sedation. The nurse standing nearby reminded him to stay very still. He nodded unknowingly, the broomstick wiggling slightly as he did so. "Don't talk to him!" the young emergency department resident hissed at the nurse, emphasizing the fact that every interaction with the boy created a reaction, and every reactive movement threatened his life. The broomstick rested securely on a short pile of hospital blankets.

The problem was that the tip of the "spear" was literally millimeters from the center of the young man's existence, his medulla. The medulla, officially medulla oblongata, is the lower portion of the brainstem, the structure that connects the brain and the spinal cord and contains the condensed centers that control consciousness, breathing, heart rate, blood pressure, and all of the pathways for movement and sensation. Pretty much everything— in a tiny concentrated package about one and a quarter inches in length, three quarters of an inch in width, and half an inch in depth.

Because the medulla is so incredibly important, nature jealously protects it in the thickest case available, the stony base of the skull. As the skull tapers down toward the spinal cord, it becomes the thick suboccipital bone, an awesome bit of evolutionary architecture, curved and dense and almost impervious to attack. The medulla is nestled within this case of bone, which is further covered by a dense column of muscle, the "capitis" muscles.

Just below the medulla, the spinal cord begins, emerging from the large hole at the base of the skull, the foramen magnum, to send impulses to the muscles of the body and to receive sensation from all of the limbs and pass these impulses back up to the brain. The spinal cord, of course, runs through the spinal column, a series of twenty-five bony rings connected by discs, joints, and ligaments that protect the nerves that send and receive their messages but allow the spinal column mobility. The rings are each completed in front by a vertebra, a block of bone that gives structure and stability to the spine. Completing the structure of the spine are the facets, joints on each side of each spinal level, which give the neck and back mobility and suppleness.

But nature permits this extraordinary machine to exist at a price. All of the vertebrae and laminae, the rings of bone at each level of the spinal column, are interconnected by relatively slender ligaments which can be torn or penetrated by trauma. Damage to these ligaments has accounted for innumerable tragedies—auto accidents, sports injuries, gunshot wounds—resulting in death, quadriplegia, or paraplegia; life-altering catastrophes occurring in milliseconds. And, of course, it makes sense that the longest of these ligaments should be at the level requiring the greatest mobility—between the skull and the spine. The heavy skull has to rotate, flex, and extend against the spine. It rests on the first vertebra, a simple ring called the atlas (named for the mythological titan who bore the world on his shoulders) and rotates on a spike extending from the second vertebra, logically named the axis.

The two brothers had been playing a fantasy game that afternoon. They were Zulu warriors engaged in a battle to the death. Their weapons were the assegai spears that made the famed African warriors so fearsome. In this case, the boys had borrowed an old broom handle they saw discarded in a trash heap. They broke the shaft in half and painstakingly whittled each stick into a sharply pointed spear. Proud of their handiwork, they danced around the back yard of their house brandishing their spears. Then the real battle began. Standing at opposite ends of the yard, they began to throw the spears at each other. Levon missed his brother by a mile. Darren's next shot cleared his brother's head by at least four feet. Levon fired back—another embarrassing miss. Then, as Levon picked up his spear and began to run back to his base, Darren launched another shot. This time, it was straight and low—and it hit Levon in the back of his neck. He fell like a stone, crying out in pain. Darren's eyes widened and his jaw dropped. He ran to his brother. "You okay, man?" Levon just moaned. Darren ran into the house screaming.

Through intuition, intelligence, and a bit of blind luck, the family, the emergency medical technicians, and the ER staff had carefully transported Levon to the gurney where he lay, without moving the 'spear.' The resident called me STAT to the ER. Just as thunderstruck as the rest of the staff, I did a cursory neurological exam and found Levon intact. Then, I shimmied an x-ray plate under the youngster's head and brought the radiology cone to the opposite side of his head to get a film of this mess. I studied it on the x-ray screen. The density of the wood and metal-impregnated dirt that covered it allowed the homemade spear to show up darkly in the x-ray that also showed the bones of Levon's skull and spinal column. And what the picture showed sent a palpable tingle down my spine. The well-carved and sharp tip of the wooden stick had not only perfectly penetrated the membrane between the skull and the atlas, neatly missing both bones, it was pointing upward, into the medulla, and about one third of the way into the foramen magnum.

I wasn't sure why Levon wasn't dead, but I wasn't about to let him die on my rotation. I grabbed a passing intern and a medical student and instructed the intern to hold the boy's head and the student to hold the spear. They were to remain absolutely still, under pain of execution. The nurse was in charge of watching them. I called the chief resident. Arthur Day was not in a particularly humorous mood. "What do you mean a spear? A stick? A stick?! Well, pull the damned thing out. What do you mean you can't? Don't make me come down there, Tom!" But come he did, sensing that there was more here than the incompetence of a junior resident confronting an absurd situation.

The chief was struck silent as he pulled back the ER curtain. The boy, lying in a fetal position, was only mildly uncomfortable in his sedated state; the intern and medical student were immobilizing the stick, their faces frozen in concentration and tension; and his junior resident nervously biting his lower lip, pointing at the x-ray box. He glanced at the terrifying x-ray and shot a quick, approving glance at the junior resident. The chief put in a quick call to a faculty neurosurgeon, who said he was on his way.

The chief walked briskly to the waiting room, where he said a few quiet, explanatory words to Levon's parents. Then, turning to the rest of the team, he said, "Let's get him to the OR." The surgical head nurse was informed that an acute emergency required her to prepare the STAT operating room, the room that was always kept empty and ready in case of just such an emergency. The anesthesiologist readied his station as the bizarre team arrived, wheeling the patient, with intern and student still holding the patient and the spear, into the OR. The protocol for sterility had obviously gone out the window.

The anesthesiologist remained serenely quiet as he gently took Levon's arm, applied a tourniquet, quickly swabbed the arm with alcohol, and deftly inserted an IV before the child could react. In seconds, he had administered a strong sedative, and a large dose of a broad-spectrum antibiotic. It was terribly tricky but crucial to pass the breathing (endotracheal) tube without changing the patient's position. Everyone held their breath as he injected a paralytic agent that would temporarily prevent any voluntary movement, slid the laryngoscope into the boy's mouth, pulled down the jaw, and deftly inserted the flexible endotracheal tube, verifying correct placement with a few puffs of air through the Ambu bag. He nodded as he connected the tube to the ventilator and taped the tube to Levon's cheek and jaw. His breathing and circulation were now safely controlled by Joe Annis, the best young anesthesiologist in the medical center, who would later serve as a trustee of the American Medical Association. And the rest of us in the room were able to breathe again.

Now, ten hands slowly and carefully lifted the child from the gurney to the operating table, responding to the cadence of Art Day. The table had been quickly prepared with chest rolls, long rolled blankets that would support the sides of the chest while allowing the excursion of the chest and belly required for breathing. At the head of the table was the ubiquitous Mayfield head holder. While everyone held the patient absolutely still, Levon was turned prone, taped to the bed, and his head was secured in the device. Now no part of the patient would move. The only frightening vulnerability was the spear. The intern and medical student were exhausted after fifteen minutes of keeping the shaft and the head absolutely immobile. Now the head was secure, and a nurse slowly and with imperceptible transition took over control of the dirty broomstick from the sweat-drenched medical student.

It was impossible to prepare the patient's head, neck, and the stick properly. So several cups of sterilizing betadine solution were poured over the whole field. The hair around the entry wound was carefully shaved, and more betadine was poured directly over the site. After the operating field was carefully walled off with surgical towels and drapes, Day and Lansen, now scrubbed, gowned, and masked, began the work of extracting the spear from their young patient.

Using a #15 scalpel blade, a small, semilunar knife on a standard handle, we made a vertical incision from the stick toward the top of the head, and another from the stick down toward the neck, each about three inches long. We cauterized the bleeding edges of the skin, fascia (gristle), and muscle beneath; Raney clips were applied to the skin and fat beneath it. Each clip was about three quarters of an inch long and semi-circular, with an open rectangle on one side and several teeth on each part of the open "mouth" on the other side. An applier was inserted into the rectangle. When opened, the mouth stretched, enclosing an area of skin and fat. When released, the clip compressed the skin and fat, stopping all bleeding from the edge of the wound. In neurosurgery, because of the complexity of the brain and spinal cord that need to be visualized and touched, bleeding is simply not tolerated. Whether it is the Raney clip, the bipolar forceps (where a small, cauterizing current passes between only the very tips of forceps when pinched together with a blood vessel between them), the Bovie cautery (an electrified probe that burns and therefore cauterizes everything it touches, named for

Harvard biophysicist William Bovie), or more modern substances, such as blood-coagulating Avitene powder, neurosurgeons have always been obsessed with a "clean, dry" operative field.

With the field completely dry, Day placed a Weitlaner retractor, a self-retaining hinged instrument with two finger holes on one side of the hinge and two metal limbs with teeth on the other. When the finger rings are pushed together, the toothed limbs pull apart against the sides of the wound, stretching the edges. This allowed surgeons to dissect further into the depths of the wound. As the dissection progressed, the nurse holding the spear leaned her elbows on the shoulders of the two surgeons positioned on either side of the patient's neck for stability. There wasn't much of an instruction manual on this case. No one in the room had ever been in this situation before. As a matter of fact, we weren't sure that anyone had ever been in this situation before.

Amazingly, the missile had struck the neck in a perfect trajectory, piercing the skin and septum of the muscles attached to the spine so that there was no injury to the muscles or blood vessels on either side. In short, it hit a bullseye—right through the center of the back of the neck. However, Day clenched his teeth as he reached the bony base of the skull. The stick had been thrown with enough force to pierce the gristle of the neck and the membrane between the skull and the spine, but it had gone further in and was lodged securely between the two bones, having spread them apart slightly. In order to free the stick, he would have to create an empty space around it; and the only way to do that was to "nibble" away the lowest part of the skull and the top of the atlas. Both of us took turns biting tiny bits of bone circumferentially around the stick. We used Kerrison rongeurs—long shafts of metal with handles whose tips were formed into sharp little jaws that bit at an angle to the operator's hand. Each bite took only a fraction of an inch of bone, so that despite the rapid action of both residents, several breaks had to be taken while the nurse or intern holding the spear was relieved and replaced.

Finally, to the relief of the whole team, the spear was loose and there was room around it to work. However, there was another problem. The tip of the stick, still right in the middle of the back of the brain, had pierced the dura, the membrane covering the brain, and was still invisible to the surgeons. We couldn't risk pulling it, in case it was stuck to a blood vessel at the base of the brain. So, we painstakingly wheeled an operating microscope into the field. The microscope, draped in a sterile plastic wrapping, was a huge affair that added considerable heat and bulk to the whole surreal scene.

For what seemed like an eternity, we carefully dissected tiny blood vessels and wisps of meningeal tissue (the delicate membranes that cover the brain) away from the piece of wood, placing small retractors as we went to hold the vital structures in place. We were on the brainstem now, and spinal fluid continued to well up in our field of vision. But again, miraculously, the spear had not damaged any of the brain and had held to a perfect line between the two sides of the vital structure.

Finally, we could see the point of the stick. It was free from the underlying tissue. Day whispered, "Alright now, pull it out, slowly." The assistants who were holding the stick withdrew it, centimeter by centimeter, until it was out of the wound and Levon was out of harm's way. Fortunately, there was no rush of blood behind it, and the rest was anticlimax. We washed the brain and the wound copiously with an irrigating solution loaded with antibiotics. We closed the delicate dura with microscopic sutures. Then we pulled the muscle, fascia, and skin together with much stronger sutures.

The next morning on rounds, Levon greeted us with a bright smile as he was devouring his breakfast of scrambled eggs, sausage, toast, and OJ. He hadn't eaten anything in twenty-four hours, and he was famished. His dressing was clean and dry, and he had no fever. He still had the intravenous line in his arm, which was delivering regular doses of high-powered antibiotics; otherwise, you might have thought he had just had his appendix removed. Levon's family was . . . grateful doesn't quite capture their mood. They were overwhelmed with relief and giddy with delight. They thanked us over and over. Art Day and I left the room and glanced at each other in disbelief. While we were gratified that our skills had gotten the youngster through this nightmare, somewhere a higher power had determined that that spear had landed so perfectly that this would not be Levon's judgment day.

CHAPTER EIGHT

Scalped

Gainesville, Florida, is a lovely, small, southern city. It has very little in common with South Florida. There are fewer palm trees, more oak trees. In the spring and summer, it is covered with a blanket of a thousand different species and colors of flowers. In the center of North Florida, the weather is temperate, not sub-tropical, so it can be quite hot and fairly cold. During the course of my four and a half years there, it actually snowed once. Okay, it was just a dusting, perhaps a quarter of an inch of white on a sea of green. But it was snow. The terrain is relatively flat, so that, combined with the climate, it is a runner's paradise. There are nearly 12,000 running trails in the city. It has been home to some of the greatest competitive runners. Olympic champion Frank Shorter and Athletic Attic founder Jimmy Carnes were there during my era.

A true university town, Gainesville is home to the University of Florida, a land-grant college founded in 1853. Currently, there are about 130,000 residents of the city, and about 55,000 students at the college. The enormous campus is dotted with cultural and athletic facilities, making it a great place to go to school or raise a family.

One wonderful advantage of being a surgical resident at the University of Florida was that, as state employees, we were given unlimited access to the brand-spanking-new Walt Disney World. About a two-hour drive from Gainesville down I-75, the route was dotted with the white-fenced horse farms of Ocala. Closer to Orlando, our senses were bathed with the beautiful sights and scents of mile after mile of orange groves (now long gone, plowed under by the developer's blade). And my daughter learned every song in the Magic Kingdom, rode every ride a million times, and slept like a princess on every ride back to Gainesville.

It was May, and I was the second-year resident on call for the weekend. I was called STAT to the Emergency Room of Shands. As I walked into Trauma Room 1, three nurses, several technicians, and a small group of surgical residents were gathered around a small form, a three-year-old child, his clothing covered with dried blood. Several bags of IV solution were attached to clear plastic lines quickly delivering fluid to the little body. A very experienced ER nurse was starting another IV to deliver a unit of whole blood. The general surgery resident in charge nodded to me and beckoned me to the head of the bed. I wasn't quite prepared for what I saw next. A small, extremely pale, little boy lay still, apparently unconscious. The incongruous part of the picture was that he had been, unbelievably, scalped. Just like a nightmare from an old Western saga, his scalp, from the top of his forehead to the back of his head, was stripped away from the pericranium, the gristly layer that separates the skin from the skull. His ears were untouched, his forehead bruised and bloody but intact.

I took in a deep breath. "Can we reconstruct it?" The general surgery resident sounded pessimistic. I looked at the flap of skin hanging from the back of the child's head. There was an old surgical rule. If the length of a skin flap was much longer than the width where it is connected, the flap won't have enough blood supply to survive. This child's scalp looked like a grisly flag hanging from the back of his head. I shook my head. "Let's call Plastics." As with most of the other medical specialties, the university was blessed with a skilled team of pediatric plastic and reconstructive surgeons. The chief soon joined us in the ER.

Meanwhile, a loose, moist dressing was applied to the denuded skull and I had a chance to do a neurological examination. I was relieved to hear the little guy moan when I shone a light into both eyes. His pupils were round, symmetrical, and briskly narrowed to the light stimulus. Another good sign. I very gently pinched his left upper arm (the last thing I wanted to do was to cause this poor little man more pain, but I needed to know if his brain had been injured, and if so, how badly). He pulled away from the pinch and pushed my hand away. He started moving his arms and legs and began to cry. My heart was touched, but my head was relieved to see that his facial muscles moved symmetrically, and that he was looking around the room at the bright lights and all the scrub-suited adults in fear. His cognition, his thinking, appeared to be intact as well.

In a few moments, he settled back into his listless state of shock, but his vital signs were holding and his blood pressure was responding to the fluids and medications that the fast-moving ER staff provided. I watched as one of the nurses simply stood staring at her little patient, gently rubbing his arm. These women

76

were amazing. How lucky we doctors and patients were to have them care about us. The chief of plastic surgery had arrived. She carefully inspected the skin flap and edges of the skin all around the wound. She moisturized the flap with sterile saline and looked up at us. Her face was grim. "I'm going to put approximating sutures to restore the flap to the rest of the scalp, but I don't like the gray look of the skin. I don't think the flap can survive. How is he otherwise?" There were no other injuries, and, neurologically, he seemed okay. I spoke to the plastic surgeon. "Do I have time for a CAT scan?" She nodded. We quickly sped the ER gurney to the nearby CAT scanner. Unlike most kids, he didn't need to be sedated for the scan. In a few minutes, I was relieved to review the films of a normal brain. No hemorrhages, no swelling, no skull fracture. He was returned to the ER, the plastic surgeon did her work, and he was quickly taken to the pediatric ICU.

I walked slowly, with the Styrofoam cup of coffee that was always welded to my hand, into the family waiting room. Two young people slumped in their chairs. The woman was silent, vacant. The man's face was streaked with dirt and tears. Every few seconds, he buried his face in his hands, and, when he raised it again, it was contorted in agony.

"Mr. and Mrs. Buford? I'm Dr. Lansen from the neurosurgery service, and this is Dr. Maher from general surgery. Can we ask you a couple of questions?" Mrs. Buford spoke first.

"The police already asked us all about it."

"I know, but we need to know some things in order to take the best care of Ricky that we can." Neal Buford nodded a couple of times, then buried his face in his cupped hands again. Finally, he sniffed hard and looked at Bob Maher and me.

"It's all my fault," he choked. "I ran him over. I ran him over with the riding mower. I killed my boy." He shook his head, unable to comprehend his own grief.

"Tell us how it happened." Buford took a shaky sip from the cup of water his wife offered him. "I was mowing the property and Ricky was playing with Waldo, he's our dog, over by the house. God, he was thirty or forty feet away from me. I was mowing around the base of our big oak tree, and . . . I guess I got distracted." He paused again, sobbing. "I put the mower in reverse to cover a patch of grass that I missed. Then I heard and felt a dull thud and saw Waldo running away from my right rear wheel, kind of yelping. And there was my boy, lying there . . . like that. Bloody and out cold." Buford threw his head back and let out an unearthly moan unlike anything I'd ever heard before.

"Ms. Buford, how is Ricky's health?"

"Always just fine. He was a nine-pound baby. He's had some colds and sore throats, but nothing else."

"All his vaccinations up to date?"

"Yes, sir. Is he alive, doctor?"

"I know it's really tough on you both, having seen Ricky's injury, and I think he's in for a long haul. But yes, he is alive, and he doesn't seem to have any other injuries. The blow from the mower blade knocked him out and tore his scalp. But otherwise, he's going to be okay." The Bufords fell into each other's arms. Neal sobbed softly against his wife's breast. He reached a grateful hand out to me.

We checked on Ricky several times each day. At first it looked like the scalp would "take," restoring the blood supply to the skin. But that was wishful thinking. By the third day, the edges of the scalp flap turned dusky and then black. Ricky's scalp would not survive. Intravenous antibiotics had prevented an infection so far. Dr. Owens made the decision. She would perform a decisive, relatively new procedure. In the operating room, she cut off the entire scalp flap and placed a loosely sutured porcine graft over the pericranium. That's right, pig skin. And she guessed right. The graft kept the pericranium and skull beneath it moist and vital.

Over the next eighteen months, Ricky would undergo many surgeries, advancing skin flaps from the adjacent, preserved scalp a few centimeters at a time, until the entire flap was replaced with his own, hair-bearing skin. By the time he entered kindergarten, he once again had a full of head of blond, albeit short, hair. And the resilient little boy had returned to his playful, healthy self. And my love-hate relationship with pediatric neurosurgery had begun. The surgery was interesting and satisfying, but the suffering of the children and their parents was unbearable.

When I left the ER at Shands after taking care of Ricky Buford that first day, stepping into the sunshine and smelling the bouquet of flowers that was Gainesville, I took a deep breath. And as I walked around the corner leading to my apartment, and saw my little girl, bronzed and blonde, playing in the swimming pool, I picked her up and gave her an extra tender hug.

CHAPTER NINE

I Have No Idea

The first two years of my residency had flown by and I was shocked at how much information I had absorbed just by being in the constant company of smart men and the relentless Socratic supervision of Dr. Rhoton. It quickly became apparent that Dr. Rhoton's teaching method was quite simple. Ask a question, receive the correct answer, ask a harder question. Ask a question, get the wrong answer, move up the ladder of resident experience until you got the right answer. No one gets the right answer? Gently suggest that everyone come back with the right answer tomorrow. Of course, being on the receiving end of this exercise wasn't just challenging—it was terrifying. Every night, after an intense day of constant activity, I'd fall asleep in my scrubs over a book or journal, trying to get the right answers. Next morning, I would hope that he had forgotten about the question. But he never did. And knowing that he always had the answer but would never tell me whether I was right or wrong was at once frustrating and infuriating. Ah, but when I knew the correct answer to one of those obtuse questions;

well, it made it all worthwhile. And, remarkably, those moments happened more frequently as I climbed the ladder of residency by reading, drilling, and osmosis; I began to learn the extraordinary world of brain science.

At night, we sometimes topped off our long day with a group psychotherapy visit to the Purple Porpoise. Then it was home for a quick dinner and an hour or two of trying to keep my eyes open to read a chapter of Youmans's *Neurological Surgery*, the enormous three-volume standard textbook of neurosurgery. We were expected not just to read it but to learn it. We were also expected to read other relevant background texts, such as Merritt's *Neurology*, several other texts in ancillary specialties, such as *Neuroradiology*, *Neuropathology*, and *Neuroophthalmology*. And, of course, we were expected to be current on the three major monthly neurosurgical journals—*The Journal of Neurosurgery*, *Neurosurgery*, and *Surgical Neurology*. Every week, we would be assigned a journal article or two to discuss at our "journal club." The peer pressure was almost as tough as Dr. Rhoton's questioning. You could always tell who had thoroughly read the week's article.

Today, neurosurgery rotations are usually quite regimented. But in the 1970s, at least at the University of Florida, the rotations were determined by the faculty, with the ultimate decisions made by Dr. Rhoton. There was a general structure. My residency lasted for four and a half years, with the residents in our program training from four to five years, depending on the needs of the program and the individual. Now, the average is six to eight years, always including a full research year (remember my comment in the prologue about neurosurgeons always being surgeons and scientists?). My residency consisted of thirty-nine months of neurosurgery, three months of neurology, three months of neuroradiology, three months of neuropathology, and six months of research. The general pattern of our neurosurgical training was three months at a time at the university hospital (Shands Teaching Hospital) or at the Veterans' Administration Hospital, with more time spent at Shands than at the VA.

In addition to evaluating and taking care of patients in the emergency room, the surgical wards, and the operating room, our learning experience was intense. There were daily resident rounds (with the senior residents teaching the junior residents, interns, and medical students) and attending rounds (with the faculty teaching the residents), weekly grand rounds and the journal club; and, of course, all the residents would gather each Wednesday morning for an early breakfast with Dr. Rhoton at the VA cafeteria. Dr. Rhoton would always enjoy a hearty breakfast as he asked clinical questions in rapid fire in his usual style, never acknowledging whether the answer given was correct or not and moving from the junior to the chief resident with each set of questions. While he smiled over his scrambled eggs, I could barely manage to nervously sip a cup of coffee, waiting for the next question to be directed at me. But the learning was constant and cumulative. By June of my second year, I knew every one of those brain arteries that had seemed so mysterious to me that first July Saturday.

My third year began at Shands. Each morning, we would start our rounds in the "Peds" ICU. We would move through the pediatric patients, the sickest and most vulnerable, then the adults. Bill McGavran was the chief resident at Shands, and Warren Wilson was his senior assistant resident. I was now the resident, and Dick Lister and Richard Jackson were my juniors. After rounds, we would split up. Bill and Warren off to the OR, Richard and Dick to the wards to do the work assigned on rounds ("tapping" the ventricles of the premature babies; performing spinal taps; changing dressings; working up new patients; cleaning up cases that were partly worked up in the ER the night before). I would either make rounds with attending surgeons on their patients or go to the OR and assist in surgery. I was now getting into the operating room with some regularity. The university hospital was very busy, and, while the chief resident was generally operating with Dr. Rhoton in one room, the senior resident was often assisting one of the other attending surgeons. Sometimes a third room would open up, or McGavran or Wilson would have to perform some other duty and I would be called in to first-assist. I began to learn the fundamentals of neurosurgery. I was always somehow tired and exhilarated at the same time. My constitution had trouble coping with the hours and the workload but my attention—indeed, my entire being—was riveted to the world unfolding before me.

Alice Baker was sixteen, pretty, and a total enigma. She had been transferred to the university hospital from a small regional hospital about a hundred miles away. Neurologically, and in every other way, Alice was a normal, teenage girl. She did seem a little quiet and perhaps overly calm . . . for someone who could remember essentially nothing about her life. It seems that Alice had gone for a swim with some of her friends at a nearby cool spring. The next morning, her mother asked her what was going on at school that day. "Ah have no ahdea," she said, in her lilting southern drawl. Her mother smiled and asked if she was going to do anything with her friends that afternoon. "Ah have no ahdea." Alice smiled with a vacant kind of stare that startled her mother. "Stop teasing,

Alice." The same vague, careless stare. "Don't be fresh, Alice." The mindless, smiling stare. Like a zombie. Three hours later, after a thorough physical and neurological examination at the emergency room, with much head-scratching and specialty consultation, the doctors at Apopka called the ER at the University of Florida.

Twenty-four hours later, Alice sat serenely on her bed at Shands, nonplussed by her situation or her rather drab hospital gown, and smiled at the group of neurosurgery residents surrounding her.

"What's your name, miss?"

"Alice. Alice Baker."

"How old are you, Alice?"

"Sixteen."

"Where do you live?"

"I have no idea."

"What day is this?"

"I have no idea."

"Where are we now?"

"I have . . . no . . . idea." The smile was simple, the answer honest.

Over the next three days, Alice Baker was subjected to a sophisticated diagnostic *blitzkrieg*. She was examined by pediatricians, neurologists, neurosurgeons, neuroophthalmologists, endocrinologists, and psychiatrists. She had a CAT scan, an EEG, and an angiogram (an x-ray study of the blood vessels of her brain). At the end of the day, she may as well not have left Apopka. Alice was a completely normal young girl . . . who couldn't remember a thing about herself or her life except her name and her age. It was clear that her amnesia and her complete lack of an emotional response to it—she wasn't frightened, not even upset, that she was in a strange place and couldn't remember a thing—were obviously and terribly abnormal. But there was no physical, metabolic, or psychological factor that could be identified that had anything to do with this. She was simply detached, and blissfully ignorant of her detachment.

Actually, it was we who were ignorant. About ten days after her admission to the hospital, the fog began to lift for Alice. First, she asked for her mother. Then, for an explanation as to why she wasn't in Apopka. Then, had she missed her English test, etc.— until everything came back. She never seemed to acknowledge how very weird this whole episode had been. She simply accepted this lapse in her life and went back to being Alice Baker, high school junior. Years later, we would learn more about Transient Global Amnesia, although it remains somewhat mysterious. Some feel it is a form of epilepsy (although three days of monitoring Alice's brain waves yielded no abnormalities), or a migraine phenomenon, or a kind of TIA (transient ischemic attack—a fleeting loss of blood supply to the brain), or the result of trauma. Whatever the cause, TGA usually disappears in a day or two, although it sometimes lasts for weeks. One interesting association is that, occasionally, it happens after exposure to cold water. Neuroscience can be baffling, right, Alice? I have no idea.

CHAPTER TEN

Vascular Malformation

At the beginning of my third year, like all of my resident family, I got a much-deserved break from the intensity of the surgical rotations. I first rotated off-service to the neurology department. My role was that of mid-level resident. This gave me a chance to learn about the non-surgical diseases of the brain, spinal cord, and peripheral nerves and to share some of my surgical insights with the neurology residents. My rotation contained not only patient care but time trying to master the mysteries of the electroencephalogram—the EEG—which gives clues to diseases by the pattern of brain waves the patient emits. These signals can demonstrate anything from a section of the brain with quiet waves as the result of damage from a stroke, increased and erratic waves from the irritation of a brain tumor or wild, rhythmic waves announcing an epileptic seizure. It got so that I could understand these patterns rather well, but I could never really master the electromyogram or the nerve conduction study. These waves could be simply observed or they could be generated by a gentle shock administered through a needle electrode. (Some patients might disagree about the "gentleness" of the shock.) These studies help to determine whether a problem arose from a pinched or damaged nerve near the spinal cord, a more peripheral nerve in a limb, or a diseased muscle (such as in the dreadful childhood degenerative disease, muscular dystrophy).

The bread and butter of the neurology service fell into three categories: strokes, seizures (usually idiopathic—unexplained—in children and caused by tumors in adults), and degenerative diseases, like multiple sclerosis or amyotrophic lateral sclerosis (ALS or Lou Gehrig's Disease). Multiple sclerosis often attacks young people, particularly young women, and its vicious plaques (areas of inflammation and destruction) can be large or small and can occur anywhere in the brain or spinal cord. Tremendous progress has been made in the treatment of MS since the days of my training, and its prognosis is much less grim. Another silver lining in MS is the fact that it can be remitting—sometimes the plaques gradually improve, along with the symptoms, and sometimes the disease simply stops. ALS, on the other hand, more common in older men, always begins with destruction in the upper spinal cord, ascending into the brainstem. It begins with painless wasting of the muscles of the arms and worsens until it impairs the ability to swallow and even to breathe. It is usually fatal in a year or two.

I quickly learned that, unlike my earlier experience with psychiatry, the science of neurology was deep and well-developed, with a long intellectual tradition that reached back more than a hundred years to Paul Broca (the French neuroanatomist who began to map what regions of the brain were responsible for what activities), John Hughlings Jackson (an English neurologist whose seminal observations were the basis of our understanding of epilepsy), and Weir Mitchell (the American Civil War doctor who learned about peripheral nerve injuries from the scores of amputees he treated). As in other fields, we were blessed with excellent teachers at Florida. Three especially come to mind. Bob Watson was a teacher's teacher. Calm and bright, he knew the answer to every question. He later became dean of educational affairs at the medical college. B.J. Wilder directed neurology at the VA. He was an easygoing, friendly man, and smart as a new coat of paint. A world-renowned epileptologist, he was an important contributor to the new generation of seizure medicines. And, of particular importance to the neurosurgery residents, he also owned the Purple Porpoise (although I never once saw him at the place). And then there was Ken Heilman. Ken, a towering intellect has given us some of our most important concepts of the understanding of memory, behavior, and speech, and their disorders.

I was surrounded by a great group of neurology residents: Anne Lowell, a descendant of the Lowells of Harvard, including the poet Amy Lowell; Robin Gilmore, terribly bright and irrepressibly witty; and Steve DeKosky, who would go on to chair neurology at the University of Pittsburgh, where he devoted his career to the study of dementia. Steve also was one of the first scientists to define Post-Traumatic Encephalopathy (PTE), the tragic consequence of brain injuries especially seen in athletes and veterans. But neurology was not for me. It was too . . . passive. There was no action, no intervention. It required patience and circumspection, two virtues that I must have missed when the good Lord was parceling them out.

Ted Barrett was thirty-four years old. He had experienced his first seizure about ten years before. He was started on Dilantin, an anticonvulsant, at that time. But he was neurologically normal and had a very limited workup. After about a year, he stopped taking the medicine. He was a big guy, dark and handsome. His young wife was quiet, friendly, and absolutely beautiful. Ted had started in his family business after college and was doing well when one afternoon, he bolted straight upright at his desk, fell to the floor, stiffened into an arched position, and flailed helplessly for about three minutes. His terrified staff called for an ambulance as he gradually stopped jerking and became quiet and relaxed. He was unconscious for several minutes. When he awakened, he was confused and disoriented.

In the hospital, the neurologist discovered that his EEG, a test that measures the pattern of brain waves, was very abnormal. Much of the left side of his brain showed depressed brain activity with occasional spikes indicating that he would soon have another seizure. Clearly, there was something very wrong happening in the left side of Ted's brain. There was no CT scanner in his regional community hospital, so he was transferred to Gainesville for a workup.

The CT wasn't hard to interpret. Two-thirds of the left side of his brain was replaced by a dark, wormy, mass—an arteriovenous malformation. Ted had been born with the malformation, which probably started as a small area where the tiny arteries and veins were directly connected. That is, in that little area, he had been born without the tiny connecting capillaries and microscopic blood vessels that slow the transition between the fast-moving arterial blood that bring nutrition and oxygen to the brain substance and the slow-moving venous blood that brings the "used" blood back to the heart. At first, this hadn't caused any problems. But the malformation gradually grew by recruiting more and more of the local blood vessels, increasing the thickness of some, dilating and thinning others. As the weird tangle of vessels grew, it began to encroach on normal brain tissue. This was particularly treacherous in Ted's case because he was right-handed, so that the movement of his right side, and especially his speech, were in danger. In retrospect, Ted and Connie had noticed that he had been getting a little "clumsy" over the past few years, and that he seemed to be having more trouble with finding the right words. They had chalked it up to stress.

Ted had two more seizures during the next week of his hospitalization until they were brought under control with a combination of Dilantin and phenobarbital. Once he had recovered to his usual state, we could tell on examination that he had some weakness of his right arm and hand and that he was dysphasic—he could speak but had trouble finding and expressing the correct words.

Ted Barrett next underwent an angiogram. Dr. Ron Quisling, a friendly and talented neuroradiologist, passed a catheter into the femoral artery in his groin and threaded it up to the arteries that fed Ted's brain. He would inject dye into each of the four major arteries, two carotids and two vertebrals. The vertebrals, which run up in two parallel channels in the cervical spine, give nourishment to the brainstem, which is responsible for the basic functions of life, and the cerebellum, the organ of coordination. The carotids, lying in the front of the neck, feed the cerebral cortex, the larger part of the brain responsible for all of our higher functions. Through carefully closing different arteries for a few moments while injecting others, Ron could not only determine the flow of each artery but how much brain territory was supported by shared blood supply, the "collateral circulation." This was important because sometimes when an artery is closed off, for example in a stroke, the other arteries can take over and prevent starvation of brain tissue, with its catastrophic outcome.

Unfortunately for Ted Barrett, the phenomenon of collateral circulation was going to work in the opposite way for him. Not only was much of the circulation downstream from his left carotid artery involved in the giant tangle of abnormal, serpiginous blood vessels that had destroyed much of the brain tissue they were meant to feed, but the malformation, the AVM, had begun to recruit abnormal vessels from the right carotid and the left vertebral circulations. This meant that we might try to remove the AVM from his brain by closing off the blood vessels of the left carotid circulation, only to find that it still survived using the blood supply from the opposite carotid and vertebral arteries.

Reviewing the angiogram, we recognized that this was what ten years later would be known as a Spetzler-Martin Grade 5 AVM. Grade 5, according to the grading system devised by two noted vascular neurosurgeons, is extremely dangerous and often inoperable. In later years, techniques would be developed that would enable "interventional" neurosurgeons and neuroradiologists to inject substances into tiny vessels near these malformations that would harden and often "starve" the AVM of its feeding vessels at serial sessions until it was harmless enough to be removed surgically or even treated with highly focused radiation. But those developments would advance too late to help Ted. And it is doubtful that even today, such a complex malformation could be substantially reduced interventionally.

Dr. Francisco Garcia Bengochea was one of those people everyone respected, as a physician and a man. Born to privilege in Cuba, he had been sent to the United States for medical education and graduated as chief resident in neurosurgery from the Columbia Presbyterian Neurological Institute in New York in 1947. He returned to Havana, where he became a key resource for neurosurgical care throughout the Caribbean and Central and South America. The Cuba of Fidel Castro was to prove brutal to the Garcia family, and the Garcias fled to the United States within six months of the revolution. Cuba's loss was to be America's gain. Garcia joined Dr. Lamar Roberts at the University of Florida in developing the first division of neurosurgery in the history of the school.

In addition to his superb surgical technique and intellectual skills, Dr. Garcia offered one unique attribute that was of incredible value to our residents. He was an absolute gentleman. In my four and a half years at the university, I never ever heard him raise his voice, curse, or lose his temper. He was courteous, even courtly, to all patients and their families, regardless of their station in life. When calling him at two or three in the morning to discuss an emergency case, I would invariably start with, "Dr. Garcia, I'm sorry to bother you at this hour," and his invariable response would be, "Tom, you do not bother me. It's never a bother."

Sometimes, Garcia would even wear an obstinate patient out with courtesy. Many times, I would accompany him to his outpatient teaching clinic, where I would do the initial evaluation and he would then discuss the case with me. We would then meet with the patient to present a plan. Inevitably, there would be occasional patients who really had nothing wrong but were convinced that they had some awful brain disease. After gently reassuring him or her that everything was going to be alright, the occasional psychosomatic patient would refuse to believe him and demand that he do more tests, give more medicine, do an operation. At this point, Garcia would say with extreme gentility and kindness, "Madame, I'm very sorry that there is no more that I have to offer you neurosurgically at this time," tugging gently at his ever-present pipe.

The disgruntled patient would then say, "Do you mean there is nothing that can be done for me?"

"No, I'm afraid there is nothing that I can do for you *neurosurgically* at this time."

"So, I need a different specialist?"

"No, there's nothing *I* can do neurosurgically for you."

"Then I need to see another neurosurgeon."

"No, there's nothing I can do neurosurgically for you."

Each repetition would emphasize a different part of the message:

'offer' . . . 'neurosurgically' . . . 'I' . . . Finally, the baffled patient would see that there was no point in pursuing the conversation further. "It was a pleasure meeting you, madame."

After lengthy consultations with the entire faculty, Dr. Garcia met with Connie and Ted. In his calmest and most caring manner, he told them that surgery was not an option for Ted. Sacrificing the major artery to his brain would probably leave him dead or devastated, and still might not even be successful in removing the AVM. The only circumstance that would bring him to surgery would be a hemorrhage into the brain.

The Barretts met this news with grace and optimism. Then they would simply go home and live their lives as if Ted didn't have this awful thing. Who knows? Maybe nothing further would happen. Garcia smiled and gently patted Ted's shoulder. "You are doing the right thing."

Unfortunately, as I was to learn many times over the next forty years, life in the arena of neurosurgery can be very cruel. About a month after Christmas, the chief resident, Warren Wilson, got a call from the ER. Ted Barrett was back. When Warren and I examined him, it was clear that we weren't witnessing another seizure. He was sleepy, expressively aphasic (unable to form speech), and his entire right side was weak. Connie sat nearby, dazed and distant. "We had a good month," she said to no one in particular.

An emergency CT scan told the story quickly. There was a fairly large blood clot deep in the left side of his brain, putting pressure on the rest of the brain and causing a "mass effect" on the right side of his brain and the brainstem. Dr. Garcia joined us in minutes.

"My dear young woman, I'm so sorry to say that we have only two choices—to leave this alone, which will almost certainly mean we will lose him, or to try and remove the AVM, which may have the same effect."

"I know Ted would want to go for it."

Two hours later, we were in the operating room, Ted was anesthetized and covered entirely in blue paper drapes, with the exception of an adhesive plastic window covering the area of his shaved scalp where we would make our incision.

The incision was large, shaped like a question mark, coming up from just in front of his left ear, then curving back almost to the back of his head, then curving up and running to the top of his head and straight forward to his forehead. We needed to expose the brain all around the AVM, not just over it. After we applied Rainey clips to the edges of the cut skin, Warren made seven burr holes in the skull, three along the left side just off the midline, two over the occipital bone, and two over the temporal lobe, just above and in front of the ear. He then connected the holes with a high-speed drill, creating a large bone flap, which we then very gingerly removed from the brain beneath. The dura mater, an opaque membrane, covers the brain. It is usually white, but Ted's dura had an ominous reddish-blue tinge.

Dr. Garcia stepped in, clad in headlight and loupes (high-power magnifying glasses—we would later bring in the operating microscope, once we had the lay of the land). His hands were rock-steady, and he brought his usual gravitas and calmness into the field. Using fine forceps and microscissors (seven inches long, with tiny blades closed by squeezing the handle of the tool), he made a tiny cut in the dura as far away from the center of the AVM as possible, then proceeded to extend it all the way around the abnormality until it was a flap held by a small pedicle. He delicately dissected the dural flap off of the brain and placed it over a moist gauze. What greeted us next was one of the most daunting sights any neurosurgeon can behold. The brain was swollen and pushing against the cut edges of the dura, and at the center of the incision was a vast tangle of matted, winding blood vessels coming right to the surface of the brain. Some of the vessels were thin, hard, and pulsatile. Others were dark purple and huge. Others still were dilated and paper-thin. We could see bright red blood swirling through the walls of this latter type. The AVM almost looked like it had a personality, and the message was clear . . . it was furious.

Dr. Garcia applied his bipolar forceps, the delicate coagulating device, to a one-centimeter area of what appeared to be fairly normal brain near the margin of the AVM. He then passed a thin metal probe to a depth of about two inches, where he knew the blood clot lay. He put a glass syringe to the end of the probe and removed about two ounces of dark red blood. The swollen edges of the brain immediately pulled away from the dura, and the brain relaxed just enough to resume its pulsations. The anesthesiologist had already given Ted the diuretic Mannitol to fight the swelling. Garcia locked his hands, arms, and shoulders into position and began to coagulate and cut each tiny "feeder"—the blood vessels leading into the AVM—gradually starving it of its fatal fuel. As Warren and I squirted small amounts of saline onto the forceps, so that they wouldn't stick and tear the blood vessels, and suctioned the irrigation away, so that the surgeon could keep a clear vision of the field, Garcia worked away, cutting literally hundreds of arteries until the AVM gradually began to lose its swelling and angry red pulsations. We continued this way, without stopping . . . for the next twenty-six hours. Warren would step in at intervals and coagulate and cut abnormal vessels, suctioning the dead brain tissue at the margins of the malformation. Every three or four hours, one of us would step away to urinate and grab a quick cup of coffee. But our entire beings, including the sixty-two-year-old Francisco Garcia Bengochea, were lost in trying to get this invading monster out of Ted Barrett's brain and give him a chance to get back to Connie, and to his life.

At hour twenty, the brain began to assume something of a normal appearance. It was pulsatile again, and the angry blood vessels were starting to look like the normal arteries and veins that we see on the surface of the brain. We had gradually defined the margin of the massive, roughly oval AVM, protecting the surface of the adjacent, normal brain with scores of half-inch cottonoids (pieces of flat, processed cotton a half inch wide and three inches long), which absorbed blood and fluid and kept the normal part of Ted's brain moist and protected. At about hour twenty-two, we were operating near the base of the AVM, deep in the posterior parietal lobe.

"There's the first feeder, men," Dr. Garcia whispered, almost to himself. A large, thickened artery, which looked the size of someone's arm under the microscope, pulsing firmly, entered the base of the malformation. He worked patiently around the entire circumference of the vessel, making sure that it didn't have a branch that went on to nourish normal brain. No, it was just dedicated to growing this terrible alien in our patient's brain.

Dr. Garcia vigorously coagulated the monster, placed two metal clips across the artery to close it, then cut across the artery between the clips. The malformation immediately shrunk by about a third, and the working end of the occluded artery pulsed harmlessly for a while, then closed off completely, lying flaccid at the bed of the AVM.

The most harrowing part of the operation was complete, but we were far from finished. We knew from studying the angiogram that there were two more "feeders," one coming into the back or posterior part of the AVM from the vertebral circulation, and another, more superficial, feeding the part of the malformation closest to the fissure that divides the two halves of the brain. This artery, like the one we had just cut, arose from the carotid circulation.

We would attack the vertebral feeder next. Time was important for two reasons. As we worked around to the back of the AVM, it began to slowly enlarge again, as the two remaining feeders took over the work of their dead comrade. Also, Ted Barrett's brain had been artificially sedated for a long time now; and, although his brain waves and vital signs were being carefully monitored, the brain was only so resilient.

After about an hour, we found the deep posterior vertebral feeder. Dissection was easier now, as the more relaxed AVM could be retracted toward the front of the brain, giving us easier access to the abnormal plane between it and the normal brain. The second feeder was almost as large and vicious as the first, but it met the same fate. Finally, the AVM, now about four cm in diameter, was held by a pedicle, like a peninsula of land, to the final, medial feeder. It was isolated, dissected, and cut. The malformation was removed and sent off to the pathologist. There was a little venous oozing on the surface of the brain where the malformation had grown, but this stopped with irrigation. The entire cavity was coated with a thin layer of Surgicel, a thin net-like oxidized cellulose polymer which discourages bleeding. Then, with three audible sighs of relief, we filled the cavity with saline and sat down in the operating room for the next half hour to make sure there wasn't another "occult," or hidden feeder waiting to erupt.

We silently closed the dura with a tiny, running suture, replaced the bone flap with wire sutures through small holes drilled at apposing locations of the skull and flap, sutured the cut edges of the temporal muscle, the galea (a grisly layer of fascia beneath the skin), and then the skin itself. We swathed Mr. Barrett's head in a large turban of surgical gauze and took him to the recovery room, still intubated and sedated. We would let the anesthesia team stabilize him, then would get a CT and an angiogram to check for blood, brain swelling, and any residual hidden evidence of malformation.

In about half an hour, we were called urgently to the recovery room. Ted had been rock stable until five minutes ago, then his blood pressure shot up and his pupils dilated. They were fixed, with no reaction to light. A deep pinch to the skin on each side of his chest brought no reaction despite the anesthesiologist's stopping the sedation. "Put him down again," Warren Wilson instructed the anesthesiologist as we wheeled the gurney to CT at a near-run. We watched in despair as the CT "slices" emerged, showing a clot that had refilled the entire surgical cavity and squeezed the adjacent brain.

In fifteen minutes, we were back in the OR. We removed the dressing, quickly removed the bone flap, opened the dura, and suctioned out the blood clot. There was brisk bleeding deep in the posterior right base of the cavity. We suctioned a small area of what appeared to be normal brain. Now the bleeding erupted, filling the cavity in seconds. With Warren and I manning two large suctions against cottonoids held against the bleeding site, Dr. Garcia, using the bipolar forceps and a third suction, gradually isolated an artery. It fed an occult part of the malformation that wasn't in the primary cavity. It was a branch of the vertebral feeder that took off farther away from the main part of the malformation—a newer child of the beast. It had not been visible on the angiogram. Garcia was able to find the artery, coagulate and clip it, and remove the last bit of the AVM, which ended as only about a half-inch ball of dark, coagulated tissue.

We went through the ritual of waiting for further bleeding,

then grimly closing the wound again. We found Connie Barrett sitting in the family room just outside the operating room. She was calm. The nurses had called her several times during the first operation, and Dr. Garcia had stepped out once to keep her posted on our progress. He had also told her why we had to go back in. "My dear, we must let the anesthetic wear off. He has been sedated for a long time. But I don't see anything that gives me much hope . . . for his survival." Connie bent her head, covered her eyes with her left hand, and tightly squeezed Dr. Garcia's right hand.

In forty-eight hours, we knew that there was no sign of neurological function, by examination or EEG, despite a "clean" CT. After a discussion with Connie Barrett, we turned off the ventilator. She stood next to the bed holding his cold hand as his cardiac tracing slowed, tapered, and stopped. My heart was breaking. Dr. Garcia understood. He had felt this wrenching feeling many times. He put his hand on my shoulder, without a word. We had known from the start that Ted Barrett had been dealt a terrible hand with this AVM and that his chances for survival had always been negligible. But we had all become so invested, and tried so hard to save this young man with such a future, such a beautiful family, such a . . . tragedy.

Years later, I would operate on a beautiful, young woman, an aesthetist who had collapsed suddenly after experiencing a piercing headache. She entered the emergency room paralyzed on the right side of her body, unconscious, and, when stimulated, unable to speak. A CAT scan showed a large blood clot in her left thalamus, deep in the dominant hemisphere. We injected contrast and repeated the scan—there were the telltale serpentine trails of blood vessels that told me it was a ruptured vascular malformation.

Margaret Cappelleri was sinking fast. Her blood pressure was climbing higher and higher, her responsiveness disappearing by the minute. The hospital where I was asked to see her was a community hospital. I wished that she had been taken to our medical center. I wished that I had time to do an angiogram that would carefully map the villain. I wished a lot of things. But that wasn't the hand that Margaret and I had been dealt.

I had a conference with her fiancé and her parents. "If I do nothing, Margaret will almost certainly die in a few hours or a few days. If I perform a brain surgery on her, she may survive or not. I may not be able to remove the source of the bleeding. If she survives, she will almost certainly have severe problems; probably paralysis of the right side of her body, and loss of much of her ability to think and to speak." Margaret's mother was crying, her father stiff and wordless. John Marchi, her fiancé, didn't hesitate. "Doc, what's the question? Of course. You have to operate. Right now." Her parents nodded.

Twenty minutes later, Margaret was in the operating room, anesthetized and intubated. After hyperventilation, Mannitol, and steroids to partly relax the brain, I performed the craniotomy quickly, getting down through her brain with retractor blades and suction. The lessons I had learned from operating on Ted Barrett years before, and many others since, guided me through the task of slowly decompressing the blood clot, knowing that the reduction in pressure would release the torrent of blood lurking in the AVM.

My assistant and the scrub nurse caught their breath as a rocket of blood shot out of the wound. I put a cottonoid pledget into the bleeding cavity and applied suction. I slowly backed the pledget away from the thickened, angry artery until I could see the bleeding source under the microscope. I coagulated it, and the bleeding stopped. But the work had just begun. That artery and two large veins that had become hybrid vessels feeding the malformation enlarged and pulsed wildly. I covered them with cottonoids, which we kept moistened with irrigating fluid. I followed the artery to its source, coagulating and cutting the parent artery. I could only pray that the artery was not "en passant," going on to supply expensive cortical real estate downstream.

The pulsations of the vessels lessened slightly. I repeated this procedure a dozen times until the vessels became normal-appearing veins again, the brain swelling diminished, and the blood clot was completely removed. I then used my suction and cautery to dissect around the outside of the malformation. There was a yellowish layer that I sought that would demarcate the lesion from the normal brain. Once in this layer, I followed it around the malformation, finally coming to a last pedicle of abnormal vessels, then coagulating and cutting them. The malformation was now a shriveled raisin that I removed from the brain and sent for pathological analysis. I filled the bed of the clot with saline and waited . . .

Margaret gradually regained consciousness. Although she remained both intubated and ventilated, her eyes clearly showed us that she was aware. The next day, she underwent an angiogram that looked good, with the exception of a tiny questionable "blush" that might be an abnormal vessel. This would bear careful watching. Two days later, her blood pressure shot up again and she became poorly responsive. An emergency CAT scan showed that there was further bleeding. After a brief conversation with her family, I rushed her back to the OR. Because she was already intubated, anesthesia took only moments; and with the cranium recently opened, I was back in the bed of the hemorrhage in minutes. This time, it was clear that there was one small area of bleeding. The microscope led me to the small abnormal artery, which I coagulated. Again, I observed the bed of the clot carefully, filling and refilling the cavity with saline. It stayed clear, and I closed the wound.

Two days later, Margaret was "extubated"—the breathing tube removed. She smiled at me as I walked in to see her on rounds. She had some slight movement of her right side. Her speech was very garbled, but she looked beautiful. I whispered a prayer of gratitude. Within a week, she was ready for discharge to rehab, and her CAT scan showed no further bleeding or swelling. At first, my pessimistic nature made me assume that, with her severe disability, her fiancé would soon move on. But, as so often, I was proven gratifyingly wrong. John and Margaret stuck together. They married. They have become my friends, and we have communicated every Christmas for almost thirty years. Margaret has a remarkable sense of humor. Although she walks with a limp and has some trouble finding her words, she remains self-deprecating and charming. Never count a good woman out.

CHAPTER ELEVEN

Amoeba

Billy Shepard was an absolutely normal, active, thirteen-year-old seventh grader in a rural northern Florida town one week. The next week he was dead.

He had been transferred to the university hospital from a local facility after his parents found him confused and complaining of a stiff neck. After he had a seizure in the ER, he was rushed to Shands. A CT scan showed a lot of swelling of his frontal lobes. A careful spinal tap was performed with a small-gauge needle. Removing a lot of spinal fluid through a large needle could shift the balance between the high pressure in his brain and the low pressure in his spine and cause the brain to literally herniate, with the cerebellum and brainstem being drawn into the upper spinal canal, where they would be compressed, resulting in a neurological catastrophe and death.

The spinal fluid showed high protein, a sign of an abnormal process in the neurological tissue or its membranes (meninges). The glucose level was very low, consistent with meningitis. But there were only a few inflammatory white cells; and no bacteria were seen or grew in culture.

Billy was started on a panel of broad-spectrum antibiotics, but he continued to deteriorate beyond control. He was given massive doses of steroids to combat his brain swelling. His seizures became more frequent despite large amounts of anticonvulsants. His heart rhythm became abnormal and his fever rose—102, 103, 105. His neck was rigid, and his entire body was in spasm. Gradually, Billy slipped into a coma, and, in five days, despite the efforts of the best minds at this major university medical center, he died.

I was not "on service" at this time. In this third year of my residency, I was rotating through the ancillary specialties that help round out a neurosurgeon's education. I would still be responsible for my on-call nights in the emergency room, but I would hand off all patient responsibilities in the morning after being on-call. Then I would spend my days working on the service that would supplement my knowledge—neuroradiology, neurology, neuro-ophthalmology, research or, at this time in my residency, neuropathology.

Bob Schimpf was the chief of neuropathology at the university. He was a well-rounded, athletic guy with a full life. He loved to sail, and I joined him one Sunday afternoon for a fast, hard sail in the Gulf of Mexico. I discovered that afternoon that clinging to a forty-foot sailboat and racing through the wind with its mast bent at 30 degrees from vertical was not a positive experience for me. I emerged green and moderately embarrassed, as Bob explained that it wasn't unusual and I should join them again when the spirit moved me. I thanked him and demurred. Board-certified in pathology and neurology, Schimpf's knowledge of neuropathology was encyclopedic. Athleticism and the outdoor life being his first passion, Bob would later leave the University of Florida for Kalispell, Montana where he would practice neurology. Why? He had tired of sailing and wanted to perfect his skiing.

It was a beautiful though slightly stifling Gainesville summer day when Billy Shepard's lifeless body was brought to the neuropathology lab. Dr. Schimpf and I were gowned, gloved and masked. Unsure of the nature of the infection that had killed this boy, we were taking no chances. After carefully positioning the body, Bob made an incision over the top of the entire scalp, from just in front of the left ear to just in front of the right. He used a Bard Parker #10 surgical blade to dissect the scalp from the surface layer of the skull, the pericranium. Both dismayed by and respectful of the tragic situation in which we found ourselves, neither of us was in a talking mood. Using a kind of power saw, he then made a cut incorporating the entire thickness of the skull, all the way around the head. With osteotomes, or sharp chisels, we pried the skull cap loose and removed it.

What we saw that June afternoon was horrifying. The dura, the brain's firm covering membrane, was depressed and slack in the front of the brain. With a surgical forceps and scissors, Schimpf grasped a small area of the frontal dura, snipped a small portion, then made a large transverse incision, folding it down toward the eyes. As we peered into the incision, we saw that the frontal lobes were . . . gone. They were liquefied, putrefied, completely destroyed. There was really no tissue to sample. Bob took a surgical swab and dipped it into the lake of purulence, applying it to a glass slide. After staining it with a reagent, he fixed the slide and placed it on the microscope stage.

Under low power, there appeared to be a fairly uniform field of cells, some inflammatory, many more of a nature more difficult to identify. Here and there were wisps of mostly destroyed neural tissue. Schimpf took a more careful look under high power. Using the observer eyepiece, I watched him focus in a large field of similar looking cells. They were unusual. Shaped like ugly, irregular triangles, they had microcysts inside, pseudopods reaching out in different directions and a kind of thin, feathery tail—Amoebae! They were everywhere, and in every field there seemed to be hundreds of them. Bob fixed more of the tissue for further staining and electron microscopy.

The next day, we met in the lab early. Bob hadn't gotten much sleep. He was still poring through his microbiology sources when he whispered something, then nearly shouted it. "Naegleria! I've never seen it before. Let's find out something about it." We went online to Medlars, the new university online resource for publications. After a couple of hours, we had learned a fair amount. Naegleria was an amoeba with pseudopods, extensions of its single walled cell that could propel it in different directions in warm, fresh water. There was only one form that was harmful to humans—Naegleria fowleri. Of course, this could be an opportunistic infection; that is, something else may have killed Billy, and this bug just jumped on the bandwagon. We'd have to do more homework. Bob needed to speak to the parents.

After explaining to the Shepards that, although there was nothing we could do to bring Billy back or ease their loss, if we could find out what had happened to him, it might help another young boy in the future. They kindly agreed to answer our questions. No, they couldn't think of anything unusual. Billy had been as healthy as a horse. In fact, he never caught colds or the flu or anything else. Had he mentioned any contact with raccoons or dogs or bats in the past few months (rabies)? How about a recent rash (measles herpetic encephalitis)? Had he fallen and struck his head recently (a skull fracture could cause leakage of spinal fluid through the nose, and bacteria could track back up into the brain, causing a brain infection—encephalitis)? Did his parents know if any of Billy's friends used drugs? No, no, no, and no. Mrs. Shepard shook her head and then stopped for a moment, tilting her head to one side. "The only unusual thing I can think about . . . and I don't see how it could possibly be related . . . is that Billy and three of his friends went swimming in Lake Stanton about a week before he got sick."

"Was Billy a diver, Mrs. Shepard?"

She smiled. "Oh yes, Billy would dive off rocks, tree branches, anything that got him a few feet above the water. He was such an athlete."

"And Lake Stanton is warm this time of year, of course."

"Not only warm, most folks say that it's fed by a hot spring."

Bob looked deeply troubled. "Listen, thanks very, very much for your help; and we are so sorry about the loss of your son."

"Hope it helps, Doc." Mr. Shepard shook Bob's hand.

I found Bob Schimpf bent over a microscope the next morning. "Went out to Lake Stanton yesterday afternoon. The water was a little cloudy. I took a sample of water from the surface in a euthermic container and it measured 76°; samples at six and eight feet were nearly 90°. Wasn't there something about Naegleria and warm water?" He had centrifuged the deeper sample and, while he didn't see any Naegleria, there were a few shadows that suggested they may have been there and deteriorated as the water cooled.

Over the next few weeks, the pathology residents and I, with guidance from Dr. Schimpf, got thoroughly acquainted with one of the nastiest little one-celled animals on the face of the earth. Nicknamed "the brain-eating amoeba," Naegleria fowleri is an amoeba that normally eats bacteria. It can survive as a cyst at very low temperatures, but in very warm fresh water, particularly when the water isn't mobile and is a little polluted so other organisms are killed, it transforms. A flagella, or tail, breaks through the cyst— this form of the amoeba can propel itself quickly. When a swimmer inhales some water containing Naegleria into the nasal cavity, this flagellate transforms again, changing itself into a trophozoite—the irregular, blob-like mini-monster we had seen under the microscope.

The Naegleria trophozoite then moves, using its pseudopod arms, to the top of the nasal cavity where it attaches to the olfactory nerves, the tiny fibers that carry aromas to the brain. The nerves penetrate the skull through small pores in the bone, where they enter the olfactory bulb and carry their impulses to the brain through the long olfactory tract, a thin nerve structure that runs from front to back along the base of the skull.

The trophozoite crawls along this path from the nose to the brain. Apparently, it's stimulated by acetylcholine, a normal brain transmitter chemical. It seems that the acetylcholine changes the appetite of the amoeba from wanting to eat bacteria to eating . . . neurons and astrocytes—the cells that make up the human brain! In the warm, moist brain, it multiplies like an alien until it eats the brain . . . and kills its victim.

This amoebic infection of the brain, known as Primary Amoebic Meningoencephalitis (PAM or PAME), is basically the product of a perfect storm. The events leading to it are so rare that in the first fifty years of our awareness of it (1962 to 2008) less than 150 cases were reported in the United States. Nonetheless, even with treatments of powerful antifungal drugs like Amphotericin B, the death rate remains at nearly 100%. In 1981, we would publish our information about Billy Shepard's case in the *Journal of Infectious Diseases*. True to our promise to his parents, we hoped that his case would build on a steady stream of knowledge that would someday eradicate this tiny, malicious animal, no bigger than a couple of red blood cells, that could kill a full-sized human in a week. Unfortunately for Billy and his family, he had the ill fortune to dive into that perfect storm on a warm June afternoon.

CHAPTER TWELVE

Road Rage

During my neurosurgery residency, we had a saying that we wanted to have printed as a bumper sticker: Train a neurosurgeon—buy a motorcycle. It was a little too grim and nasty for us to actually do it, but you get the idea. The state of Florida doesn't have a "helmet law," so driving bareheaded is perfectly legal. Florida is not the only state with this custom. Only nineteen states require all motorcyclists to wear helmets whenever they're riding. In Florida, anyone over twenty-one years of age with $10,000 of medical coverage is eligible to ride helmet-free.

This law isn't as frivolous as it appears at first. There's a lot of conflicting evidence about the effect of wearing a helmet while riding a motorcycle. Some serious studies suggest that wearing a helmet dramatically reduces the incidence of serious head injuries. But other studies say these statistics are too high, that motorcyclists wearing helmets tend to ride less safely, that (for some reason, maybe reduced peripheral vision) helmet-wearers are struck more frequently than those without and that, per capita, head injuries are closer in frequency to bicyclists and pedestrians than to car passengers. Also, it has been suggested that, while reducing serious head injuries, helmets do nothing to prevent catastrophic neck injuries. I certainly am no expert on this. Wearing a helmet just always seemed like it made common sense to me.

During my 'off-service' year, I completed several months of research in Dr. Rhoton's Gildred Microsurgery Laboratory. Here, we learned to take apart and put together every piece of an operating microscope, and we learned to perform microscopic operations on the blood vessels of lab rats. We would spend hours dissecting their tiny carotid arteries, then severing them, sewing them back together, and transposing the vessels—attaching the end of one cut artery to a cut in the side of another. This was accomplished under high power microscopy, twenty or more times normal size. We used jeweler's forceps to manipulate the blood vessels, microscissors to cut them. To suture the vessels together, we used curved needles that could barely be seen by the naked eye attached to nylon strands that were the thickness of three red blood cells placed side by side, much finer than a human hair. These sutures were so small that we could place ten of them, cut and tied, around a vessel the size of the "o" in "In God we trust" on a dime. These were not large structures, if you know what I mean.

In addition to this practical training, I was involved in research on the anatomy of three small blood vessels at the base of the brain: the posterior inferior, anterior inferior and superior cerebellar arteries. This wasn't particularly difficult research, just making observations on the shape, size, position and variations of these arteries in human cadavers. But these observations, along with many others by Rhoton and his students on the anatomy of the human brain, over many years would result in the production of his masterwork, *Cranial Anatomy and Surgical Approaches*, possibly the world's best-selling neurosurgical text.

The third benefit I received from my work in Dr. Rhoton's lab was the friendship of two wonderful men, David Hardy and Kiyotaka Fujii. Both men were young neurosurgeons spending a year or two in Dr. Rhoton's lab. Their research was much more productive than mine, but I had the great pleasure of spending time with them discussing techniques, comparing cultures, playing pinball and enjoying a few pitchers of beer. David, a native of Edinburgh, was brilliant, surgically talented, and incandescent. His Scot's temper was matched by his generosity. He would go on to become consultant at Cambridge University and president of the Society of British Neurological Surgeons. Kiyo Fujii, a quiet man with a wicked sense of humor and great pinball skills, was extraordinarily gifted both surgically and intellectually. He would become professor of neurosurgery at Kitasato University, the first Japanese medical school established after World War II, and chairman of the board of trustees of the Kitasato Institute.

The days spent in the lab were idyllic, without the pressures of clinical work and with time for family, friends, and, of course, reading in preparation for the written board examination. The "writtens" were Part IV of a series of national medical exams; the first at the end of the second year of medical school; the second at the end of the fourth year; the third at the end of the internship. Part V would be the oral examination, usually taken after two or three years of post-residency practice, when six examiners would review the cases you had done and ask you a daunting series of questions over the course of a day. More about this "interesting" experience later.

At the end of my lab rotation, I returned to Shands as chief resident. No more fun and games. Every day and every night were meant for work—taking care of patients, "rounding" with the residents and attending surgeons and nearly nonstop surgery, case after case, honing the skills that would be essential for a life in neurosurgery.

So, what does all of this have to do with motorcycle helmets? Every learning experience in neurosurgical training is a building block. On a fine, warm, April, Saturday afternoon, I was sitting at the nurses' station sipping coffee and trying to digest the latest issue of *Journal of Neurosurgery*. My beeper suddenly went off— STAT page to the ER. I entered Trauma Room 1. The nurses and ER staff were hurriedly starting IVs in a young, dark-haired woman. Her jeans were ripped at the knees, her denim jacket torn. She had a lot of scrapes and bruises but no obvious compound fractures or massive lacerations. Her pulse was thready and fast but regular. Her belly was soft and didn't react with pain to deep pressure. She had been briefly sedated so that the anesthesiologist could get a breathing tube in her, but that was wearing off. She pulled her arms and legs away in response to our pinching her to check her reactions.

She'd been on the back of a motorcycle racing down Interstate 75 when a car changed lanes abruptly, forcing her driver to turn sharply to the right. He managed to get control of the bike, but, as he slowed down, the bike fell and skidded on its side. The young woman, nineteen-year-old Brenda Owens, was tossed from the bike, hitting her head and scraping along the roadside to a stop about forty feet from the bike. Unconscious, she was brought by EMS directly to the Shands ER. When she came in, she was unresponsive, but, after intubation, she had begun to move her arms and legs spontaneously. I spoke to her boyfriend, a twenty-one-year-old from a nearby town. No, he didn't know where her parents lived, maybe Georgia. He was sullen, a scrape and bruise above his right eye. He took out a cigarette. "Not in here," I said. He put the cigarette to his mouth, then smiled slyly at me and got up and walked out. His two friends fell in behind him, giving me dirty looks.

"Tom, c'mon back in. I don't like her right pupil." Tanya White was a very experienced ER nurse, and I wasted no time. Brenda was not moving now, and her body was rigid—spastic. I quickly shone a light into both of her eyes. The left pupil reacted quickly, shrinking to the stimulus of the light. But the right—nothing. Wide and dilated, it was unresponsive. I pinched her right arm, and it slowly pulled away; but nothing on the left. It didn't move. She was paralyzed on the left with a dilated right pupil. This had all happened in about five minutes. "Tanya, she's got a Foley, right?" The catheter would drain her urine, conscious or unconscious, and I ordered 100 grams of Mannitol, a powerful diuretic that would reduce swelling in her brain. But that left me with a huge decision.

The epidural hematoma is one of the most lethal injuries a human can experience. Generally, what happens is that someone experiences a sharp blow to the head—a fall, a car accident, an assault, a sports injury. This results in a skull fracture. If that fracture is over one of the major blood vessels that run through the dura—the thick, elastic membrane that covers the brain—the blood vessel can be caught in the fracture and torn. Then, since the blood is arterial, with high pressure, it rapidly creates a blood clot that pushes harder and harder against the brain until there's no place left for the brain to go. The pressure squeezes the brainstem, where all the vital activities occur, and death quickly follows. One of the signs of this pressure on the brainstem is a dilated pupil on the same side as the clot, resulting from pressure on the third cranial nerve, the oculomotor, which comes out of the brainstem just where the swelling brain pushes over a membrane, the tentorium, that separates the upper two thirds of the brain from the lower third. The classic case is the high school football player who gets caught in a hard tackle and loses consciousness. He passes out due to a concussion and wakes up in a few minutes. He sits on the bench for ten or fifteen minutes, feels better, and asks the coach if he can go back in (this, of course, before the current concussion initiative was implemented at all levels of play). The coach looks at him, waves him back in, and, ten minutes later, he collapses on the field in a coma. The epidural time bomb has gone off. He is rushed to the nearest hospital, where he is dead on arrival.

Brenda Owens was in that critical moment. She was dying in front of our eyes, and I didn't know how long we had. I looked down at my shoes for inspiration, and I didn't hear anything. Then I looked at the girl. She was young, her short black hair shining against the bright overhead light of the emergency room. Every minute I waited could be her last or could steal some important function from the rest of her life if she survived.

"Tanya, please get me a drill set." Along the walls of the emergency room were dozens of wire racks, each with stacks of sterilized instruments covered in the standard blue-green hospital wraps and sealed with off-white paper tape. Somewhere in that jungle was what I needed. Tanya was back in 60 seconds.

We quickly washed our hands, bathed them in betadine sterilizing solution, and put on sterile gloves. I took a sterile razor from a prep kit and shaved a patch of Brenda's hair, about three inches in diameter and just above her right ear. "Tanya, you'll assist. Get a sterile suction tube. Mike, put that burr hole tray on the bedside stand next to me," I said, speaking to the intern who had joined us. "Okay, open it. Peel the leaves of the cover away from the tray in all directions without touching the contents. And Mike, before you do that, get a mask on." His face reddened briefly and he complied. "Mike, I'll also need a disposable Bovie." The go-to tool of neurosurgery, the Bovie is a wand that transmits electrical energy to whatever it touches. The tip is an elongated bit of thin metal, about half an inch long and a few millimeters wide. It was encased in a plastic sleeve about the shape and size of a pencil. The disposable version had a limited life but was very helpful in situations like ours.

"Tanya, please turn her face to the left and hold it there." I took a box of gauze sponges, poured betadine over them, and swabbed Brenda's shaven skin with six of them, one at a time. Then I folded two sterile towels and placed them over her head, leaving a square aperture that fit the shaved area. I injected a large area of her scalp with a combination of lidocaine to anesthetize the area and epinephrine to discourage bleeding. I fitted a #10 Bard Parker blade onto a handle and made a vertical incision about two and a half inches long. I carried the incision right down to the skull. My patient didn't feel anything. She was comatose now. The edges of the skin and muscle beneath bled modestly, and I touched the Bovie to the bleeding points, quickly stopping them. I placed a toothed retractor in the wound and opened it, exposing a circle of bone just over two inches in diameter. In the middle of the incision was a jagged, irregular skull fracture, its center discolored a dark blue by blood beneath.

I attached a drill bit to a manual drill. The tip of the bit was a centimeter wide, and the drill was a rather primitive affair—about eight inches long. Its center portion was U-shaped and its handle rotated freely. I held the handle with my right hand and twisted the drill with my left. The sharp bit quickly ate a hole in the skull just next to the fracture (I didn't want to make the hole through the fracture, since that might push fragments of the broken bone into the brain beneath). What I saw immediately justified my concern. A large gelatinous blue blood clot lay just beneath the bone and was already pulsing through the hole. I took a Leksell rongeur—when I squeezed its handle, two half-centimeter cups came together and bit pieces of bone around the edges of the burr hole. Using the Leksell, I expanded the hole to almost two inches. Now the clot began to "express," pushing out of the skull like a newborn baby through the birth canal. I removed about three ounces of clot with the suction tube. When most of the fresh clot had been removed, a spigot of bright red blood shot from the wound about six inches above the skull. Applying the suction tube to the area of fresh bleeding, I could see the culprit. A branch of the middle meningeal artery that supplied the dura had been torn by the skull fracture. I grasped the dura containing the nasty bleeder with a pair of sharp metal forceps and applied the Bovie's current to the forceps. The dura that I held quickly blackened and shriveled, the artery blanched and stopped bleeding. As I sutured the edges of the muscle, galea, and skin, Brenda began to stir. I was gratified to see that she was moving all four limbs.

We quickly took her to the operating room upstairs where we prepared her in more conventional fashion, with anesthesia and assistants. After draping the patient, we removed the sutures and expanded the incision to about five inches, curving the upper end forward to allow greater retraction. I slid a power saw with a protective tip against the edge of the burr hole I had made in the ER and removed a large circular piece of bone over the entire temporal lobe. There was a moderate amount of clot adjacent to the original hematoma. This was removed with suction, but there wasn't a lot to do. The torn artery was fully coagulated. We cleaned up the area, tacked the dura to the adjacent bone and the center of the bone flap with small silk sutures, and returned the bone flap to its site using "dog bone" plates and small self-tapping screws. The plates were about a centimeter long, with expanded ends containing holes for placing the screws—they looked just like . . . well, you know . . . dog bones.

The next morning, we visited Brenda in the ICU. She was awake and alert, moving all of her limbs, and breathing on her own. Two days later, she was sitting up and taking nourishment in a regular hospital room.

"How are you feeling, Brenda?"

"I want a cigarette."

Explaining that there was no smoking in the hospital rooms, she shot me a nasty look, more like a sneer. You're welcome, I thought. Her boyfriend, sitting on her bed, and his two friends lounging nearby laughed. I didn't.

"Brenda, wouldn't this be a good time to quit smoking?"

"Why don't you mind your own business?" The look on her face was cold. There was a big piece of me that wanted to inform her how close she was to death three days before and how our team saved her life. But I knew it wouldn't even register.

"We'll get you out of here as quickly as possible," I said with more than a twinge of sarcasm. Later in the afternoon, I was told that she had signed out against medical advice. "I'm tired of this bullshit" were her exact words to the nurse in charge of the unit. Her gratitude warmed my heart. Unfortunately, my experience suggested that she would probably end up in another emergency ward because of another accident, abuse by her boyfriend, or a drug overdose.

Fortunately, progress is being made in making head injuries rarer and less lethal, at least in the area of sports. Rules are now in place that mandate taking a youngster out of the game after a concussion, where he or she can be closely observed. Safer helmets in football have appeared, as well as discussions about making head contact rarer in that sport by safer tackling and setup techniques. Training of coaches in injury assessment is now routine, and there is a much greater awareness, thanks to studies of the delayed effect of post-traumatic encephalopathy, of the potential of even seemingly trivial head injuries to have lasting effects on thinking, mood, and memory. But motorcycles still defy our efforts.

CHAPTER THIRTEEN

A Tumor Made of Pearls

After a very busy tour as chief resident at Shands, I rotated to the chief residency at the Gainesville VA. The pace was slower, but the responsibility great. It was true that some of the vets largely used the hospital for routine care and to buy cigarettes and cheap clothes at the PX. Oh yes, and some were malingerers. But many of the vets were really hurting. As I outlined in a previous chapter, often there wasn't a particular pathology that we could identify. They "somaticized"—the back pain kept them from being able to work but the exam and the CAT scan were normal. The headaches were unbearable, but there weren't any neurological findings. Many of these fine men were victims of what we would later identify as Post-traumatic Stress Disorder, often not manifesting any physical abnormalities, but an illness just as real and devastating as any other. At that time, we didn't have the insight or the science to make the diagnosis, but we were generally sympathetic to the real pain that these veterans were feeling.

Terry Stankowski was fifty-three years old. He was a wiry

little guy with a ready smile and a great sense of humor. Like most guys of his generation, he always had a cigarette hanging out of the corner of his mouth. Just now, he wasn't in a laughing mood. He had developed headaches that started at the base of his skull, then worked their way up over his ears to his temples and forehead. They were pounding and relentless; and worse, they were happening more and more frequently. They were blinding headaches and were barely touched by Tylenol or aspirin. And there were a couple of other strange things that were beginning to bother him. His left cheek was starting to tingle a little bit, and his voice was getting a little hoarse. Once in a while, he thought he was seeing double when he looked to his right, and that was before he'd had even one bourbon.

Terry had been a young man in his twenties when he volunteered for the Korean Conflict ("Hell, doc, that wasn't no conflict—it was a nasty, bloody, fightin' war!"). He had a good job as a heavy equipment mechanic, but his older brother had been a Marine in the big war, wounded in the Pacific in 1945. He idolized his brother and somehow felt that he'd been cheated out of his share of the glory. So, when things started to heat up in the Korean peninsula, well, this was his chance. "But there wasn't nothin' glorious about it, doc. It was cold as a witch's tit on the shady side of an iceberg. And them KPAs were real fighters. You'd think you got aholt of a hill, and there'd come a stream of 'em, tough as nails. Me and my buddies barely made it out at the Chosin Reservoir. Seoul changed hands between the North and the South four times. And our generals knew it was a real war; but Harry Truman kept calling it a 'police action'. Hell, I didn't see any police over there. There were winter nights there, when our platoon was isolated, and I could hear 'em creeping up on us. I was scared damn near to death. But it slowly changed. Our Air Force was so dang tough that we drove the North Koreans and the Chinese back above the 38th parallel. And that's where we are today—still at war, no treaty, stalemate— after twenty-seven years." Terry shook his head slowly, wistfully.

"There wasn't no big victory parades when we got back, not like '45. No girls meetin' the trains. No bands. Nothin'. It's like everybody was just kind of ashamed. 'Cause we didn't win. But that didn't help my nightmares. It was just as much of a war to me as WWII. I could still see my platoon lieutenant—hell, he was probably younger than me—take one from a sniper right through the side of his head. He crumpled like a house of cards. And Corporal Jenkins. A negra fella. Tough as nails. Fell on a grenade. Took it for the team. He just laid on it, holdin' onto his helmet. Then there was muffled boom . . . I can still hear it. His body jumped up about a foot and a half. Then he came back down, blood spreading in a pool all around him. He never moved again. Dead as a stone. Yeah, doc, it was a real war.

"So sometimes those dreams would wake me up, and I'd walk around half the night sweatin' and smoking cigarettes and drinkin' bourbon. My ex said I wasn't wrapped too tight. And I guess she was probably right. But anyway, I've always felt good, you know, physically. Oh, I know, too many cigarettes and too much booze. But I've never really been what you'd call sick. Then these damn headaches started. At first, I thought I really was goin' off my rocker, like my ex always said, with all this other stuff—the tingling on my face and seein' double. But nobody's that crazy. So, I figured I better get to the VA and find out if there might be somethin' else going on."

I told Terry that I thought he'd done the right thing. We sat and talked for a while. I told him that my Uncle Jim was in Korea and that he brought me back one of those embroidered silk bomber jackets. I thought it was about the coolest thing I'd ever been given. And it felt to me that people were starting to understand the sacrifices that these guys had made and the costs they had paid.

We headed to the PX and got a couple of nineteen-cent packs of cigarettes, then headed to the commissary, where we had a cup of coffee. Getting the sense that I understood what he'd been through, he told me a few more stories about his war—the fear, the carnage, the isolation, and how he'd had to button it all up when he got home. "My folks just couldn't understand why I wasn't the same funny kid who left them two years before." His eyes welled up, then he gave his head a rough shake, snuffled loudly, and smiled. "Jesus, what're you, some kind of fuckin' shrink?" I just chuckled back.

We went back up to the emergency room, where I did a neurological examination on Terry. His cognition was fine. He knew the date and place, could count backward from 100 by sevens, knew the names of the president and vice-president. He could balance on each foot. His strength was fine, he could resist the pushing and pulling of all his limbs. The sensation of his arms and legs was equal, and his reflexes were all normal. Then we started to evaluate his cranial nerves, the nerves that come out of the base of the brain and brainstem, emerge from small holes in the skull and supply everything from vision and smell to hearing and facial expression. His vision was good, his pupils reacted briskly to my flashlight and accommodated to looking at my finger when I held it close to his face. I asked him to close his eyes and held a cigarette under his nose. "Tobacco," he correctly identified. Then we ran into trouble. When I asked him to look to the right, his left eye moved perfectly, but his right eye couldn't get past the middle of the socket. His right sixth cranial nerve, called the abducens nerve because it abducts, or pulls, the eye away from the midline, wasn't functioning. The left nerve was okay. I stroked his cheeks with a wisp of cotton—he felt the right, but not the left. I touched the cotton to his right cornea—his eye blinked shut normally, but nothing on the left. The fifth cranial nerve, the trigeminal, named for the three divisions it breaks into as it emerges from the skull, was out of whack on the left, the opposite side from the faulty sixth nerve. I asked him to close his eyes tightly against the resistance of my fingers. The left gave good resistance, but I was able to open the right eye easily. The seventh, or facial, nerve was not functioning properly. His hearing and balance were okay; these were functions of the eighth nerve, the auditory and vestibular. I asked Terry to open his mouth widely. He stuck his tongue out as asked, and it pointed to the right. The strength of the left side was good, but not on the right. The right twelfth nerve, the hypoglossal, was damaged. I touched the back of his pharynx with a tongue depressor. No gag. His ninth nerve, the glossopharyngeal, wasn't working. And finally, I knew from his hoarseness that the tenth nerve, the vagus, was also involved.

I was alarmed. And stumped. Here was a healthy guy, up and about, acting fine, with debilitating headaches and various cranial nerves from both sides of his brainstem malfunctioning. And the headaches. He was clearly having the effect of some kind of pressure on his brain, just not enough pressure to affect his consciousness or his strength or movement. I knew one thing. Whatever was happening to Terry Stankowski was affecting some very expensive real estate—the base of his brain.

I admitted Terry to the hospital. I told him that there was something serious going on in his brain, and we had to find out what it was and what we could do about it (if anything, I thought). He met the situation with his usual aplomb. "Figures," he said and shrugged his shoulders (well, at least the eleventh cranial nerve, the trapezius, that elevates the shoulders, was working).

The CAT scan whirred for several minutes (in those days, the machine took a comparatively long time to take an x-ray of a particular point in space, transmit it to a computer and place it as a pixel on a display. It would then create a mosaic of those pixels that would make up a picture of each "slice" of the brain from the base of the skull to the top of the head). As the machine created slice after numbered slice, we watched the monitor. There was something there all right. Or more accurately, there was a "nothing" there. What appeared to be a dark, empty space was pushing Terry's brainstem away from the base of his skull, stretching all the cranial nerves and making them misbehave.

We paused the machine and injected an iodine-based dye into a vein. The dye would enter blood vessels which would then "light up" on the scan. It was called a contrast-enhanced study. We repeated the scan, and this time saw several delicate strands traversing the dark space. It looked like a dark honeycomb. As Terry left the scan, he asked, "See anything interesting, doc?"

"This one's going to take some studying, Terry."

"Like I said, nothin's ever simple with me, man." He flashed his best Southern smile, hiding the anxiety that I knew he felt.

The next morning, we presented his case at our resident

conference. As we ascended the ranks in our questions about the case and its likely diagnosis, we got a variety of opinions. With Dr. Rhoton quizzing the junior residents about the pathways of the cranial nerves, the circulation to the brainstem and the senior residents about the correct surgical approaches to the lesion, we didn't have too much time for getting opinions about what this strange-looking thing actually was. One of the attending surgeons took a shot.

"I think this might be an old hematoma, clot from a burned-out vascular malformation." But it must have grown to progressively involve the cranial nerves. "It's slowly expanding because spinal fluid is being drawn into it because of its density." And the "strands" within the tumor? "Vascularized scar tissue." It was weird but thought out quickly and well. Parker Mickle, the faculty member who had been on call when Terry came in and would be performing the operation with me, had obviously had more time to think about the case. "I think it's an epidermoid." One of the other attendings shook his head, but Dr. Rhoton was impassive. It was a stretch. Here was a fifty-something guy presenting with fairly recent symptoms of a brain lesion. The CAT scan picture was certainly good for this tumor, a cystic tumor formed by the shedding and accumulation of keratin and cholesterol, as the epithelial (basically, skin) cells that formed the margin of the tumor broke down. This would explain the 'hollow' or empty appearance on the CAT scan—cysts aren't solid. The location was right, too. Epidermoids often occurred in the middle of the base of the brain. The problem was that epidermoid tumors are thought to be congenital tumors, formed when the neural tube which creates the brain and spinal cord closes and leaves behind a small group of ectodermal (skin) cells, which gradually expand. These cysts grow very slowly and don't create symptoms until they start pressing on important structures. But fifty years is pretty darned slow. Nonetheless, I agreed with Parker Mickle.

"Dr. Rhoton?" I asked.

"I'll wait until next week's conference."

"But we're doing the case tomorrow."

"Exactly." He beamed his best Kentucky grin as we all laughed.

J. Parker Mickle was a brilliant and affable young neurosurgeon. Only five years my senior, he had studied at Vanderbilt University Medical School and done his residency at Harvard while also doing neuroscience research at MIT. He joined UF's department in 1979, just before I became chief resident. One of the things that attracted him to Gainesville was his athleticism. Parker—he insisted that the residents call him Parker; no formality, no Dr. Mickle, even for the first-years—was a competitive runner. He had run a bunch of marathons, and Gainesville was home to a lot of runners; amateurs, collegians, Olympians. Humble and self-effacing, he always seemed to be smiling. He was also a history buff, which automatically endeared him to me.

The following morning, I met Terry Stankowski just outside the operating room in the holding area. "Well, doc, here goes nothin'." I wasn't playing games this morning. "Terry, we are going to take the best care of you that we possibly can." He teared up for a moment. "I know you will, doc." Parker spoke briefly with him, reviewing the plan that we had all agreed on with Terry.

A few minutes later, the patient was asleep. We were doing the surgery with the patient in the sitting position, so a catheter was placed through a vein into the right atrium to catch any air bubbles that might escape from the wound into the circulation. This was necessary because, if enough air got into a vein, it could create a fatal "air embolus." We secured the patient's head in the pins of the C-shaped clamp that would hold his head absolutely still during the operation. Using a series of cushions and tape, we gradually maneuvered the electronically-controlled operating table into the sitting position. We removed the top portion of the table on which his head rested so that he was now sitting bolt upright with the back of his head and neck exposed. Using an electric clipper, then a straight edge razor, we shaved the back of the head and neck clean, then prepared it with an antiseptic solution and draped every bit of the field except for an area four inches wide and eight inches vertically, which was covered with sterile clear plastic.

We made a vertical incision seven inches long, down to the bone, and used a periosteal elevator that looked like a flattened spoon, with a sharp circular margin to elevate the muscle and periosteum, the gristle that covers the bone, away from the skull, holding it in place away from the exposed skull with self-retaining retractors. Using the power perforator, we made three burr holes over the left side of the skull to work on the side of the brain where most of Terry's deficits were noted and connected them with a power saw. After removing the piece of bone disconnected from the rest of the skull, we used Leksell rongeurs, thick bone-biting instruments, to extend the edges of the exposed dura until we had about a four-inch oval of exposure.

Next, we attached a long metal bar to the base of the operating table. To this were attached several Leyla retractors. These were snake-like metal devices of various lengths. When tightened, they assumed whatever location and position was required, remaining rigid and tight. Legend has it that one of the great founders of modern neurosurgery, Mahmut Gazi Yasargil, a Turk who became his adopted Switzerland's gift to surgery, was once watching his little daughter Leyla string beads onto a string and noticed that when she secured each bead by pinching the string just beyond the last bead, the string of beads became stiff. He used the same concept, placing a short articulating rod between each metal sphere, with all of them strung over a wire cable, so that when the end of the cable was tightened, the retractor would assume any shape and length desired. Retractor blades of various lengths and widths could then be attached to a connector at the end of the Leyla and used to safely and securely pull brain structures out of the way of a target. The Leyla retractor quickly caught on with neurosurgeons around the world and has become an indispensable item in the brain surgery toolbox.

The operating microscope was brought into the field and covered safely with a large plastic drape tightened to a lens cap that sterilely covered the working end of the microscope. Using a tiny blade, a nick was made in the dura, which was then opened into three leaves, which were sutured to the retracted muscle. Now the cerebellum, the large cortical structure responsible for balance and coordination, was exposed. As Parker Mickle supervised and observed, I elevated the left "tonsil" of the cerebellum—an appendage that hangs from the bottom of the larger organ—with a hand-held brain retractor, exposing a film of arachnoid, the thin membrane that encloses the spinal fluid. Carefully holding a bit of the membrane with forceps, I stabbed it with a slender knife, after which a jet of spinal fluid gushed out then wound down to a steady drip, allowing the cerebellum and the brainstem, which lies just in front of the cerebellum, to relax. We waited five or ten minutes while the spinal fluid continued to slowly drain, and the Mannitol we had given at the start of the case worked to dry the brain even further.

I then introduced a long, thin retractor, elevated the cerebellum, and retracted it to the right, tightening the Leyla device. I adjusted the microscope to high power and pulled the retractor a bit tighter. As I focused on the depth of the operating field, I saw something that I had never seen before or since. The memory of what I saw is as fresh four decades later as it was then. I can only inadequately describe it as a fistful of shiny pearls. The tumor filled most of the left side of the base of the skull, and it was composed of a field of bumps that were intensely white and opalescent.

Holding my bipolar forceps in my right hand, ready to coagulate the blood vessels that were expected to be torn when I entered the tumor, I held a small metal suction tube in my left and touched it to the tumor. To my surprise and relief, there was no bleeding. Instead, a small hole widened into a little cavern as the tumor instantly disappeared into the suction. I turned to Parker Mickle. He wasn't surprised. "That's an epidermoid, all right." His preoperative diagnosis was correct. "They're like bits of popcorn, airy and light." He was right. I became more vigorous in my suctioning. An occasional tiny vessel needed coagulating, but generally the field was "dry." I widened the field of each attack on the tumor from a few millimeters to nearly a centimeter at a time. As the tumor disappeared, I began to see the outline of the stretched cranial nerves that had brought Terry to our attention. The nerves five through twelve were stretched and displaced by the tumor that had grown so slowly but relentlessly. The nerves had to cross the empty space between where they emerged from the brainstem to the small holes where they exited the base of the skull. Parker and I traded off, suctioning section after section of the tumor. At one point, we followed it across the midline of the brain, accounting for its effect on both trigeminal nerves. After about five hours, the tumor had essentially vanished up our suction tubes. There were multiple tiny wisps of tumor and membrane attached to the cranial nerves and the brainstem. I was reticent to try to pick these bits off of the sensitive neural tissue, and Parker was reassuring. "This tumor is so slow-growing, those little specks will never grow back in his lifetime." We slowly removed the mass of cottonoids, the strips of fabric that protected normal brain during our dissection, and prevented the contents of the tumor, which could be very caustic, from mixing with the spinal fluid and irritating the brain.

When they had all been removed, we vigorously irrigated the entire field with saline and removed the retractors. The cerebellum and the cranial nerves gradually found their way back to their normal locations. We closed the dura with a running suture of 6-0 silk and placed a large piece of gelfoam, a thin artificial membrane that was nonporous and hemostatic (preventing bleeding) over the dura, then replaced the bone using small dog-bone struts secured with tiny screws to the bone. The muscle and galea were closed with sutures and the skin with staples. The wound was dressed and Terry returned to the supine position.

Since anesthesia had been so long, over seven hours, we opted to keep Terry sedated and intubated, breathing with the assistance of a ventilator for several hours. The next morning, he was extubated after the sedation had worn off. By late afternoon, he was just slightly sleepy, and it was fairly easy to examine him.

He was moving everything in response to my requests, and the cranial nerves were already improved in their function, although the sixth nerve that moved his eye was still stubborn—it was the most delicate of those affected by the tumor. Three months later, Terry had regained about 90% of his function. He smiled at me with his usual pluck. "You didn't take out anything that I need, did you, doc?"

CHAPTER FOURTEEN

The First Aneurysm

I was never quite sure how George Sypert felt about me. He was a brilliant guy who had left his native Texas to train in basic neuroscience and neurosurgery with Arthur Ward, one of the towering figures of American scientific neurosurgery, at the University of Washington in Seattle. He had come to Gainesville bringing government grants for his ongoing investigations in brain science. He spent equal amounts of his time doing clinical surgery and, in his lab, investigating the cellular physiology of nerves in the hope of developing breakthroughs in the treatment of spinal cord injuries. He held my junior resident, Bill Friedman, who would ultimately succeed Dr. Rhoton as chairman of neurosurgery at Florida, in the highest esteem. Bill was doing serious research with Sypert as a beginning resident while the rest of us were trying to catch an hour of sleep between operations. He had little patience with most of the residents. "I can teach a monkey to operate," he would say, "I'm trying to train brain scientists who can operate!" I knew that I could never measure up to George's standards, but I tried my best to increase my fund of knowledge enough to avoid embarrassing myself in front of him.

George would tease my friend and co-resident Bruce Woodham and me. He would variously accuse one of us of being "born without a cerebellum" (the organ of coordination) and the other of being "born without a thalamus" (the organ that transmits sensory information to the cortex). It didn't seem funny to either of us at the time, but he would then flash his disarming grin and we couldn't stay angry with him. At teaching conferences, he was brutal. He would lash out mercilessly at residents for not knowing things that we thought were arcane and he thought were ridiculously fundamental. Generally, Dr. Rhoton would tolerate these teaching moments. However, even George was not above the boss's reach. In an era when the neurosurgical uniform, particularly at national meetings, was grey flannel slacks, blue blazer, and school tie, George favored leisure suits and bell-bottom pants. One morning, Dr. Rhoton came to conference with a brown paper bag filled with copies of a single paperback—John Molloy's best-selling *Dress for Success*. He insisted that every resident and every faculty member take a copy. There was no mystery about the target of the sartorial lesson.

Bruce and I became obsessed with making sure that George would not be able to outwit us when it came to clinical information. And, as we progressed as surgeons, he began to show us grudging respect. I even occasionally detected what might have been a trace of affection. But I was very surprised at what happened one September afternoon near the beginning of my chief residency.

A middle-aged man had collapsed at the school where he served as assistant principal. He had mentioned to another teacher that morning that he didn't feel well—a little nausea and a dull, right-sided headache. About an hour later, while sitting at his desk, he grabbed his head, shouted out, and fell to the ground, where he began shaking uncontrollably in a grand mal seizure. The staff called for an ambulance as his assistant cradled his head in her arms. By the time the emergency workers arrived, the seizure had stopped and William Timmons was lying on the floor, calm but confused, wincing every once in a while from his headache. His right arm reached behind his neck, which he massaged slowly.

"Does your neck hurt, Bill?" His secretary was visibly upset as she described what had happened to the ambulance crew. "How do you feel, Mr. Timmons?"

". . . Pain . . ." He pointed to his head. The emergency tech flashed a light at his pupils. His right eyelid was a little lower than the left. The patient was getting a bit more lucid with each passing minute. "God, what a headache! And my neck is so stiff!" The tech lifted his head slightly—his neck was stiff as a board. He lifted the patient's drooping right eyelid. The right eye was looking outward while the left was looking directly at the examiner. The right pupil was wider than the left and reacted poorly to light. Timmons passed the rest of the exam with flying colors. He now knew his whereabouts, the date, and the people around him. His limbs moved strongly, his sensation was fine, and his reflexes reacted perfectly.

The third cranial nerve, the oculomotor nerve, translates rather easily from Latin. It is the nerve that gives motion to the eye. Two other nerves are also involved: the fourth, or trochlear nerve, helps the eye rotate; the sixth or abducens nerve, pulls, or abducts, the eye from looking straight ahead to looking to the side. But the rest

136

of the activity of the eye, looking up, down, and towards the nose (medial motion) and opening the eyelid, are all the responsibility of the third nerve. The nerve comes out of the brainstem and runs along the base of the front of the skull until it reaches a small hole called the superior orbital fissure, where it emerges and divides into various divisions supplying the eye. Just before it leaves the skull, though, it runs right next to the carotid artery, which is passing in the opposite direction, entering the skull to give the brain its blood supply.

This anatomical relationship between the carotid artery and the oculomotor nerve led to one of the most important discoveries in the history of neurology. The great arbiter of sudden death from brain hemorrhage is the "berry" aneurysm, an expanding, usually round bubble emerging from the wall of an artery. These aneurysms usually occur when a smaller artery branches off from a larger one. One of the most common sites for this to occur is just after the entry of the carotid artery into the skull, where the small posterior communicating artery, one of nature's wonders, emerges.

In 1664, Oxford physician Thomas Willis published a study of brain anatomy with the aid of illustrations by the famous polymath, Sir Christopher Wren, who was also a physicist, astronomer and, most famously, the architect who designed St. Paul's Cathedral in London. Arguably the most important revelation in the book would become known as the Circle of Willis. This bit of natural ingenuity involves a circular connection of eight arteries beneath the base of the brain. They are all connected: the left carotid artery connects to the anterior communicating artery; in turn to the right carotid artery; then the right posterior communicating artery; the right posterior cerebral artery; the basilar artery; the left posterior cerebral; the left posterior communicating and back to the left carotid. What's the point? If one of the four major arteries (the two vertebral arteries in the back of the neck joining to form the basilar) from the neck to the brain closes off, the Circle of Willis can allow blood from the other three to supply the territory of the fourth and prevent a stroke! This system of "collateral circulation" isn't perfect and doesn't always work, but that it has developed at all is certainly one of the most remarkable achievements in human evolution.

In 1829, neurologist John Adams published a report in the British medical journal *Lancet* explaining that an enlarging berry aneurysm at the junction of the carotid artery and the posterior communicating artery could press on the oculomotor nerve, creating a dilated pupil, an outwardly deviating eye and a sagging eyelid. In 1927, the Portuguese neurologist, Antonio Egaz Muniz, developed a technique for injecting an iodine-based dye into the arteries entering the brain that would then project white on a dark x-ray background. This test, the cerebral angiogram, allowed us to see the blood vessels of the brain and, of course, aneurysms for the first time in living humans. In 1949, Egaz Muniz would win the Nobel Prize for his discovery. Only seven years after Egaz Muniz's discovery, in 1934, the great Johns Hopkins neurosurgeon, Walter Dandy would operate on the brain and, for the first time, place a small metal clip across the base of an aneurysm, obliterating it without sacrificing the artery itself.

Which brings us back to Bill Timmons. The ambulance bringing him to Gainesville from Ocala arrived within one hour of his having a seizure. The neurology resident examined him and quickly concluded that the oculomotor paralysis and the stiff neck were caused by a ruptured right internal carotid aneurysm at the takeoff of the posterior communicating artery. She concluded this because, first, this had come on suddenly, pointing more toward a rapidly expanding aneurysm than to something growing slowly, like a tumor. Second, the stiff neck. This occurred because the leakage of blood from the tip of the aneurysm had flooded the spinal fluid chamber that bathes the brain and spinal cord. Spinal fluid (more correctly cerebrospinal fluid, as both the brain and the spinal cord float in it) is contained within a beautiful translucent membrane known as the arachnoid, for its resemblance to a spider web. Sidebar—one of my first colleagues in New York was Kenneth Gang, an urbane and witty sophisticate. One day, we were operating on a brain clot when he spotted a spider descending gently over the operative field on a silken thread. Gang quickly noted that we must be operating on a "subarachnoid" hemorrhage.

To double-check her diagnosis, Anne Lowell rushed Mr. Timmons to the CAT scan, where a thick, white, blood clot at the base of the brain (fresh blood shows as white against the dark gray shadow of the brain on the CAT) and a thin layer of white coating the entire brain confirmed the hemorrhage. Finally, she nimbly introduced a long needle into the spinal canal in his lower back, performing a lumbar puncture—a spinal tap. The spinal fluid emerged under fairly high pressure with a persistent pink tinge. Yes, she was sure the patient had ruptured an aneurysm. He was one of about sixty percent of patients who survive to this stage. She loaded him with an anti-convulsant to prevent further seizures.

In minutes, I had answered Anne's page, done a quick examination of the patient, and reviewed the CAT and the spinal tap results. He was in otherwise good health, and, if we acted quickly, he stood a fair chance of survival. If the aneurysm had a chance to bleed again, his chances would drop dramatically. I called Ron Quisling, the brilliant, young neuroradiologist who had joined the faculty from the University of Michigan, having completed his training only four years before. Ron was smart, well-read, and unflappable. He would have the angiogram suite ready in ten minutes. Twenty minutes after that, we had our answer. The first film was developed. It was a lateral view of the patient's skull. Against the dark background and faint light tracings of the bones of his skull, the white internal carotid artery and its branches stood out dramatically. Just behind the back of the right orbit, the eye socket, the artery divided into its first branches. The first branch, the ophthalmic artery, headed straight toward the eye. The second, the posterior communicating artery, headed to join the Circle of Willis. At the junction of this takeoff, we saw a pea-sized white balloon pointing straight upward. It was wider and round at the top and tapered to a thin base where it took off from the parent artery. I nodded at Anne. She had made the right diagnosis from the start. Now it was my job to use every minute of the time Anne had saved by her mental acuity to save this guy's life.

We slammed through the routine lab, EKG, and chest x-ray workup, and got him type and cross-matched for a blood transfusion (he might need it—these operations could get a little dramatic). His wife had arrived by now, and, as we walked his gurney through the halls toward the elevator that would take us to the operating room, I asked her about any background that might be helpful: allergies (we'd want to give him antibiotics as an anti-infectious precaution); was he a smoker (that would certainly make his extubation—the removal of the breathing tube after surgery—riskier); any other major illnesses (it would be quite a surprise if we learned that he had terminal cancer after this hazardous surgery)?

Within two hours of his arriving at the Shands Emergency Department, Bill Timmons was lying on the operating table. Anesthesia was given. We quickly changed into scrub suits, surgical caps, and masks. After he was sedated to unconsciousness, he was given a paralytic agent that could be reversed but would keep him from moving a muscle (or his head) during the critical microscopic dissection that was about to occur. We gently rolled the patient on his side. I sterilized his low back and inserted a small needle into his spinal canal. A catheter was then threaded through the hollow needle into the spinal fluid space. Clear, pink-tinged fluid emerged under a fair amount of pressure. I secured the catheter to the skin with a bandage and tape, then connected the end of it to a tube with a valve. I could turn the valve and halt the flow of fluid. The tube was in turn connected to a bag where we could collect the fluid. It was a closed system (there was no exposure of the fluid to air, where bacteria could invade and cause meningitis).

We turned Mr. Timmons onto his back, or the supine position, again. The modern operating table is ingenious. It is a series of flat panels supported by an outer metal frame. The panels are connected at junctions and the junctions contain gears that allow the panels to be separately elevated or lowered. The panels are "radiolucent," so x-rays can be taken of any body part without the image being blocked. At the beginning of my career, the gears were turned manually, but very soon they were controlled electrically. I first elevated the largest panel, the one behind his back, about thirty degrees. Next, I raised the lower panel to elevate his legs slightly, then lowered the bottom panel a bit. This bent his knees slightly, taking the pressure off the muscles at the back of his legs. Surgery could take a long time, and we wanted his position to approximate nature as nearly as possible.

With this maneuver completed, my assistant resident held the patient's head while I unscrewed and removed the top panel of the table. With his neck and head now completely free, I applied a Mayfield head holder to the skull (named after another of the great innovators of neurosurgery, Frank Mayfield, founder of the Mayfield Clinic in Cincinnati; the device ensures that the patient's head remains absolutely still during surgery). As I've described earlier, it's basically a U-shaped metal clamp. One tip of the U has a sharp tapered pin, the other tip has a rotating arc in the shape of a C, with two pins at either end of the C. By placing the patient's head in the U, turning a knob at the base of the device causes the pins to close in until they are firmly attached to the skull through the skin. In Mr. Timmons's case, his head was turned toward the left and the solo pin was applied to the left forehead, about two inches above the eye. The rotating arc was lined up to conform to the curve of the right side of the back of his head, and its two pins were applied so that the front one was about an inch above the right ear, with the back one about four inches behind, penetrating the scalp at the back of the right side of his head. With all pins tightened, the head and the clamp are one unit. When the clamp is mounted by a gear to a bar that is secured to the base of the table, there can be no movement of the skull during surgery. The device sounds a bit gruesome, but it is fundamental to brain surgery.

Holding each of the arms of the clamp in my hands, I rotated the head so that it was turned 60 degrees to the left, then tilted the head back so that the highest point of the operating field would be the malar eminence, the cheekbone. I locked the clamp in place. With an electric shaver, I trimmed an arc of hair from the middle of the forehead to just behind the top of the right ear. Drenching a small white towel in a combination of betadine sterilizing solution and saline, I moistened the patient's scalp where I had shaved it, then took a straight edge razor and close-shaved the area I had trimmed. Advancing residents take pride in the fact that they don't leave a nick or cut behind during this process. I guess this emphasizes the kinship between modern neurosurgeons and medieval surgeons, who were always barbers.

While I left the room with Dr. Sypert for the scrub sink, the assistant resident began a time-tested tradition. With latex-gloved hands, he took several of the small cotton towels and gently scrubbed the shaven portion of the patient's scalp for ten minutes with betadine soap. Then he took a long clamp that held folded gauze sponges, dipped the sponges in betadine solution, washed the prepared area, discarded the sponge and repeated the process three times. George Sypert and I came back, our hands elevated from the elbows, still dripping slightly but carrying the water away from our sterile fingertips. We took sterile towels and dried our hands. The scrub nurse passed the surgical gowns over our arms, the circulating nurse tied the gowns behind us, and we tied a sterile waistband in front. We then folded sterile blue towels and placed them around the circumference of the prepared skin. We secured them to the skin with staples. A steel table was wheeled from the bottom of the table until it stood at the level of the patient's neck. It was lowered to about three inches above his shoulders. Now sterile blue sheets were used to wall off the surgical field from the rest of the room. Taking a blue sharpie, I drew an arc on the skin from the right side of the forehead just above the right eyebrow, up and back for about three inches, then down in front of the right ear and across the right zygoma, the bone that runs back across the temple from the cheek. Finally, a large "aperture" sheet, about six feet in diameter, was placed over the entire area. In its center was a clear plastic sheet, slightly less than a foot in diameter. The underside of the plastic was adhesive and it stuck firmly to the skin, further isolating but exposing the operative area. The edges of this drape were brought down over the surgical table and to IV poles at either side of the area to isolate the non-sterile personnel, including the anesthesiologist and all of his machinery. This routine, which I've described at the beginning of this story, in combination with our careful hand washing and cautious movements and preoperative intravenous antibiotics, was our best defense against postoperative infections.

The assistant resident finished his scrubbing and joined us at the head of the table. Two clear tubes were advanced to the head of the table and clamped there. Their tips were attached to small angled metal suction devices. These metal tubes had small handles near the top with slits in them. By sliding a thumb over more or less of the slit, the surgeon could control the exact amount and intensity of the suction to adjust to the delicacy of the tissue and the amount of blood or fluid to be removed. Next, a Bovie cautery was brought in. Named after the inventor and physicist who worked with Harvey Cushing, the father of American neurosurgery, the device conducted an electric charge that, when triggered by a button, could coagulate blood vessels or cut tissue. Then a Malis bipolar forceps, a more delicate coagulation device invented by Leonard Malis, chairman of neurosurgery at New York's Mt. Sinai Hospital, was prepared.

This type of forceps applied current only between the tips of the forceps so that one could place a small blood vessel between the tips of the forceps without damaging any of the surrounding tissue. The wires from these tools were passed off the field to generators outside the sterile area. Two plastic bags were secured to the top of the overhead table. One suction tip and the Bovie were placed in one of the bags, another tip and the Malis in the other. This would make the tools readily accessible yet prevent them from falling below the surgical field, where they would be considered contaminated. The complexity of these invariable rituals and the names of the many pioneers who invented the instrumentation were testimony to the devotion of countless surgeons and nurses to climbing the mountain that was brain surgery. We neurosurgeons are all familiar with the stories behind each of these instruments, and justifiably proud of our neurosurgical heritage.

Taking a #10 bladed scalpel, I traced the pathway that I had drawn with the sharpie. A tiny line of blood expanded from the line, like the icy path of a speed skater's blade. The blade was a curved scimitar about an inch long and half an inch wide, mounted on the end of a handle to which the disposable blade could be snapped on or off easily (if you were a particularly dexterous scrub nurse), exchanging it with smaller blades as the operation became more microscopic. With the assistant resident pressing a gauze sponge on one side of the cut edge and Dr. Sypert doing the same thing on the other side, bleeding was kept to a trickle. As they pulled the skin edges slightly apart, I applied the tip of the Bovie cautery to the tissues beneath the skin: the galea, a layer of gristle that lay under the scalp. As I moved from front to back, I encountered the temporal fascia, a thicker membrane covering the temporal muscle.

Now we took time to coagulate a few larger arteries beneath the skin. Then we applied Raney clamps to the skin edges. These were small plastic jaws that were expanded by their applier device, enclosing the skin and the blood vessels beneath it. When the applier was released, the jaws closed, stopping all bleeding while not damaging the skin. These would be removed sequentially at the end of the surgery when it was time to close the wound. Our wound was about five inches long, and we used about twenty Raneys. Finally, I used the Bovie to cut through the pericranium, the last membrane covering the skull, and the temporal muscle.

Using a Cobb elevator, a metal tool with a flat, spoon-like tip about an inch in diameter, I pulled the pericranium and the temporal muscle on the inferior side (closest to the chin rather than the top of the head) away from the skull until I had created a flap of skin, membrane, and muscle, exposing the base of the skull over the frontal and temporal lobes of the brain. A moist gauze was placed over the inner surface of the flap, and it was retracted downward using skin hooks. These were literally two-pronged hooks attached to springs which connected to alligator clips. The alligator clips were attached to the drapes near the patient's shoulder, keeping the skin flap folded down and away from the skull.

Now, with the temporal and frontal portions of the skull exposed and dry, I held a large pneumatic drill in my right hand, bracing its tip with my left. The tip of its drill bit was about 2/3 of an inch in diameter. I rested it against the frontal bone, just to the side of the forehead and above the eye, a precise location known as MacCarty's keyhole, after neurosurgeon Collin MacCarty of the Mayo Clinic, who described his landmark in 1961. Putting slight pressure with my right hand, I depressed a hand lever, and the drill spun into motion. It quickly bit through the bone, making a neat hole in the skull. By a brilliant engineering design, the drill bit sensed when it had gone through bone and was touching soft tissue and jerked quickly to a stop. Withdrawing the drill, I could see the dura mater at the base of the hole. The dura, or "tough," membrane is the opaque outermost layer of three that protect the brain. Beneath the dura is the arachnoid, or "spidery," membrane, a softer translucent layer that retains the spinal fluid. Finally, the pia mater, the most delicate and barely visible of the three, adheres to the surface of the brain.

As the cut edge of the bone oozed a bit of venous blood, I used a Freer elevator, a long metal stick ("long" being a relative term in the tiny world of neurosurgery—in this case, about 7 inches long) to apply a dollop of bone wax (a combination of beeswax and paraffin) to the cut bone edge. This soft wax pushed into the small holes in the bone that contained the bleeding veins, compressing them and stopping the bleeding. Next, I made another burr hole in the temporal bone just above the zygoma and in front of the right ear. Then, using a dural elevator, a small hockey stick-shaped tool, I pushed the dura away from the undersurface of the bone at both burr holes.

Now it was time to "connect the dots." The scrub nurse exchanged the drill bit at the end of the pneumatic handle with a rotating triangular blade. She then screwed on a cover that ended in a small cuff fitting over the tip of the blade. I slipped this blunt cuff beneath the rear of the front burr hole. Again depressing the handle and pulling the saw in a semicircle, I connected the frontal and temporal burr holes. Sliding the saw out of the temporal burr hole, I inserted it into the inferior part of the frontal burr hole and pulled it toward the base of the skull. The bone became very thick here, and I couldn't cut across it, so I performed the same maneuver from the temporal burr hole forward until the two lines created by the saw were very close. Dissecting the dura away from the undersurface of the bone flap, I took the Cobb elevator, slid it under the back of the arc I had created, and pulled up firmly, cracking the small island of unconnected bone. This allowed us to remove the free plate of bone, oval and about three inches in diameter, exposing the entire surface of the lower frontal lobe and the anterior superior part of the temporal lobe of the brain, covered by dura, of course. Taking a piece of bone wax, I rubbed it along the entire cut edge of the skull where I had removed the free flap of bone, stopping all bleeding from the bone.

Exchanging the pneumatic saw blade for a one-millimeter-wide drill, we made a series of angular holes that entered at the top of the bone and emerged through the cut edge. These were placed at intervals around the circumference. Then, tiny sutures were placed through the dura and "tacked up" to the bone so that bleeding couldn't occur between the bone and the dura after the surgery. Taking a #11 blade, a thin scalpel tapering to a sharp point, and long forceps, with small teeth at the tips, we pulled up a bit of dura and pierced it with the blade. Holding the cut edge, we used a blunt scissors to create a semicircular flap of dura the same shape as the bone flap but just inside its circumference. Pulling this toward the base of the skull and sewing it to the muscle we had pulled away earlier, we now saw a landscape of brain—the lower part of the frontal lobe and the front and top of the temporal lobe covered in a thin layer of pink. The blood from the ruptured aneurysm had spread over the surface of the brain beneath the delicate pia-arachnoid membrane. The blood had insinuated itself into every sulcus and over every ridge of cortex, giving the brain an angry, swollen appearance. I could see the reason why the brain was so insulted by the hemorrhage.

Now that the brain was safely exposed, the anesthesiologist removed over an ounce of spinal fluid through the catheter we had placed at the beginning of the case. Dr. Sypert took the #11 blade and pierced the arachnoid membrane where it was stretched between the temporal and frontal lobes. A gush of pink-tinged spinal fluid emerged. As we suctioned it away, holding our suction tips against a small, cottonoid pledget that we placed on the surface of the brain, the angry swelling subsided and the brain fell away from the edges of the dura. We introduced two, thin, brain retractor blades, one beneath the frontal lobe and one at the tip of the temporal lobe, securing them with Leyla retractors. Pulling on these blades very gently, we locked them in place. This exposed a bit of the base of the skull. We brought in the operating microscope and focused it in high power, making the tiny structures at the base of the brain appear twenty times their normal size. We then opened the Sylvian fissure, the cleft between the frontal and temporal lobes, with microscissors, very small blades attached to long handles manipulated by squeezing them between the thumb and index finger. We gradually cut the arachnoid membrane between the two lobes for about a one-inch length (which seemed about a mile under the microscope). This allowed us to readjust our retractors, pulling the lobes further apart. We could now see the right optic nerve. Following this nerve toward the hole where it emerged from the eye into the brain, we now entered the danger zone.

As we elevated the frontal lobe a bit more, we could see the right carotid artery, one of the four major arteries supplying blood to the brain. As it entered the brain, it hugged the outside of the optic nerve. The first branch emerging from the outside of the carotid is the posterior communicating artery. As I mentioned earlier, it "communicates" between the circulation of the front and back parts of the brain. Now, going to even higher microscopic power, we encountered the enemy. At the junction of the carotid and posterior communicating arteries, we could see the base of an oval membrane. The membrane was thin, thin enough to see arterial blood swirling angrily inside. The aneurysm.

George Sypert stood up from the stool he had been using to perform the microsurgery to this point. He looked in my direction. "Are you ready?" I knew what he meant and slid wordlessly into the seat. We exchanged instruments. He took the microsuction and I the bipolar forceps. We were now a single organism; me dissecting the aneurysm, his hands an extension of mine, ready to assist or take over in a millisecond. I now took a second microsuction in my left hand and an angled ball probe in my right. This was a thin rod, 7.5 inches long, tapering to a thin point, which then angled at 40 degrees on a probe about as thick as a few human hairs, ending in a small metal ball. This was an ideal dissecting device, as it could round corners and open microscopic passages without cutting or tearing any structures. Placing the suction tip at the base of the aneurysm, I worked the probe around the crotch between the "distal" base and the carotid artery, then between the aneurysm and the posterior communicating artery, the "proximal" portion. Moving the probe millimeter by millimeter, the probe rode on the pulsations of the carotid, like waves on a shore at this magnification. The dome of the aneurysm, where it had ruptured, was stuck under a leaf of dura and not visible to me. As I worked around, a few wisps of clotted blood went up the suction, and, pulling a series of small adhesions, like diaphanous scar tissue, away from the neck of the aneurysm, I was able to mobilize it all around the circumference. I finally saw the oculomotor nerve, which had caused the paralysis of the patient's right eye, pushed to the side and stretched by the aneurysm.

The neck of the aneurysm was now completely free of any other structures. The blood swirling through the wall was clearer and clearer, and I knew that freeing its neck was making it more mobile . . . and more dangerous. It would burst at any moment, flooding the operating field in a sea of blood and critically obscuring our view. Sypert had quietly exchanged his suction tip for a much larger version, ready to clear the field in the event of rupture. I quickly exchanged the probe for an aneurysm clip. "A gentle curved clip, please." Communications were minimal at this point. The experienced scrub nurse knew what I meant. She took a tiny clip, a device with two curved apposing blades attached to a spring coil, and inserted the coil into an applier, a long-handled device that held the coil. I tested the clip by applying a little pressure to the applier. The blades of the clip opened, then closed tightly as I released the pressure.

Each blade slid into the proximal and distal crotches at the base of the aneurysm's neck as the blades were spread apart. The blades were slightly curved to conform to the curve of the carotid artery. I gently pushed the base of the clip against the neck and began to release. As the blades started to close, the dome of the aneurysm bulged and thinned. The dome enlarged and suddenly the field was filled with blood. I placed the tip of my suction near the dome of the aneurysm, clearing the blood just enough to finish closing the blades of the clip. The bleeding stopped. Removing the clip applier from the field, I handed it to the scrub nurse and took a long 27-gauge needle in my right hand, the smallest-bore needle in my armamentarium. With all the courage I could muster, I punctured the dome of the aneurysm and suctioned the rest of the blood from it. The dome collapsed into a tiny shred of torn tissue above the blades of the clip. Taking a microscopic blunt freer, a small spatula on the end of a thin rod, I explored the base of the aneurysm's neck and found that the clip was snug against the carotid artery, obliterating the aneurysm but not compromising the flow of blood through the carotid. Looking at the tips of the aneurysm clip, I made sure that it wasn't touching the posterior communicating artery or the oculomotor nerve. They were clear.

"Nice work." George Sypert was terse in his compliment, but it meant the world to me, as he had never before given me anything like a compliment. Although he said, "nice work," I heard "life's work," as I realized that this surgery was what I wanted to do with my career. By the time I hung up my spurs years later, I had clipped 450 aneurysms.

For the next several minutes, we irrigated the operative field and the basal cisterns (the spinal fluid spaces around the base of the brain) with sterile saline. I then injected a small amount of papaverine (a vasodilator, originally derived from the opium poppy, to help prevent the development of vasospasm—the constricting of the brain arteries due to their exposure to combined blood and spinal fluid) around the surface of the carotid artery and the small blood vessels near the aneurysm. After injecting the papaverine, we cut the sutures holding the dura up and sewed it to the dura around the edge of the bone with a 4-0 silk running suture (less than a half millimeter in diameter). We tacked up the dura by placing a 4-0 silk through the center of the dura, threading each end through two small adjacent holes drilled through the bone flap, and tying the suture outside the flap. This would hold the dura against the bone flap, again, to prevent a blood clot from developing between the dura and bone after surgery. We then secured the bone flap to the adjacent skull with the 'dogbone' plates and screws. Since the bone flap no longer had a supply of blood for nutrition, it would not be likely to fuse, or knit back together, with the skull around it.

Next, we brought the edges of the muscle together by suturing the cut edges of its fascia, the strong gristle on the surface of the muscle. Then we brought the edges of the galea, the fascial layer beneath the skin, together with absorbable sutures and stapled the skin edges with a skin stapler.

Mr. Timmons awoke a few hours later. He was oriented to time and place and moving all his limbs. He still had the right eyelid lag, and his eye was still off to the right when we elevated the lid. The day after surgery, we did an angiogram. It showed that the aneurysm was gone and the blood vessels around it looked quite normal. A few months later, he was back at work, the eyelid working just fine and the right eye a bit "lazy" but starting to move normally (his brain still had to remind that third cranial nerve to work properly). His wife mentioned that he still wasn't quite as sharp as he had been, so he was working half days. But they were both grateful to God that he was alive and well.

CHAPTER FIFTEEN

Sleigh Ride

As my neurosurgical training drew to a close, I examined my options. Dr. Rhoton mentioned the possibility of my staying at the university and taking additional training in pediatric neurosurgery. Although I greatly admired J. Parker Mickle, Gainesville's pediatric neurosurgeon, and would have enjoyed working with him, my heart was not in that subspecialty. If I was going to stay in academics, I wanted to do aneurysms, and Art Day was firmly ensconced as the faculty member doing that work. Bruce Woodham and I had talked about going to Orlando together. It was a booming, young city with lots of opportunity and only three neurosurgeons (another Rhoton suggestion to us). However, Bruce wanted to go back home to Alabama and return to give service to the people who were his roots.

So, I gave serious thought to New York. I had enjoyed my years there and missed the cosmopolitan lure of Gotham. I decided to return to New York and joined Anthony Brittis, a fine man, board-certified in both neurosurgery and physical medicine and rehabilitation. We moved to Bronxville, New York, in January of 1980. I joined the staff of four community hospitals and the faculty of New York Medical College in Valhalla. Our office was in Bronxville, as was our busiest hospital, Lawrence Hospital. I quickly made close and lasting friendships among the surgeons and internists there, and my practice grew rapidly. I also covered the emergency rooms of all the hospitals. Life was exciting, but a total whirlwind. I wouldn't look up and evaluate my life and its values for thirty years. During that time, I would part ways with Anthony Brittis (we saw the direction of the practice differently), join three other neurosurgeons in the Neurosurgical Group of Westchester in White Plains, see our group grow then split as two of us, Sam Kasoff and I, became full-time faculty at New York Medical College and established a neurosurgical residency training program there, with Sam as chairman and me as vice-chairman.

During those years, I would devote myself to neurovascular surgery, operating on aneurysms and publishing articles based on research on these cases.

The winter of 1980-81 was a cold one, and there was plenty of snow in Westchester. Another important issue to recall about that year is that we were still fairly deep in the Cold War with Russia. The Russian Mission Residential Complex was a large bunker-like high rise in the leafy Riverdale section of the Bronx, immediately adjacent to Westchester County. Arguably still a listening post for the Russians, it was a very clandestine place.

About five o'clock on a cold, February afternoon, I was called for an emergency at St. Joseph's Hospital in Yonkers, one of several community hospitals that I covered. I arrived to find a very alert, frightened, six-year-old boy sitting on a gurney. His mother was holding a bloody towel against the top of the left side of his head while three men in suits stood nearby. There was quite a bit of blood on his parka and play clothes beneath, but he was alert, and I noticed that he was moving his arms and legs normally. I smiled at him. He managed a furtive grin. His mother was very anxious and began to speak to me, urgently and desperately, in perfectly fluent Russian. I raised my hands, palms up, and tilted my head. "Allow me, Doctor." The shortest and stockiest of the three men stepped forward. He had short black hair and wore black-rimmed glasses. The suit was well-fitted, but his black shoes were clunky and industrial. "I am Dr. Boris Boriskaya." His English was heavily accented but excellent. He extended his hand. "Tom Lansen." As I shook his hand, he explained that the boy's mother wanted to know if he would live. I turned to her, smiled, and nodded. A tear coursed down her wide Slavic cheek. She kissed her son. Dr. B explained to me that the boy had been sledding with his schoolmates down the long lawn of the compound, lost control of his sled, and smacked firmly into a large tree. As far as he knew, the child had not lost consciousness. He walked with me to the gurney.

"Will you translate for me?"

"Of course."

I spoke to the mother. "I need to examine your son. What is his name?"

"Nicolai."

"Please take the towel away from his head." Both mother and son winced as she did so. He shot her an angry glance. A little blood oozed from the edges of a jagged, three-inch cut. I washed my hands and put on a pair of sterile gloves. Using a gauze, I gently pushed away a few strands of blood-matted blond hair to evaluate the wound. It was horizontal, about two inches behind his hairline. Very gingerly, I introduced my index finger into the wound. The lad was game—he winced but didn't cry. I felt a depression of the skull beneath the center of the wound. Sometimes a blood clot beneath the pericranium, the gristle that coats the outside of the skull, could simulate a skull fracture. Removing my finger and taping a gauze loosely over the wound, I did a neurological examination. I palpated the back of his neck.

"Does your neck hurt, Niki?"

"Nyet." I had him bend his head forward and back. No discomfort. Dr. Rhoton had taught me a thousand times that any blow strong enough to cause a head injury was strong enough to injure the neck. Missing a neck fracture or dislocation could have disastrous consequences. His vision and eye movements were normal, as were his sensation and reflexes. His strength was good, and he followed all commands like an old trooper. I liked this kid.

Unfortunately, our luck ran out there. A front and side x-ray of his skull showed that this was not a hemorrhage under the pericranium but a depressed skull fracture. A circular fracture about an inch wide, with a vertical line through the center, was depressed beneath the adjacent skull. The vertical line created a V-shaped secondary depression that was pushing about half an inch into the boy's brain. The area of the brain affected would be expressive speech.

"How does his speech seem to you, Dr. B?" Boris was hovering near me, as he had from the first minute of our meeting.

"Just fine."

"He's going to need surgery. But first we have to get a CAT scan."

Computerized Axial Tomography was still in its relative infancy at this time, and there were few units in community hospitals. St. Joseph's was no exception. We packed Nicolai into an ambulance and drove him a couple of miles to the nearest scanner.

"May I come to the console room with you? I've never seen one of these studies." We watched the monitor as the study was slowly reconstructed from digital data into white, gray, and black pixels that gradually turned into pictures of slices of the child's brain at one-centimeter intervals. The process took about thirty painstaking minutes (now the whole thing is done in seconds). We watched anxiously as the slices around the area of injury appeared. There was the white of the bone with the sharp V pushing against the gray representation of brain tissue. Fortunately, so far, there was no hemorrhage within the brain. Nonetheless, I knew the fracture had to be elevated or it would do damage. Even if it didn't, it would become a focus for possible seizures later.

Back at St. Joseph's, Niki had fallen asleep on the ER gurney. I asked Boris if there could have been any other cause for the injury, my eyes conveying the obvious question. He was stern and direct. "No possibility." I trusted him, but, as Ronald Reagan said, "Trust, but verify." The police who had stood patiently by since Niki's admission would take care of following that up. Then I spoke with his mother, flanked by the two quiet suits. Boris told me she was a UN official and had been in New York for three years. "Ma'am, we're going to have to take Nicolai to the operating room. We'll put him to sleep, shave a little hair around the cut. I'll have to enlarge it a bit so that I can get in, elevate the fractured bone, and repair it. If I can, I'll use tiny plates to secure the fractured part back to the normal skull. If I can't, I'll replace the broken piece with resin that will harden to be just as strong as the skull. Anything can happen in surgery, even brain bleeding or damage. But the broken piece needs to be fixed, and I need to have a look at your son's brain underneath to make sure it's okay." After translation, she nodded as she dabbed a tear from her eye. I handed her the permission sheet for signature. One of the suits took it from my hand.

"She does not have the authority to consent," he said tersely. Then he signed the document and handed it back to me.

"And you are . . . ?" He acted as if he had not heard my question. I asked Boris if this guy was legally in charge. He assured me that he was. This complicated things for me. If something went wrong and this guy didn't have the authority to consent to the surgery, I would have created an international incident. On the other hand, if I pressed them, surgery could be delayed and the child put at risk. I had to trust Boris. The other suit motioned to Dr. B, and the three walked to the corner of the room. One of them spoke quietly to the doctor, who reddened and shook his head, whispering vigorously. The man's voice rose slightly as he spoke slowly and emphatically.

It seemed a rather bizarre Cold War fantasy was taking place. Dr. B walked back to where I stood and explained that they needed him to be with me at all times. This included the operating room. I wanted the reason. "Because they are concerned that you will place a monitoring device in the boy's head during surgery." I couldn't help but laugh out loud. The suits were not amused. Boris lowered his head for a moment. Even he couldn't swallow this tripe. Then our eyes met.

"Look, doctor, I'm in a tough spot here. My wife is a consular official. I was allowed to join her here about four months ago. Any failure on my part will send me home. Please."

"Boris, do they really think that I quickly and covertly called CIA and asked them to speed a listening probe to me? Or am I an agent, too?" He cocked his head to the side and just looked at me.

"I know you're not. But more importantly, they don't." His face stayed pointed at mine, but his eyes gestured in the direction of the suits. I sighed.

"Boris, are you a surgeon?" He shook his head. "Well, don't pass out, and stay out of the way." His grin betrayed an endearing gap between his front teeth.

Nicolai was asleep and intubated. I had placed the back of his head on a donut head rest, elevated it slightly, and shaved about a half inch of his hair all around the wound. I injected diluted epinephrine into the skin near the poles of the wound to reduce bleeding. I then extended the cut a half inch beyond both ends. The slight bleeding was controlled by placing a flat, self-retaining retractor in the wound and spreading it until the edges of the fracture were completely exposed. I cleared away the shreds of pericranium clinging to the fracture, then used a high-speed pneumatic drill to make a small hole just adjacent to the fracture. Using a pneumatic saw, I made a circular cut through the skull around the outside of the fracture, beginning at one end of the burr hole and ending at the other side. Through the hole, I then introduced a dural separator, a paper-thin, slender, rectangular probe attached to a long hexagonal handle. I gently rotated the probe, carefully separating the dura from the depressed fracture. As I approached the linear fracture that ran through the center of the depression and marked the deepest part of the fracture, where the dura might be stuck or even torn, I worked very slowly and meticulously. If the dura was torn, a false move here could cause the probe to go under the dura and possibly injure the brain. Fortunately, the dura separated fully from the fracture. I put in a #3 dissector, a larger curved probe. I elevated the depressed segment and the cuff of bone I had created and removed it from the skull. A clean, circular hole in the skull remained. I applied bone wax to the cut edge of the skull and inspected the brain. The dura had a small, irregular bluish bruise; in the center was a small tear in the dura. With an Adson forceps, I grasped the dura by the edge of the torn area and elevated it. With a tiny blade, I extended the tear a few millimeters in both directions. This allowed me to see the surface of the brain. The view pleased me. There were no bruises or cuts on the surface. It was pristine. I quickly sewed the edges of dura watertight.

Turning my attention to the piece of removed bone, I was able to re-contour the depression to its normal curve. The edge of the fracture was secure to the cuff of bone I had made. I placed a suture through the center of the dura and drilled two small holes near the center of the fractured medallion of bone. I brought the ends of the suture through the holes and tied them at the surface. Similarly, I tacked up the edges of the dura to the adjacent skull through small drill holes I made in the circumference of the skull defect, using tiny silk sutures. These maneuvers would prevent a blood clot from developing between the dura and the skull after surgery. Finally, I placed the medallion of repaired bone back into the defect and secured it with three of the familiar small, dog bone plates, thin titanium plates about one-third of an inch long with holes at each end to allow me to drill 3 mm screws into the skull and the fractured medallion, permanently securing the fragment. I quickly closed the wound using 4-0 vicryl sutures to approximate the galea in order to prevent bleeding under the scalp, and 4-0 transparent nylon to close the skin. The wound was bandaged, Nicolai was awakened and taken to the recovery room. As I made sure that he was neurologically intact, I placed my hand on his mother's shoulder. She quietly held her boy's hand. The suits were unmoved.

After a night in the ICU, Niki spent a day on the pediatric floor, relishing the ice cream treats and none the worse for wear. I saw him one week later in my office for suture removal . . . with the mother, Dr. B, and, of course, the suits. As I bade Nicolai farewell, having instructed the doctor regarding further post-operative care, the boy shook my hand and smiled. "Thank you for make me better, doctor." His mother beamed at his mastery of English.

In 1983, I took my oral boards. This was the final test, the culmination of the lengthy series of national examinations that had begun in my second year of medical school. All the other tests were written exams, and I dreaded the thought of an oral test. Very nerve-racking. The oral examination required building up a substantial log of operations after the completion of the residency. After passing the last written examination, during your residency, you are Board eligible. When you pass the orals, you become Board certified. But passing is not a cinch. First, there is the psychological pressure—several hours of questions and answers one on one with six renowned experts, two at a time for three sessions. Second, there is the knowledge of how important board certification is, and the fact that this is the last exam of hundreds that you've taken throughout your educational career. Finally, a substantial percentage of candidates failed the exam. Of course, you could take it again. But if you failed again, you were required to take the written examination again before applying for the oral.

My old friend, Bruce Woodham, and I decided to do a full court press on this one, as we would be taking the exam at the same session. We left our practices and families for several weeks and studied our texts, our cases, and grilled each other on every bit of subject matter back through all the years of our residencies. As our confidence grew, we considered the variables. One obvious factor was the venue. Our test was to be given at the LSU Medical Center in New Orleans, hosted by Dr. David Kline, the chairman of the Neurosurgery department and the world's expert on peripheral nerve disorders. One of the most daunting challenges to any resident is mastering the anatomy of the peripheral nerves—the brachial plexus, the lumbar plexus, the lumbosacral plexus. Each group of nerves united, branched, reunited in different patterns. And each level and section, in roots, cords, and nerves, had separate names and locations. It was a gargantuan task, and very few surgeons specialized in this discipline. But David Kline was one of them . . . the best one. So, we drilled and drilled on the peripheral nerves, until we would dream about them.

We arrived in NOLA on a muggy April day. Is there another kind of day in New Orleans? Bruce and I splurged. Each of us rented a suite in one of the most famous hotels in the city, on Bourbon Street in the French Quarter. We were both too nervous to enjoy it, but as I recall, it was quite elegant.

The Oral Board examination was divided into three one-day sessions. Bruce was assigned to Day 1, I got Day 2. The first thing we learned on arrival was that Dr. Kline was hosting the tests but was not going to be one of the examiners. All of that cramming about peripheral nerves could have been used on re-mastering more relevant information. However, true to form, Dr. Woodham sailed through the exam and the next morning he was elated when his office called to tell him that a telegram had arrived to let him know he had passed. Now, I began to fantasize like Walter Mitty. I would fail, humiliated in front of my colleagues, the word spreading like wildfire across the country to my old fellow-residents, instructors, and most terribly, to Dr. Rhoton. Inevitably, the time for the interviews came.

I walked into the LSU neurosurgery department as if I were going to the gallows. I faced each pair of experts with my best attempt at bravery; they included a famous aneurysm surgeon from the University of Minnesota, a renowned microneurosurgeon from Chicago, an epilepsy expert from St. Louis, one of America's leading surgeons from Pittsburgh, a senior and universally acknowledged academic from Boston and an accomplished pediatric neurosurgeon from San Francisco. I don't remember much about the rest of the day. I patched together my answers as best I could, leaving with the impression that I had got most of the answers correct, particularly in the section of cerebrovascular surgery—aneurysms, my favorite topic. Nonetheless, I left LSU with a feeling of dread. Bruce and I spent the rest of the evening at the hotel's bar, he euphoric, I catatonic.

The next morning, I got a call from my office. I had passed. I was officially certified by the American Board of Neurological Surgeons and would be allowed to join the American Association of Neurological Surgeons. I was tremendously relieved. First, I tried Woodham's room but then I realized that he had taken the first flight that morning back to Alabama. I walked over to the window and opened the large French doors that looked out onto Bourbon Street. Sanitation workers were busily sweeping up the detritus from last night's inevitable massive party. As I looked across the narrow street to the building opposite mine, I saw, looking back at me, a rather obese gentleman, his chin on his right hand, his elbow resting on the railing of his veranda. I also could not help but notice that his head was shaved, and he was wearing large, gold, hoop earrings and an off-the-shoulder, pink, taffeta evening gown. I turned around, walked over to my suitcase, and murmured, "I gotta get outa here!" It would be twenty-five years before I set foot in New Orleans again.

CHAPTER SIXTEEN

Looks Like a Baseball

Neurologist Ron Silverman was not a man given to exaggeration. Educated at Albert Einstein College of Medicine and trained in neurology at New York's Mt. Sinai Hospital, he was bright and quiet, with a gentle sense of humor and a calm, direct method of diagnosing and treating patients. We became friends as well as colleagues almost as soon as I arrived in New York. So, when Ron called my office and told my assistant that I was to see a consult at Lawrence Hospital urgently, I knew that it was serious.

Margaret Robbins was a lovely, fifty-two-year-old, high school math teacher. She had no children of her own but was absolutely devoted to her students. So, it was horrifying to them when, standing at the blackboard one spring afternoon, she suddenly stared into space for a moment, then fell to the ground like a dead weight. She lay there shaking violently for several minutes, blood dripping from the corner of her mouth—she had bitten her tongue. Students stood trembling. One screamed. Two others ran for help. Mrs. Robbins had suffered a grand mal seizure. The violent shaking gradually subsided with occasional small bursts continuing, like the aftershocks of an earthquake. Then she was calm, as calm as death. She had kicked off one of her shoes and her blond hair was disheveled, the band at the back partly dislodged, strands of hair going in all directions.

Suddenly, the principal and the school nurse were hovering over her while a knot of students stood by with tears in their eyes. Then she slowly opened her eyes and rolled from her side onto her back. She stared and looked around uncomprehending. Her lips began to move and her garbled speech started to clear.

"What . . ."

"Take it easy, Peggy." Joe Carvacchio touched her shoulder gently. He had been principal of Eastwood High for only three years, but they had worked together and been friends for twenty.

As the paramedics lifted her gently to the stretcher, her focus and her words cleared. "What happened, Joe?" She touched her tongue where it was sore and saw the blood on her fingertip.

"You fell, Peggy. You fell." She looked at him quizzically as they rolled her to the ambulance.

Ron Silverman had left a message for me: the patient had a large mass. This was a catch-all term for anything occupying space in the brain where it shouldn't be—a tumor, an abscess, anything that pressed on the brain.

I was surprised when I met Peggy Robbins. Of course, she was nervous, still not knowing what had happened to her or why. But otherwise she was intact. Her speech was a little clumsy because of her now-swollen tongue but she was alert and oriented to time and place. She couldn't remember anything from lunch onward—nothing about her class that afternoon, nothing until she was being taken to the ambulance. She was experiencing retrograde amnesia, a loss of memory for everything that happened before the seizure. This is a common occurrence, whether with a seizure or a concussion. Had she had any strange feelings or sensations before blacking out? Seizures are often preceded by an aura—a sense of unrest, an uncomfortable feeling in the stomach, a strange smell or taste. No, she didn't remember anything like that.

I tested her cranial nerves. No loss of visual field, no double vision, no loss of facial sensation or facial weakness. I asked her to hold her hands straight out in front of her and close her eyes. There was no downward drift of either limb to betray subtle weakness, or an upward drift, a clue to a loss of sensory awareness of the arm. These would give me some idea of where the lesion was irritating or even damaging her brain. Her strength and reflexes were normal and symmetrical. I stroked the sole of her foot with the pointed tip of my reflex hammer. Her toes bent downward; there was no Babinski's sign. Joseph Babinski, a 19th century French neurologist, had found that an upward thrust of the toes to stimulation of the bottom of the foot was normal in newborns but a sign of pathology in the brain or spinal cord in adults. Finally, I asked her to walk in tandem along a tile line in the floor and to touch her fingertips to her nose, alternating the left and right hands. This would be a sign of a problem with the cerebellum, the brain's organ of coordination. Her performance was flawless. If I hadn't been told that she had a grand mal seizure two hours before, I would have been wondering what she was doing in the hospital.

A word about seizures. While there are lots of varieties, for our purposes, there are four basic types: grand mal, petit mal, focal and complex partial seizures. Grand mal, or generalized seizures, are the most disturbing to the observer. They are marked by a loss of consciousness and generalized, rhythmic shaking called tonic-clonic activity. This vigorous shaking can cause the victim to bite their tongue, bruise their bodies, even break a bone. The natural reaction of the well-intentioned observer is to put a spoon or a tongue depressor into the person's mouth. This can actually cause serious injury. The right thing to do is to gently turn the victim on their side so that they don't breathe in their saliva or blood and wait for the seizure to subside. It will almost certainly stop on its own. On very rare occasions, the seizure won't stop, in a condition called status epilepticus. The only hope here is to get the person to the hospital as quickly as possible, where intravenous anticonvulsant medication and muscle relaxants can be given as a life-saving measure.

Seizures are caused by electrical "short circuits" in the pathways of the brain. Often starting from a small area of abnormal brain tissue—a "focus" that can be something we're born with or an area of brain irritated by a blood clot or the local pressure of a tumor on brain cells—it can remain localized, causing a focal seizure, where there may be a rhythmic twitching of the opposite hand or a staring episode with turning of the head away from the focus, or develop into a generalized seizure, recruiting circuits throughout the brain into a massive outburst of firing electricity.

The generalized, or grand mal, seizure doesn't give us many clues to the site of the seizure or its cause, although an old medical maxim says that a grand mal seizure in an adult is the sign of a brain tumor until proven otherwise.

The other three seizure types are a little more helpful in giving us clues. The petit mal, or absence (pronounce it the French way—

"ab-sonse") seizure is usually a short spell of inattention, staring into space and a complete indifference to one's surroundings. It occurs commonly in children and is associated with the brain's deep structures. Sometimes these spells simply resolve, or they can evolve into episodes of grand mal seizures—classic epilepsy.

Focal seizures can give us the best clues of their origin. For example, a seizure that causes only shaking of the right hand points us to a lesion on the lower rear part of the outside of the left frontal lobe.

Finally, complex partial seizures; these are seizures marked by complicated activity of which the victim is completely unaware. They may stare into space and turn their head while lifting one hand and licking their lips. These spells usually localize to the temporal lobe.

These days, seizure disorders are increasingly controllable with a variety of anti-convulsants. In Peggy Robbins' case, a combination of Dilantin and phenobarbital prevented any further activity. And, although I was pleasantly surprised by her absolutely normal exam, I maintained a cautious sense of pessimism, knowing that she'd just had a grand mal seizure and getting Dr. Silverman's message about her MRI scan. But nothing could have prepared me for the jaw-dropping shock of seeing her MRI. By the late 1980s, imaging technologies had come a long way.

In 1895, Wilhelm Roentgen, a mechanical engineer and physicist, discovered that electromagnetic radiation, x-rays, could be absorbed in different degrees reflected by the density of the tissues they passed through. The first x-ray picture he took was of his wife's hand. When she saw her skeletal fingers on the image, she exclaimed, "I have seen my death." The cathode rays were soon absorbed onto photographic film and x-rays were born. The next great breakthrough was achieved in 1927 by Portuguese neurologist Egas Muniz, who injected a contrast agent, very opaque to x-rays into arteries and veins, allowing the blood vessels to be outlined clearly against the relative pallor of the surrounding tissues. This angiography gave surgeons the ability to outline aneurysms, vascular malformations, and tumors—now we knew exactly where the villains were and where to operate to remove them. In 1967, just eight years before I began my neurosurgical training at the University of Florida, Sir Godfrey Hounsfeld leapt lightyears ahead with his invention of computerized axial tomography. The computer allowed an x-ray source to spin around the brain (or any other organ), sending radiation to small receptors. The data of all these individual beams was then collated and analyzed by a computer, for the first time rendering an amazing anatomic picture of the brain at each "slice" or level of inspection. It was as if we were cutting the brain into one-centimeter-thick sections, showing each slice as if it were demonstrated in a pathology lab. We could see the grey matter, the white matter, the ventricles, and, yes, brain tumors as if we were looking at them in the lab. The first time I saw one of these studies, in 1973 at NYU, I was astonished. It had revolutionized medicine.

But I was learning about the brain in a magical era. Only a few years later, in the early 1970s, just as I was leaving New York for the University of Florida, physicists Peter Mansfield and Paul Lauterbur (who would be awarded the Nobel Prize for their work in 2003) discovered that they could magnetically stimulate tissues, and that different types of cells would "relax" from this stimulation at different rates. These different rates of relaxation could be detected by receptors and analyzed by a computer. The differences could be assigned a different visual "intensity." The different intensities could then be assembled into a picture of each slice of the brain. Magnetic Resonance Imaging, MRI, was born. The addition of intravenous contrast agents would allow computers to portray brain tissue and abnormal tissues as precisely as an anatomy book. The *coup de gras* occurred when, a few years later, stereotactic surgery became a reality. This allowed us to take a metal probe, with small radioreceptors attached, and correlate its radio waves with the MRI. We could now touch the probe, in real time, to a point on the patient's scalp, and identify exactly where to enter the skull to find our nemesis, the brain tumor. It even allowed us to outline the tumor, telling us how large the bone flap had to be to encircle the edges of the tumor—not a centimeter too large or too small. Paul Broca, the great 19th century neurologist, and Wilder Penfield, a 20th century Princeton football star turned Montreal neurosurgeon, had given us the ability to generally localize brain tumors based on neurological findings. Hounsfeld, Mansfield, and Lauterbur had now given us the tools to take a patient who had a grand mal seizure, place them in a diagnostic tube for a few minutes, and emerge with a picture of the exact location, extent, and probable nature of the tumor.

Peggy Robbins was an early beneficiary of this extraordinary technology. As I sat with South African neuroradiologist Alan Danziger and scrolled through the photographic films of her brain, he gave me a sidelong glance and a raised eyebrow. "Looks like a large baseball, don't you think?" Alan had become thoroughly Americanized in his New York years. Her contrast-enhanced MRI showed us a huge, bright, oval lesion that occupied about two-thirds of the right side of her brain. The tumor had compressed the underlying brain tissue and shifted its contents from right to left. The ventricles, the spinal fluid-containing chambers of the brain, were compressed and pushed into the left side of the skull. We realized at once the reason that she had survived without symptoms. The brain tumor was all a single, bright color. This was a benign tumor, a meningioma. If it had been a malignant tumor, such as a fast-growing, life-ending glioblastoma, or a metastasis from a cancer spread from somewhere else in the body, it would have a mottled signal, with areas of dead tissue showing dark against the bright background. It had grown so slowly that it tricked the brain into accepting it as a normal part of its surroundings. But it had now irritated the adjacent brain tissue enough to trigger a seizure. This had given us a signal of the tumor and had saved Peggy's life. I was almost certain that her tumor was a benign meningioma, although I had treated few malignant meningiomas, which were as fast-growing, relentless in their recurrence, and capable of metastasis like any other cancer.

I explained to Peggy Robbins that I was not comfortable doing this surgery in a community hospital. I felt that, despite the excellence of the nurses and anesthesiologists at the hospital, this surgery required a team that did complex brain surgery on a regular basis, and that she would require careful monitoring in a neurosurgical intensive care unit, with resident physicians and intensivists available twenty-four hours a day.

That evening, I sat with Peggy and her husband, Edmund, and explained what we were up against. She had a tumor, the largest I had ever seen. The good news was that it was probably benign, non-cancerous. The bad news was that it had to come out, and its removal was not going to be an easy task. We would have to remove a piece of her skull that would extend over most of the right side of her head, and we might not be able to put that piece of skull back if her brain swelled too greatly in reaction to the removal of the tumor. The tumor would have stolen blood vessels from most of this part of her brain. It would have to be removed, piece by agonizing piece, over many hours. The miniscule blood vessels would have to be separated from the brain microscopically. Some would have to be sacrificed, and these could share blood supply to parts of the brain that could steal function from the brain itself, causing a stroke. Finally, removing the tumor from her brain could upset the delicate balance that the tumor's growth had caused over years, causing massive swelling and even risking her life. Peggy was frightened, tearful. Edmund was somber, withdrawn. I was . . . concerned. I knew that this was the kind of surgery I had trained for over many years. I could remove this tumor, but the outcome could be catastrophic for this fine lady who meant so much to so many. I hoped that this thought hadn't been read by the patient. We all knew that we had no choice. We transferred her to the Westchester Medical Center, the region's major academic medical center, where she was prepared by the neurosurgical team.

Mrs. Robbins was asleep and intubated. I shaved her scalp (she had decided that so much was going to have to be shaven that shaving the whole thing would let her hair grow back at the same rate, or she could wear a wig for a while). I gently turned her head to the left, careful to coordinate with the resident elevating her right shoulder to avoid hurting her neck. We placed her head in the head holder and secured it with pins. I studied her MRI again and calculated where the tumor would project onto the surface of the skull. I planned a curvilinear incision from the hairline above her right pupil, back along the middle of the scalp to a place just behind her right ear, then curved down to the ear, then forward and down again, to the zygoma, the horizontal bone running from the ear to the cheekbone (maxilla). The contours of this incision would make enough room to surround the tumor. We sterilized her scalp, went to the scrub sink outside the OR, gave our hands and arms a ten-minute scrub, returned to gown and glove, drew the anticipated incision with a sterile marker and draped the entire field except for the area around the surgical incision, which was exposed through the plastic adhesive window in the center of the drape. The suction tubing, Bovie, and bipolar cauteries were secured and their ends passed off the field. The trays with all of the instruments that we anticipated needing were placed. We injected the course of the incision with a dilute solution of saline and epinephrine to reduce bleeding, then opened the incision and applied the Raney clips for quick control of bleeding. It was remarkable that, with a great deal of experience and a coordinated operating team, an incision this large, about 25 cm in total length, could be made with only about an ounce of blood lost.

Using a Cobb elevator, we elevated the skin and pericranium and folded the resultant flap of skin forward and downward, rolling it over a lap pad (a cotton pad thicker than the 4 x 4-inch surgical sponges we used in cranial surgery and more often used in abdominal laparotomies; hence the name) to prevent the skin flap from being folded over itself too acutely, which could close the blood vessels and starve the skin flap of its blood supply. This could create a catastrophe; the skin flap could actually die, requiring multiple surgeries and skin grafts to replace it—one of a neurosurgeon's worst nightmares. Remember little Ricky Buford in Chapter 8? Fishhooks—yes, fishhooks, although with blunt tips—were then inserted under the base of the turned skin flap. Each was attached to a rubber band. Five of these were collected and secured with a surgical tie, which was then clamped to the drape of the overhead table, securing the skin flap.

Next, we addressed the fan-shaped temporalis muscle, its broad end secured to the skull and its narrow end diving deep to the zygoma, where it attached to the jawbone, the mandible. Using a Bovie, we cut a line parallel to the broad end, about a centimeter from the edge. We then used the Cobb elevator to undermine the muscle, again elevating a second flap, which we secured to the undersurface of the skin with 3-0 silk ties—sutures a fifth of a millimeter in diameter. We covered the ensemble with moist, surgical gauze, again, to keep the skin and muscle from drying out during the procedure, endangering its blood supply.

Now we could finally see all of the skull that we would need to temporarily remove. Placing burr holes around the circumference, we connected them with the pneumatic saw until the bone flap was free. Then, using first a dural separator then the curved Penfield #3, part of a set of brain surgery instruments devised by Wilder Penfield, founder of the Montreal Neurological Institute, we separated the dural membrane from the undersurface of the skull. But perhaps a word about Penfield is in order.

Born in 1891 in Spokane, Washington, Penfield played football at Princeton and then received a Rhodes scholarship to Oxford. Returning to study medicine at Johns Hopkins, he then trained under Harvey Cushing at Harvard. He began his career at Columbia University in New York, where he embarked on his goal of mapping brain anatomy and function (he would stimulate a small area of a sedated patient's brain during surgery and record where the response occurred—a movement of the hand, a feeling on the tongue or the foot) and the surgical treatment of epilepsy. In 1928, he accepted an invitation to become the first neurosurgeon at McGill University in Montreal. His efforts attracted the attention of David Rockefeller, and, in 1934, the Rockefeller Foundation funded Penfield's Montreal Neurological Institute, which he would direct until his retirement in 1960, making myriad scientific contributions, developing cranial surgeries and instrumentation, as well as training generations of brain surgeons.

Using the Penfield #3, we gradually separated the dural membrane from the skull flap until it was free. By good fortune, the tumor, although it had grown through the dura, had not invaded the skull. We could remove the bone freely. Had the bone been invaded by the tumor, we would have had to remove the portion involved and fill it in with a wire mesh or resin cranioplasty to take the place of the natural bone. But that's where our luck ended.

The tumor was not happy to be bothered by us. It had grown over the space of years to about the size of a medium baked potato, about four inches long and three wide. It indented the brain to a depth of about three inches. It was now pulsing and swelling, with the brain around it also starting to swell, pushing at the edges of the cut skull. At the beginning of the case, we had known that this was likely to happen, so we had given her a large dose of steroids and Mannitol to combat the swelling. It hadn't been enough.

We gave her another diuretic and asked the anesthesiologist to hyperventilate her—increase the frequency and depth of oxygen supply to her lungs. This would reduce her level of carbon dioxide, which promoted brain swelling. It worked. For at least a little while, the brain pulled away from the skull slightly. But we had no time to savor our little victory. I knew what had to be done, and quickly. The tumor had to be "gutted" to reduce its mass effect on the brain.

I outlined the tumor with the stereotactic probe and then made a small cut through the dura, just beyond the junction of the tumor and the adjacent brain. With a scissor—the tip of its deeper blade flattened and dulled (to avoid lacerating the tissue below)—I cut the dura all the way around the tumor. Along the way, I encountered and coagulated several large meningeal feeding arteries that ran through the dura and had nourished the tumor as it grew from the base of the dura and pushed into the brain.

Keeping the tips of the irrigating Malis bipolar cautery forceps separated about five millimeters apart, I quickly coagulated the small blood vessels that covered about an inch of the surface of the tumor. Taking a small "fifteen blade," I made a long cut into the tumor. The chief resident held two brain retractors against the cut edge, spreading them slightly to give me access to the interior of the tumor. I then took pituitary forceps—a scissors-based device with apposing cups at the working end. Grasping a piece of tumor about a half inch long and an eighth of an inch wide, I passed it to the scrub nurse for a "frozen section" analysis by the neuropathologist. We really didn't need confirmation of the nature of the tumor, though. It was clearly a meningioma, as suggested by the MRI. Firm and not terribly vascular (bloody), it couldn't be easily removed by suction like a primary glioma arising from the brain tissue itself would be.

After a few more "bites" of the tumor had been taken, and

applying the Malis bipolar to the small blood vessels cut by this activity, I knew we were on a very limited clock, and that the tumor and brain would soon overcome the effects of the steroids, diuretics, and hyperventilation and start their angry swelling again. So, I resorted to a technique that was over seventy-five years old. Removing the blade of the Bovie cautery, I replaced it with a wire loop. When the Bovie was activated, the loop would be completely electrified, enabling me to cut through a swath of tumor and scoop it out like a warm ladle in frozen ice cream (for some reason, neurosurgeons—particularly this neurosurgeon—are afflicted with food analogies).

This technique was much more successful, and I found that I had been able to remove about three more ounces of tumor over the next fifteen minutes. Now we were moving. Nonetheless, great care was still warranted. As the unipolar wire loop came closer to the edges of the tumor in the deep areas where our visibility was limited, it might approach the surface of the brain adjacent to the tumor where its current could be transmitted to damage normal brain, with obviously devastating effects. So, the deeper I went, and the closer I thought I was to the brain, the thinner the slices I made with the wire loop. A year or two after I operated on Ms. Robbins, stereotactic localization techniques would be commonplace. With them, we would merge the preoperative MRI scan with intraoperative points of reference on the patient's scalp and face. A probe could then be coordinated with an antenna and it could be used in real time to identify the exact point of its tip. Voila! We can touch the tip of the probe to the deep part of the tumor and know exactly how close we are to the adjacent brain.

Every few seconds we would stop to coagulate "bleeders,"

assess the amount of tumor removed and estimate the size of the tumor that remained. An hour . . . two . . . three had passed—I was oblivious of the time—and the tumor was now a hollow shell. We shifted our attention to the outside of the tumor, the capsule. I slowly peeled the rim of the tumor away from the brain, inserting tiny cottonoids between the brain and the tumor capsule until there were scores of these pledgets around the tumor. Finally, after nearly five hours of dissection, the last bit of tumor was peeled away from the brain. There were more than a hundred cottonoids covering the exposed brain. While the resident gently irrigated the cottonoids with warm saline, I gingerly lifted each one away from the brain. When we finished, there was a cavity in the brain that looked like the crater of a small volcano. We filled the cavity with saline three or four times, coagulating an occasional, bruised microvessel betrayed by a wisp of blood in the clear irrigant. We filled the cavity one last time with saline and watched it for about fifteen minutes. The fluid remained clear, telling us that there were no more hidden vessels that would bleed after we closed the wound. The brain was soft and pulsatile, relaxed now that the invader had been removed.

We replaced the large piece of dura that had to be sacrificed with the tumor with a porcine (pig) graft, sewing it to the adjacent normal dura. Passing a tiny probe through the suture line to rest on the surface of the brain (it would measure the pressure in the brain after surgery to detect any swelling), we brought its terminus out through one of the burr holes, returned the bone flap into place, and secured it with micro-screws and plates. The galea was brought together with 3-0 monocryl absorbable suture and the skin edges with 4-0 blue nylon suture, using several single sutures in a running, locking pattern. We dressed the wound with a strip of thin gauze impregnated with an antibiotic, several folded 4 x 4-inch gauze pads, and a head wrap of two layers, very soft Kerlix, then a roll of three-inch-wide gauze. These were applied very gently and without traction to prevent any tension on the wound.

Mrs. Robbins very gradually awakened from anesthesia. After a total of six hours under sedation, it took her most of that evening to begin to respond to voices. However, by morning, she was fully awake and, thank God, completely intact. The intracranial pressure monitor was removed on the second day, and her sutures were taken out five days later. When I saw her for a two-week postop visit, her hair was growing back and her anxiety was much reduced. She returned to her math class in the fall.

Two years later, on a routine follow-up MRI, a pea-sized recurrence of tumor was picked up at the edge of our dural suture line. Fortunately, by this time, no surgery was required to treat the tiny lesion. A revolutionary technique called stereotactic radiosurgery had become available that enabled us to obliterate the tumor without making an incision. More about that later. Two generations of modern technology had resulted in a very grateful patient and a very happy surgeon.

And so the years passed, from case to case, hospital to hospital. I took on leadership roles, becoming chief of neurosurgery at several of the hospitals in Westchester County. In 1997, I served as president of the Westchester County Medical Society, the second-oldest in America, and used the opportunity to examine the archives of the society and to write its history—from 1797 to 1997.

CHAPTER SEVENTEEN

You Call Yourself a Cardiologist?

Hydrocephalus translates from the Latin as "water brain." The translation is quite accurate. There are four chambers, or ventricles, in the center of the brain connected to each other by small canals. These ventricles manufacture and contain cerebrospinal fluid, or CSF. Small tufts of tissue in the chambers, the choroid plexus, make the CSF, which then drains down and out over the spinal cord and back over the surface of the brain to be absorbed into large veins through filtering devices called pacchionian granulations. The system is a beautiful machine—unless it fails.

The two most common means of failure are in newborns and the aged, respectively. Noncommunicating, or obstructive, hydrocephalus is usually detected in utero or at birth. The baby's head is large, and ultrasound imaging shows that it is filled with massively distended ventricles, often with the cerebral cortex reduced to a compressed rim against the inner surface of the skull. The most common cause of this type of hydrocephalus is the failure of the full development of the cerebral aqueduct, a long slender channel between the third and fourth ventricle. This was demonstrated experimentally by the great Johns Hopkins neurosurgeon, Walter Dandy. This blockade of flow causes strong pressure to build up relatively quickly in the brain. This can obviously lead to profound brain damage. However, the increasing sophistication of imaging and microsurgery has allowed this pressure to be diverted by placing a shunting device that drains the excess fluid into the abdomen, the chest or a large central vein. Another technique allows the drainage of CSF from the inside to the outside of the brain by microscopically creating a hole through a very thin membrane at the base of the brain. These procedures can result in the re-expansion of the brain, and normal function. Unfortunately, many babies affected with hydrocephalus have other congenital problems, such as spina bifida, which can result in paralysis and spinal deformities. Any way you size it up, these little folks start with a tough series of challenges. And, once in a while, it makes them stronger than the rest of us. But more on that later.

Communicating, or normal pressure, hydrocephalus is generally more subtle and sneaky in its onset. Although it occasionally develops after blood is spilled into the CSF by a ruptured aneurysm or head trauma, the more common onset is in the elderly. One theory holds that small traumas in life to the brain, or even viral infections, gradually accumulate proteins that get stuck at the base of the brain or in the pacchionian granulations. This process slows the flow of CSF and very slowly increases the pressure in the ventricles until symptoms of this pressure emerge. With modern imaging such as MRI, the slow seepage of fluid through the walls of the ventricles can be seen as a change in signal or color of the brain tissue where it touches the ventricles. However, the size of the ventricles in communicating hydrocephalus almost never reaches the size of those in infantile hydrocephalus.

This version of hydrocephalus is known as communicating, as there is no distinct area of blockage seen, such as the cerebral aqueduct. It's also called "normal pressure" hydrocephalus, or NPH. This is because, when a spinal tap is performed in non-communicating hydrocephalus, a manometer connected to the needle shows a very high pressure of spinal fluid. But in communicating hydrocephalus, there is no distinct blockage, so the pressure may be normal or only slightly increased.

In NPH, the most common symptoms are confusion or dementia, incoordination with a "wide-based" stance and gait, and urinary incontinence. These symptoms are the result of the pressure first affecting the nerve fibers that control these functions near the surface of the ventricles. One of the pioneers in the treatment of this disease, Dr. Salomon Hakim, a neurosurgeon from Colombia with a Harvard PhD, developed many of the early devices which, although refined over the years, are still what neurosurgeons use today for infantile and adult hydrocephalus. And, although great progress has been made in early diagnosis and surgery, it's still estimated that over ten percent of the aged in assisted living settings may have hydrocephalus.

The "shunt" operation is conceptually straightforward, like so many great inventions. An incision is made on the top of the front of the head about an inch from the midline and just in front of the coronal suture, a line that represents the closure of the frontal and parietal bones in infancy. A burr hole is made beneath the incision, and a small nick is made in the dura mater. A thin catheter, tapered to a dull bullet shape at its tip, with multiple tiny holes in the deepest part, is placed through the brain, usually into the right lateral (largest and first) ventricle. The emerging part of the tube is then connected to a valve—a small plastic chamber that can be readily accessed in case the fluid needs to be sampled to evaluate blockage or infection of the system. The valve also has a certain amount of resistance so that too much CSF isn't drained out of the brain by the shunt. The other, distal, end of the valve is then connected to a long tube, open at its end. This tube is then threaded underneath the skin of the scalp, the front of the neck, chest, and abdomen. Small one-centimeter "advancing incisions" are usually required to allow the tube to be pulled along under the skin. A slightly larger incision is then created at the abdominal end to allow the introduction of the tube into the peritoneal cavity, where the intestines reside, so that the CSF is drained into an area where it can be absorbed by the omentum, an apron of fatty tissue that is usually responsible for sweeping the abdomen clean of irritants. It's then excreted into the venous blood stream.

While the operation is not technically difficult, it is not without potential complications. Often, the drainage of the CSF from a somewhat atrophied brain will cause the shrunken brain to pull against veins over its surface. If these veins break, a small or sometimes large collection of blood can accumulate between the dura and the brain, exerting enough pressure to cause damage, or even death. When these subdural hematomas are drained, the shunt must be temporarily closed while the brain re-expands.

Another problem with shunts is infection. The plastic shunt is a foreign body, and even in modern surgery, where the tubing is impregnated with antibiotics, bacteria can be introduced into the system, fester there, and create an infection. This can be serious enough to result in meningitis. If infection occurs, generally the entire system must be removed, a ventricular catheter used to flush the spinal fluid chambers with antibiotics and intravenous antibiotics added for good measure. After the infection is cleared, a new shunt must be placed. Occasionally, in the elderly, initial placement of the shunt "jump starts" the drainage system, and infection or bleeding does not require placement of a new shunt. But infants almost always become "shunt-dependent" and require lifelong shunting. Unfortunately, the immature immune system and other sources of infection often require a child with hydrocephalus to undergo several shunt replacements in the first year of life.

On the bright side, many victims of hydrocephalus, old and young, regain normal function with the placement of a ventriculoperitoneal (VP) shunt. But sometimes, particularly in the elderly, the confusion and unsteadiness are caused by several factors, including stroke and Alzheimer's disease. One way of testing is to do a "therapeutic" spinal tap, taking off a couple ounces of spinal fluid. If the patient's symptoms improve for a brief period, it is possible that a shunt may help. And there are imaging advances such as the RISA scan (explanation a little lengthy for our purposes) that can further home in on the diagnosis.

We weren't so lucky with Rose Cilento. Rose was a seventy-eight-year-old woman who had been hearty and sound until about two years before I met her. She was feisty and bold, with a great laugh and a wiry frame, all five feet of it. Unfortunately, she had almost no idea of what was going on around her. Her husband, Don, was an extremely patient and loving man. At over six feet, he towered above her but constantly and gently held her hand. They had been married for fifty-seven years, had two attentive children and had looked forward to a retirement filled with the joys of friends and family. But it was not to be. At seventy-six, Rose became forgetful and cross, suspicious of everything that Don did. By the next year, if Rose said she was going for a quick walk by herself, Don would have to talk her out of it or risk spending several hours with the police combing the neighborhood. "Don't be silly," she'd say, "I knew exactly where I was going. Now which house is ours again?"

Kind of like the old joke about the elderly couple in bed:

"You know, I could go for a quick snack. I'm going to grab a glass of milk and a couple of cookies. Want anything?"

"You know, I think I'd like a bowl of ice cream."

"Want anything on it?"

"Yes, I'd like a cherry and some nuts. But write it down, honey. You know how your memory is."

"Nah, I can certainly remember that. Anything else?"

"Maybe a little chocolate syrup. But write it down."

"Don't be silly. I can remember that." Half an hour goes by and the old guy walks into the bedroom with bacon and eggs. She looks at him disapprovingly, shaking her head. "You forgot the toast."

Funny, but not for the exhausted caregivers or the frightened, confused victim. Rose Cilento was an enigma. She responded slightly to a spinal tap, and her CAT scan showed enlarged ventricles, but there was also a fair amount of atrophy, or wasting, of the brain, which could be due to strokes or other chronic disease, or just old age. Her family was desperate, and I felt that there was at least a modest chance of success, with minimal risk.

The surgery went well, without complications, although there were regular recriminations from Rose, who wanted to know what I was doing in her room and that I had done a terrible job of styling her hair. The first few post-operative visits at my office gave me some hope for signs of improvement. But after six months, and after I had made sure that the shunt was functioning properly, it was clear to the Cilento family and to me that the surgery had not done what we had hoped. After the last visit to the office, as Don Cilento kindly led his wife out of the office, she turned sharply to me and said, "You have done nothing for me." I looked at her apologetically. She said, "And you call yourself a cardiologist!" Anxious looks spread among the other patients waiting to see me.

Harry Gross had been a very successful advertising copywriter with a large Manhattan firm. He had created some memorable TV and radio ads, and, since his retirement ten years ago, he had done some serious writing and was working on having his first novel published. Harry had always been a flamboyant character with a fast, caustic sense of humor. But over the past few months, his wife, Sarah, had begun to suspect something more was going on than his usual craziness; looking at her quizzically when she asked him how his dinner was the night before, cursing over a misplaced set of keys or the checkbook, being shorter with her than he usually was. She finally managed to bring it up to their internist of thirty years. "Oh, for God's sake, Sarah, that's just Harry." She finally convinced the doctor to refer them to a neurologist at a major center in Manhattan. The mental testing was fine—serial 7s, eye-hand coordination, fund of knowledge, etc. Yes, his gait was a little off, but he was eighty-one and had a little arthritis.

"Any problems with controlling the urine?"

"Of course not," Harry snapped. Sarah rolled her eyes. The doctor met with Sarah privately. "Frankly, Mrs. Gross, I just don't find anything wrong with your husband that would justify a lot of painful and expensive testing."

"Doctor, I know my husband, and I know there is something wrong."

"Perhaps you're both just a little uncomfortable with the notion that you're getting older?" He smiled sympathetically. She wanted to punch him.

Over the next few months, Harry definitely declined. Nothing terrifying, but alarming, nonetheless. Three times he had called her Sadie, his mother's name. He had to call her from the post office for advice on how to get home. He had fallen twice and had wet himself several times. Maybe it was old age, maybe it was Alzheimer's, but Sarah Gross wasn't going to let the love of her life slide into oblivion without a fight. She began to read everything she could find about confusion and imbalance in the elderly. Most roads led to Alzheimer's or another problem currently without a cure. But what if he had a brain tumor or something that could be treated?

I assessed Mr. and Mrs. Gross across my desk. She was obviously cagey, and maybe a little suspicious of doctors. He was a little less tidy and put together than the average retired executive, but she had explained that he had always been "arty" and a bit eccentric. His neurological examination was unremarkable, but there was something about him. He walked a little unsteadily; although he was eighty-one, he was a good eighty-one. He'd had a minor heart attack in his late 60s, but Sarah had guided his diet and exercise, and he seemed to be in good health. When I asked him who the vice president was, he laughed and said, "that idiot," but he didn't answer the question. Sarah handed me the CAT scan report that she had demanded be done. I looked at the report and at the films themselves. It concluded that he had atrophy of the brain "consistent with age" but added that there were bifrontal periventricular lucencies (fluid in the brain next to the ventricles) and the ventricles themselves were "borderline enlarged." A syndrome was emerging.

"Doctor, I'm convinced that my husband has normal pressure hydrocephalus." She handed me a folder of articles she had collected about the disease. I placed it on the desk. "My wife, my dear doctor, is a card-carrying hypochondriac; and she is desperate to sign me up." He laughed. She stayed focused on me. "I think you may be right, Mrs. Gross." She first shot me a skeptical glance, then beamed triumphantly. "I told them, I told them all. And I told you, Harry." Harry smiled condescendingly.

The therapeutic spinal taps and RISA study were unquestionable. Not only was the flow of spinal fluid slow, it was actually backing up into the ventricles, slowly building the pressure on the depths of the brain. As we got to know each other, Harry confided that his memory loss was worrisome to him, and that his loss of urinary control was embarrassing.

The shunt I used for Harry was a newer variety that allowed us to program the amount of spinal fluid removed from the brain by increasing the resistance to flow through the valve. This could be done at any time after surgery. A small hand-held device was placed against the skin over the valve and a setting chosen. The device then "dialed down" a metallic arm within the valve magnetically, partially closing or opening the size of the channel shunting CSF. The resistance could be set high in order to reduce the outflow and lessen the chance of the pressure falling too quickly and allowing a subdural blood clot to develop. If set lower, the flow would increase. This could be the strategy, if symptoms of NPH increased or a CAT scan showed enlarging ventricles. The surgery went well, without complications, and, within a week, Harry and Sarah both knew that he was back. He told me that he hadn't realize how cloudy his thinking had become. His walk was brisk and confident, and there were no more embarrassing bladder problems.

A year later, he returned to his consulting business and was thriving. But his wife wasn't so sure. She noticed that he was having trouble with the checkbook and paying the bills. She called me and asked if a CAT scan was in order. I had appreciated her perception and sensitivity from the beginning, so I had a scan done the next day. Sure enough, the ventricles were slightly increased, and there was a bit of fluid seeping through the ventricular wall. I brought Harry into the office and programmed his valve to a lower setting. After a week, we repeated the scan. It was unchanged, and his symptoms were getting a little worse. Sarah said that his walking was getting a little unsteady again.

After sterilizing the skin over the valve, I introduced a very thin needle into the valve. I pulled on the syringe gently and was able to get about a cc of fluid out . . . then it stopped. I injected a couple cc's of sterile saline. It flowed in easily. I tried to withdraw fluid again, with the same result. The answer was clear—there was a blockage in the shunt. It wasn't in the tubing that went to the abdomen because the injected saline went into the valve with ease. The fact that I couldn't get any CSF out meant that there must be a block between the valve and the ventricle in the brain.

The next day, I took Harry to the operating room. After preparing the incision over the burr hole, I re-opened it. I detached the tubing going into the brain, the ventricular catheter, from the valve. No CSF came out of the end of the tube. Slowly, I withdrew it from the brain and discovered the problem. The deep part of the catheter was clogged with dense tissue. The excess of protein in the system had coagulated, closing the path for drainage. I replaced the tube with a new ventricular catheter, and CSF quickly emerged from the end of the tubing, under pretty high pressure. I reconnected the tubing to the valve and pumped the valve with my finger a couple of times. I could see the CSF swirling through the clear plastic dome. I closed the incision and watched Harry in the ICU for a couple of days. He was discharged on the fourth day and got right back to baseline.

The shunt did not fail again. Sarah called me five years later. Harry had died of a heart attack at age eighty-six. He was sharp to the end. She thanked me for taking care of him . . . and believing her. I thanked her for her inspiring love and attention that had saved her husband.

CHAPTER EIGHTEEN

Little Boy, Big Aneurysm

From 1987 to 1997, I served on the full-time faculty at New York Medical College, where I was vice-chairman of the neurosurgery department and chief of cerebrovascular surgery. After 1997, I would remain on the faculty, but would help start a large multi-specialty group with my friends Jack Stern, Ed Kornel, Seth Neurbardt, and Kent Duffy. This group would combine academic and community practice. I also joined the Yale neurosurgery faculty.

Raoul Soto was nine years old in 1988 when he started to complain of headaches to his mother. The Sotos were Portuguese and had emigrated to join the large Portuguese community in Yonkers, New York. This always seems to happen in our great melting pot of a country. A family or two immigrates to a random place in America—Minneapolis, Dearborn, Yonkers—and the message goes viral back home. There's gold in the streets. Like this story all over the United States, the first generation of Yonkers Portuguese were laborers, hospital attendants, servants. The second and third generations now include doctors, lawyers, and accountants.

The Sotos were no exception. Joao Soto had started as a bricklayer's assistant but now had a small landscaping business and was prospering. His wife, Maria, still worked as a housekeeper to help make ends meet. They were emblematic of a centuries-old American tradition—honest, hardworking, humble, ambitious. Raoul was cut from the same cloth. Bright and handsome, he was a curious and energetic nine-year-old. Until the headaches began.

There is a maxim in pediatric neurology. Young kids don't get headaches unless there is a real, structural problem. So, when pediatric neurologist, Ron Jacobson, saw Raoul, he was concerned. He examined him carefully. He was neurologically intact, but he didn't brush off the headaches as school anxiety or neck strain. He ordered a CT scan.

"Tom, Ron Jacobson. I have a youngster with a bad problem. He has a giant aneurysm in his right temporal lobe." I was surprised. Children rarely develop aneurysms, particularly large ones. "Let's bring him in for an angiogram, Ron." By this time, my career had transitioned from community neurosurgery to full-time academics at New York Medical College, and I had finally become able to concentrate on the specialty of cerebrovascular disease, as I had hoped since residency days. I was in my early forties. The most productive time for a neurosurgeon is between forty and fifty-five—old enough to have experience and confidence, young enough to feel invulnerable. My opinion on this still holds. So, this case was right up my alley. I just wished it hadn't been a nine-year-old boy.

Raoul was scrappy. Self-confident and outgoing, he had no fear. I was already proud of him. He and I were going to be partners in this challenge. His parents were understandably terrified.

"Is he going to be alright, doctor?" Maria asked.

"We need a lot more information, Mrs. Soto. But I promise you that I am going to do my best to solve Raoul's problem." It was little comfort for this mother. Fortunately, I had Michael Tenner. Mike was, and is, the most gifted neuroradiologist I have ever known. A native of Baltimore (BALdimmer, as he would say), Mike had trained at the best institutions in America and had settled down in New York, where he gained a lifetime of experience and an extraordinary citywide reputation. There is nothing about brain and spine anatomy that Mike doesn't know. And, like so many polymaths, he has a million interests. For one, he is a masterful sushi chef . . . go figure.

Mike Tenner injected all of the major arteries to Raoul's anesthetized brain, inside and outside the skull. He then "subtracted" the films so that the arteries showed up as black channels against a pale background of the brain and skull. The result of the study was impressive, and daunting. There was an enormous aneurysm in the child's right temporal lobe. Remember, an aneurysm is basically a balloon filled with blood that occurs where an artery in the brain branches into two smaller arteries. It gradually enlarges until its wall becomes so thin that it can rupture, sending high pressure blood into the brain and spinal fluid. Up to 60% of the people who experience this aneurysmal rupture die or are permanently incapacitated by the consequences of the hemorrhage to the brain.

Raoul's aneurysm emerged from the first branch of the right middle cerebral artery. The problem was twofold: it was enormous—about five centimeters, nearly two inches, in diameter, and it had no neck. Most aneurysms, as they emerge from the "parent" artery, have a slender neck. This allows us to either inject microscopic coils into the aneurysm, filling it and rendering it harmless, or to place a metallic clip across the neck surgically, depriving the aneurysm of its blood supply, effectively defusing the bomb. But this aneurysm was a killer—too large to coil, no neck to clip.

Years before, at Gainesville, Albert Rhoton had taught me a technique called the EC-IC (extracranial-intracranial) bypass. It was a technically exquisite, physically challenging operation. Devised to supply blood to the brain when the carotid artery closed, usually due to atherosclerosis, the idea was to take an artery from the scalp, the superficial temporal artery, dissect it, open the skull, and anastomose it (plug it in) to a major artery in the brain, the middle cerebral artery, bypassing the main carotid artery and giving life-saving blood to the brain downstream. In cases like Raoul's, it was possible that the only way to kill the aneurysm would be to sacrifice the main artery that supplied it, the middle cerebral artery. Unfortunately, this artery was also giving blood supply to most of his right cerebral hemisphere. Closing off the artery would most probably cause a major stroke and, in all likelihood, death. But if I could close the artery just as it entered the aneurysm and supply blood to the same artery just distal, or downstream, to the place where I closed it, I could kill the aneurysm and save the brain. No problem, right? I couldn't find enough saliva for a good swallow.

I was entertaining the thought that the EC-IC bypass might just be the solution to our problem. I searched the neurosurgical literature. There were a number of cases of giant aneurysms treated in this way, but not a single case of a child. The situation was obvious: This was possibly the only chance we had to save this boy, but there was no data. Nothing that would reassure us that the EC-IC technique would work or that, if it did work, that the effect would last into adulthood.

Sydney "Skip" Peerless, a professor in London, Ontario, was a master of microvascular neurosurgery. He had done more microvascular bypasses than anyone, and, fortunately for me, he had been a visiting professor at Gainesville during my residency. I called him. He remembered me from his time at the University of Florida and from our visits at neurosurgical meetings. I presented Raoul's case. I asked if he had done the bypass on any children. "No, Tom, I haven't; and frankly, I don't know that anyone has." My heart sank. "Having said that, I would apply the same principle to this child as I would to an adult and say forge ahead. I don't see that you have a lot of choices here. If you don't attack the aneurysm, it will kill him. If you do the operation and you lose him, you will have given him the best chance he could have." Dr. Peerless's comments left me feeling alone, standing on an icy, windy precipice, holding Raoul by the fingertips.

"Joao, Maria, we have to have a very serious talk. As you know, Raoul has a large brain aneurysm. It may explode and kill him. It may continue to grow and impair him. It could even stay the same and cause no harm. So, we have two choices—leave it alone or fix it. The risk that leaving it alone has is that it may grow or explode. This worries me because he only started to complain about headaches this year, and that makes me think it may be growing. If we try to fix it, we have two problems. First, there could be problems from the surgery. I mean bad problems. He could die, or have a stroke, or an infection. Or the surgery might not work. I have to be honest with you."

The silence was deafening. The three minutes of silence felt like an eternity. I knew that I would never pressure these parents. I would live with whatever decision they made. Maria Soto spoke.

"Doctor, may we call you later today or tomorrow?" I was humbled by her courage. "Of course, Mrs. Soto."

The next morning, Joao Soto's response was terse and eloquent. "Doctor, we have decided that our Raoul cannot live beneath the pendulum of doubt. He, and we, cannot worry that tomorrow, or next week, or next year, he may be stolen from us. We understand that we are all taking a risk—we, and Raoul, and you. Let us take it together." I began to plan what was to be the most challenging brain operation of my life. To my knowledge, the complex surgery I planned had never been done in a child. I was on a very high wire indeed, with no net.

Maria Soto kissed her boy's forehead and stroked his hair. Lying on the gurney on the way to the OR, Raoul was stoic and silent. He had already been through a lot for a ten-year-old. He had undergone numerous tests, drawing of his blood, IVs, even the cerebral angiogram, which was daunting for many adults. As he was positioned on the operating table, I leaned over and smiled. "When you wake up, this will all be over, Raoul." His lips tightened into a nervous smile. In a few moments, he was asleep, not with a general anesthetic but with deep conscious sedation. This was our choice because if our interference with his brain circulation was in doubt, we could bring him to a higher level of consciousness during the operation to make sure he could move the left side of his body. A large central venous line was passed into his heart, particularly in the event that we had a sudden loss of blood and he required massive fluids and transfusion.

We prepared and draped the right side of his scalp and his right cheek. I spent the next hour using a tiny ultrasound probe to follow and dissect the right superficial temporal artery down to the zygoma, the bone running back from the cheek to the ear. After the artery was completely free, with a generous cuff of soft adventitial tissue around it, I wrapped it in a saline-soaked sponge.

Then, retracting the incision that I'd made, we split the temporal muscle and made a burr hole in the front of the temporal area and expanded this slightly using rongeurs (bone-biting tools). This exposed the dura, which we then cut in "cruciate" (cross-shaped) fashion, retracting the four edges of the dura with small sutures. A pristine expanse of brain was now visible, about three centimeters in diameter.

After opening the dura, I found a generous middle cerebral artery branch that was running up into the brain, just after the place I knew I would find the aneurysm. I turned back to the donor artery and dissected about a half-inch length of it completely clean of tissue until only the wall of the beating artery remained. Next, I opened a small area, about a centimeter of arachnoid, the silky translucent membrane that encloses the brain in spinal fluid. Using high power microscopy, I dissected the wisps of tissue around the recipient vessel for about one and a half centimeters, then took a small piece of latex cut from a sterile glove, about the same length and width, and tucked it beneath the artery, making a stage on which I could work. Next, I closed the superficial artery down near the zygoma with a temporary vascular clip, strong enough to stop the flow of blood through it but soft enough to discourage the artery from permanently closing over the next twenty minutes or so. Then I cut the dissected end of the superficial artery with a microscissors, giving me a long, free pedicle, with the dissected free cut end of the vessel available for me to use.

I cut a half-centimeter length of soft plastic tubing, so thin it was barely visible to the human eye, on the bias so that both ends were pointed. I placed two vascular microclips across the middle cerebral branch about a centimeter apart, then made a longitudinal cut in the artery with a microknife. The cut was slightly longer than the diameter of the donor vessel. A few drops of blood went up the microsuction device. Using a jeweler's forceps, I slid the tiny plastic tube into the artery. This gave the artery's wall some strength so that I could manipulate it. With the middle cerebral artery now closed, I knew that I would have no more than thirty minutes to complete the anastomosis that attaches the vessel from the scalp to the brain artery. If you can't do it in that time frame, your patient dies or is devastated by a stroke.

Cranking up the microscope to maximum power, I could see red blood cells glistening against the strong light of the microscope in the blood vessel just beyond the clips I had placed. It was a majestic sight. As I had often thought over the years in these situations . . . this is where we live, this is life. Again, using jeweler's forceps, I lined up the tip of the superficial artery perpendicular to the cut in the middle cerebral artery. Now, the two blood vessels, each a millimeter in diameter, look gigantic, like Lincoln Logs. Fingers would be far too massive to allow any vision of the field, so the instruments we use are long and slender, with tiny working ends, keeping hands out of the picture. Next, using a microscissor, I 'fishmouthed' the tip of the donor artery, opening it slightly to increase the size of the anastomosis, and therefore, the amount of blood delivered to the middle cerebral artery branch. Then, I sutured the donor artery to the recipient, placing a dozen sutures around the circumference of the junction. The diameter of each suture is about the width of two red blood cells side to side (it's

10-0 gauge nylon, about a hundredth of a millimeter in diameter).
The needle carrying the sutures is so small . . . well, let's put it
this way: If you stuck it into your finger, you would never feel
it. It's rounded and tapered at the end so that it doesn't tear the
artery when it passes through. The first two sutures (each pre-cut
by the operating nurse to a length of one inch and secured to its
own needle) were placed at the ends of the cut in the recipient
artery and through the donor artery. Then, five sutures were placed
on either side, through both arteries, at regular intervals until the
anastomosis was completed. Prior to tying the last knot, the plastic
stent was removed.

I removed the three vascular clips. A high-powered stream
of bright red blood shot from the anastomosis. Either one of the
sutures wasn't tied properly and had come loose, or there was too
much distance between two or more of the sutures. I replaced the
vascular clips, irrigated and suctioned the area, and found the area
where I had left slightly too much room between two sutures. I
placed another between these, placed a cuff of coagulating gelfoam
around the suture line, and removed the clips again. The anastomosis
jumped to life. The superficial temporal artery stiffened and
pulsed; the middle cerebral artery enlarged and beat beautifully. If
all worked well, the anastomosis would further enlarge and mature
over the next week or two as it took over supplying blood to most
of the right half of Raoul's brain.

But we weren't quite finished yet. Under high power microscopy,
I dissected gingerly around the massive aneurysm that filled much
of the area that should be occupied by Raoul's right temporal lobe—
the middle fossa of the skull. The aneurysm was not enjoying being
disturbed. It pulsed angrily. I could see the blood swirling inside.

It was like a sleeping monster, waiting to be poked. But my goal was not to disturb it. My goal was to strangle it. Seconds turned into minutes as I crept down the Sylvian fissure—the cleft between the frontal and temporal lobes—until I reached the artery that fed most of the blood supply to the right half of the brain, the carotid artery. I followed this toward the aneurysm until it branched into anterior and middle cerebral arteries. The middle cerebral was the artery that fed the sleeping monster. I came as close to the base of the aneurysm as I dared, then applied a Drake tourniquet to the artery. This device, named for the great pioneer aneurysm surgeon, Charles Drake, Skip Peerless's mentor at London, Ontario, was basically a noose to encircle the artery. I slid a thirty-centimeter length of 3-0 Prolene suture—a smooth, fairly thick nylon—around the artery, then threaded the two ends of the suture through a ten-centimeter-long polyethylene tube that I brought out to the surface of the brain. I tested the device by putting slight pressure on the artery by pulling gently on the suture, then put a clip on the suture to keep up that slight pressure. Dr. Mike Tenner, who had placed a catheter into the carotid artery at the base of Raoul's neck at the beginning of the procedure, now injected dye into the artery. As I'd hoped, slightly less dye entered the aneurysm but flowed vigorously through the anastomosis. We let Raoul regain consciousness a little, and he was able to move his left arm and leg well.

When I saw this result, I let out a long breath and began to close the wound, replacing the bone after I had removed enough of it to allow the polyethylene tube egress from the brain, and adequate to allow the superficial temporal donor artery to enter the skull unimpeded. After dressing the incision, I went out to the family room to explain to the Sotos that we were successful in our plan—so far. They physically sagged with relief.

Several years before this operation, I had applied an earlier standard technique in the case of an elderly lady. In that case, she had presented with a series of small seizures, then a mild temporary stroke called a transient ischemic attack, or TIA. The giant aneurysm was inoperable, and its parent artery was unapproachable by the "Drake" technique. So, I applied a slender vice-like device to her carotid artery in the neck. Over three days, I screwed down the clamp slowly, watching her strength and neurological examination closely, until the carotid artery was closed. On an angiogram the next day, there was no flow through the carotid artery, but, as preoperatively, the other arteries in the brain appeared to be providing adequate circulation to the entire brain (collateral circulation) while allowing very little dye to enter the aneurysm. One week later, she rapidly deteriorated; her CAT scan showed a massive stroke. Two days later, she died.

While Raoul's case and the surgical technique weren't exactly the same, I still got very little sleep over the next week. Each day over the next four, we repeated a CT-angiogram, which gave us a picture of the flow of blood through the anastomosis and how much blood was still getting into the aneurysm. If the anastomosis wasn't adequate, either on the CT or on Raoul's exam, I would release some of the tension on the noose around the middle cerebral artery. If everything was okay, I would tighten the noose a bit more. On day four, no blood was filling the aneurysm, and the anastomosis was filling the entire right brain with circulation. On day five, I opened the incision under local anesthesia and placed a large metal clip on the plastic tube deep beneath the surface of the wound, fixing the position of the tube and the "noose." Then I cut the portion of the tube emerging from the wound, and closed the incision. The die was cast.

A month later, Raoul and his parents walked into my office. I teased him about how quickly his hair had grown back. Flashing a self-conscious smile, he handed me a beautifully-wrapped package that contained a plaque with a touching message thanking me for saving his life. Work, and life, didn't get much better than this.

Thirteen years later, his family wrote me a letter. They had moved back to Portugal and wanted to let me know that Raoul had just won a national motor racing championship. I like to think that his surgery had taught him two things: Life can take crazy turns, so be ready; and don't be afraid to take a risk.

CHAPTER NINETEEN

Spasm

Over the years, I gained confidence in my ability to operate on brain aneurysms. I felt a certainty and comfort in the microscopic technique, the gentle retraction of the brain, even the occasional rupture of the aneurysm when the clip was about to be applied. I felt I could get out of pretty much any situation with these dangerous time bombs. By the mid-90's, I had operated on hundreds.

There's an old saying: *Pride goeth before a fall*. Donna Parkinson brought me off my horse.

Donna was a thirty-eight-year-old mother of three. She was beautiful, intelligent, and kind. Her husband and family adored her. Her husband was terrified one autumn morning when she stood near the breakfast table, cried out, and fainted. Not able to rouse her, he ran to the phone on the kitchen wall and dialed 911. His hand shook as he explained to the EMS dispatcher what had happened.

Half an hour later, Donna lay on a gurney in the medical center's ED. She was awake now, albeit drowsy. As I bent over the young woman and said her name, her eyes slowly opened, and she winced.

"I have a headache."

"Donna, can you raise your arms out in front of you?"

She did so, slowly but accurately. She was able to tell me her name, the date, where we were. Her neurological examination was normal, with the exception of a stiff neck and a problem with her right eye. Her right pupil was slightly dilated, and she couldn't elevate the right eyelid quite perfectly when she tried to open her eyes widely.

As I have discussed, experience told me the answer. She had ruptured an aneurysm of the right internal carotid artery, where the posterior communicating artery emerges from it. The suddenness of her symptoms and her stiff neck suggested a hemorrhage in her brain. The lag in her right eyelid and dilated pupil identified injury to the right third cranial nerve, the oculomotor nerve. The most common cause of this situation? The aforementioned "PCommA" aneurysm. Donna's CT showed a fair amount of blood in the basal cisterns, the spinal fluid space around the base of the brain. The angiogram confirmed the diagnosis. The diameter of the aneurysm was about one centimeter, a third of an inch, and it had a well-defined neck connecting it with its parent artery.

With unbridled hubris and immodesty, this was my favorite brain surgery. First, I was most comfortable, and therefore most adept, at aneurysm surgery. Then, this particular artery tended to be the easiest to dissect and access. Finally, these aneurysms often had well-defined necks, across which I could place an obliterating clip. I explained the problem, the dangers of the surgery and of the hemorrhage itself and the possibility of long-term neurological problems from the hemorrhage to Mark Parkinson. I told him that there was a real possibility that Donna could have serious residual effects or even that she could lose her life. Inside, I really didn't believe a word of it. I was confident that surgery would go well, that I would defuse the aneurysm, and that her outcome would be good. My explanation was pro forma.

The goal was to get in quickly, clip the aneurysm, wash out as much blood from the spinal fluid (subarachnoid space) as possible, apply both intravenous and direct anti-spasm medication, papaverine (dripped right onto the parent arteries), and then challenge the system with fluid to keep those vessels wide open. The reason: Even when the aneurysm is quickly clipped, blood has already been spilled into the subarachnoid space. The blood breakdown products, bound with iron, were very irritating and caustic to the brain arteries, causing them to go into "vasospasm" and contract. If they contracted, they could stop providing adequate nutrition to the brain, causing a stroke or even death. Vasospasm was a delayed curse, occurring three to nine days after the initial hemorrhage. About a third of patients experienced vasospasm, and at least one third of these suffered a neurological consequence. I wanted to get Donna, like all of my patients with subarachnoid hemorrhages, into the OR as soon as possible.

The surgery was "routine." By this time, I had operated on over 400 aneurysms—the placement of a spinal drain, the curvilinear incision, the opening of the skull and the dura. As we approached the base of the brain, we encountered a fairly thick layer of blood. This was gently irrigated and suctioned until the brain, although stained by blood, was identifiable and clean. Microdissection carried me to the optic nerve, which I followed to the carotid artery, then to the origin of the posterior communicating artery.

There it was. The dome of the aneurysm was peeking out from under a layer of dura, the tentorium. It was pulsing angrily. As I gently elevated the dome, the neck of the aneurysm was clear. Holding the dome with a Rhoton dissector (a long-handled probe with a small spatula at its end), I used a Spetzler suction tube (after Robert Spetzler of Arizona's Barrow Neurological Institute, a giant in aneurysm surgery) that had a gently blunted tip (less likely to strike and rupture the aneurysm) to remove the last vestiges of blood from the field and define the circumference of the artery. I analyzed a series of aneurysm clips for size and shape and ultimately chose a seven mm, curved, Sugita clip.

Kenichiro Sugita was professor and chairman of neurosurgery at Nagoya University. He was born into a family of physicians. Sugita was a true Renaissance scholar. As a young man, he was a painter and cellist. As a neurosurgeon, he invented everything from his eponymous aneurysm clips to surgical head clamps, tables, microscopes, and instruments. Fittingly, he was founder of the International Society for Neurosurgical Technology and Invention. I met Dr. Sugita at a gathering of aneurysm surgeons in Japan in 1987 (seven years before his untimely death in 1994). After a long day of discussions, some of us gathered for a nightcap at the elegant hotel bar. As I listened to the strains of a lovely classical melody from the grand piano in the room, I suddenly noticed that the pianist was Sugita. I listened for a while, then walked over to the piano. "Dr. Sugita, that's beautiful. Is it Liszt or Chopin?"

"Neither," he replied with barely a glance. "It's Sugita."

I applied the Sugita clip to Ms. Parkinson's aneurysm. The sac immediately sagged. I pierced the dome with a tiny, twenty-six-gauge needle and aspirated the blood filling it. The aneurysm collapsed and did not refill. The papaverine was applied to the local blood vessels, the wound was closed, and Donna Parkinson was taken to the recovery room, vital signs stable.

The morning after surgery found Donna awake and alert. Removing the pressure of the aneurysm on her third cranial nerve had resolved her eye issue. She was doing so well that we anticipated her discharge from the hospital after four or five days of observation. I discussed the agenda for her discharge and follow-up with her husband confidently. But day four dawned with storm clouds on the horizon.

The residents on rounds that morning found Donna drowsy and incoherent. Over the next several hours, she became less and less responsive. It was possible that she had developed acute hydrocephalus from blood clogging the circulation of spinal fluid in her brain. Or perhaps I hadn't placed the clip properly across the neck of the aneurysm and she had bled again from the aneurysm. We rushed her to the CAT scan. No, there was no hydrocephalus, and there wasn't a blood clot. Just a mild but ominous diffuse swelling of the entire brain. I had seen this horror movie before—vasospasm. An emergency angiogram confirmed my fears. Essentially, all of the blood vessels of her brain were narrowed irregularly, as if a mad gnome was running through the brain randomly squeezing the arteries. Our interventional neuroradiologist, Imre Weitzner, and I studied the angiogram. We were surprised at how severe the vasospasm was, given the relatively modest hemorrhage the patient had experienced, along with our prompt intervention. But the pictures didn't lie.

Imre took her back to the radiology suite and re-introduced

the catheter into her system. He visualized each of the major blood vessels of Donna's brain and injected a dilating agent into the arteries. While the vessels dilated somewhat, the effect wasn't as dramatic as we had hoped. We brought her back to the ICU, where we continued intravenous Nimodipine, a calcium channel blocking agent introduced to treat high blood pressure but a promising drug to fight vasospasm. We also used "triple-H" therapy: hypertension (elevating the blood pressure to try to "force" blood into those constricted arteries), hemodilution with fluids (diluting the blood so that it would flow more freely), and hypervolemia (extra fluid to again challenge the narrow vessels). We added steroids to try to reduce the swelling in her brain. These, and a host of other therapies, failed.

By late that evening, the outcome was clear. As Donna Parkinson's coma grew deeper and deeper, her life signs failed. At 7:30, she died. My own pain became even more intense as I watched her young husband, his hand holding hers, his head bobbing gently as he sobbed into her lifeless lap. I had been so assuring, so confident of the outcome. Although I had recited the risks of her illness and surgery when we first met, I honestly had no idea that, five days later, he would be a widower with three young children.

When I started my neurosurgical residency, we were challenged by this mysterious killer. Over the next thirty-five years, brilliant researchers have devoted years to identifying who was most vulnerable to vasospasm, what caused it, and what agents or techniques might defeat it. To my knowledge, we still don't have the final answer.

CHAPTER TWENTY

Now I Know How You Feel

On a cold February day in 1984, I was called to see a very ill, young, Haitian immigrant at one of our community hospitals. He was in isolation, as he had a fever and a chest x-ray had shown he had pneumonia. His sputum was cultured and grew a rare organism, pneumocystis carinii. He had painful ulcers in his mouth, and on his right shin was a dark, ulcerated lesion. Biopsy showed this to be a Kaposi's sarcoma. Why was I called? In his downward spiral, he had developed left-sided weakness. A CAT scan showed a large round tumor deep in the right frontal lobe and a smaller, similar tumor in the left parietal lobe. The young man had acknowledged that he had used IV drugs.

Because he was in isolation, I donned the mandatory gown, gloves, and mask and entered the room to evaluate Rene. He was very sleepy but opened his eyes when I spoke to him. He followed my instructions drowsily, and I confirmed that he had left-sided weakness, a hemiparesis. Rene moaned softly, indicating that his mouth hurt. I placed a straw to his lips and he sucked a bit of water. It didn't help. The nurse said that she'd give him more IV narcotics. Soon he was sleeping in relative comfort.

A conference was held among the Infectious Disease (ID) specialist, the neurologist and myself. The patient had been given multiple antibiotics but didn't appear to be gaining ground. The ID was concerned about the possibility that this man might have a "new" disease that had been reported among gay men in Southern California and New York, and among some Haitians.

The disease had been called the Acquired Immune Deficiency Syndrome (AIDS), as the immune system became ineffective in fighting infectious diseases, and rare infections emerged in these patients. Later, the infecting virus would be identified and named the human immunodeficiency virus (HIV), scientists concluding that it originated in Africa, where it had crossed from chimpanzees to humans.

By the end of 1984, more than 7,000 Americans were infected and more than 3,000 died. By 1999, AIDS would become the fourth most common cause of death in the world, the most common cause in Africa. It soon became clear that the disease was not limited to gay men and IV drug users but occurred in male and female partners through sexual transmission and in the children of mothers infected with AIDS. Urged by the gay community, governments around the world, the World Health Organization, the United Nations and the pharmaceutical industry attacked the disease. While still a major health challenge, the death rate from AIDS has dropped dramatically, and the percentage of people being successfully treated with antiviral agents and living in good health has steadily climbed.

But in 1984, its cause and treatment were largely a mystery, and most physicians, including yours truly, were completely ignorant of the syndrome. So, on the day when I examined Rene, I took the usual isolation precautions, but I, and the rest of the staff, did not react with the same dread and even hysteria that would later accompany an encounter with a patient suffering from AIDS.

At the urging of the medical team, I performed a biopsy on this mutilated, tired man. Under general anesthesia, I made a small incision on the right side of his scalp over the frontal lobe, where the CAT scan told me the lesion hid. I made a burr hole through the skull, cauterized the dura with the bipolar forceps, and incised it with a cruciate incision about five mm in length. Cauterizing the arachnoid membrane beneath the dura, I made a tiny stab incision into the surface of the brain with an 11-blade, a needle-pointed scalpel. Using the CAT scan to measure the depth and trajectory of my approach, I passed a six-centimeter metal cannula, with side holes at its tip, to a depth of two-and-a-half centimeters, about an inch from the surface. I felt resistance—this was the capsule of the lesion, and I pushed with a little force. The tiny metal tube broke through, and I held it steadily with my left hand as I attached a five-centimeter syringe to the tube. I gently drew back on the syringe, and a stream of pearly thick liquid emerged into the syringe. I sent the fluid to the lab, and the answer quickly returned—a rare fungus had invaded Rene's brain.

Rene stumbled on, lasting another month before the rare bacteria and fungi that had invaded his organs and overcome them, due to his inability to develop any successful immune response to them, finally caused his death.

We brain surgeons joined the growing phalanx of physicians, nurses, and social workers fighting in the front lines against this frightening tsunami that became the AIDS epidemic. Soon there were wards full of HIV-infected patients reminiscent of the tuberculosis wards of the 1920s and the polio wards of the 1950s. Ultimately, brilliant researchers would wrest control of this disease, as they had the others.

On a September Saturday evening in 1995, I was called into the medical center by the chief resident. He had admitted a Central American immigrant, semiconscious and emaciated. The CAT scan revealed a large lesion in his cerebellum, the organ of coordination, pressing on his brainstem, in the area that controlled consciousness. Among the tests that were acquired on admission was an HIV test.

The chief resident discussed the case with me, and we agreed that there was no time to waste. Get him to the OR. I got to the operating room with dispatch. He'd already had the patient prepared, anesthetized, draped, and was ready to make the incision. The patient was placed in a semi-sitting position, and we made an incision from the base of the back of his skull down to the upper part of his cervical spine. With my assistance, the chief resident quickly dissected the tissues of his skull and neck until the bones were clean and exposed. He made several burr holes in the base of the skull and connected them with a high-speed saw. He removed the resultant piece of skull, about three inches in diameter. The dura was stretched with pressure. It was cauterized and cut. The cerebellum angrily forced its way toward us, and we quickly brought the operating microscope into the field. Cauterizing the surface blood vessels, we suctioned a substantial portion of the herniating cerebellum away. There, we confronted the capsule of a large abscess. We broke the surface of the capsule and suctioned its pearly, viscous contents. Then we dissected the margins of the abscess and removed it totally. The brain swelling soon subsided, and the cerebellum regained its normal appearance.

We "cleaned up" the surface of the cerebellum where the abscess had lurked and watched the scene to make sure there was no bleeding or undue swelling. Satisfied that we were out of the woods, we quickly closed the wound. We exchanged comments about how we would manage the patient postoperatively and engaged in idle talk. We had started steroids to reduce brain swelling and broad-spectrum antibiotics to begin the attack against what we were certain would be an HIV-related disease.

As the chief resident closed the muscle layer of the surface of the wound with 3-0 Vicryl sutures (an absorbable firm suture) using large, curved needles, I felt a sharp stab in my left index finger. I had been inadvertently in the way of the needle. Blood filled my glove. I stepped away from the field as the chief continued the closure, clearly concerned with me. Pulling my glove off, the circulating nurse doused my hand with disinfectant. It was a deep stab, and it bled for several minutes. The Infectious Disease team was immediately called. The resident was terribly upset, though it was neither his nor my fault.

There was no choice. They immediately started me on AZT, Zidovudine, the only hope that we had against my infection with the HIV virus.

I drove home that night with a feeling of dread. I would now join the sad ranks of men and women dying of this modern plague. Like the doctors and the priests of the Black Plague of the Middle

Ages, I would become a victim of this mysterious curse that I was trying to cure.

When I got home, I stumbled into the library and poured myself a large Scotch. I slugged it back and sank into the sofa facing the warming blaze of the library's fireplace. Our dinner guests, my dear friend, Michael Fareri, a real estate developer, and his companion were sitting in front of the fire with glasses of wine. As I sat staring into the fire, they immediately sensed my distress. My wife, holding a glass of Chardonnay, pulled an ottoman close to my chair and placed her hand over my wrist. She was not used to me being like this. I usually kept my hand tightly to my vest when it came to my work, and I was pretty reserved about my experiences. I had met Tara at Lawrence Hospital. She was a young nurse but had immediately impressed me with her intelligence and organizational skills, and her quiet, responsible manner. Although I barely knew her, we were taking care of Dan Manganero together. Dan was dying of metastatic prostate cancer, and I was using high doses of medication to try to control his pain. One morning, when Tara was on duty, Dan said to me, "Doc, your wife was just here." I smiled, indulging his drug-induced confusion. Later, Tara came into his room and he said, "Tara, your husband came by this morning." That afternoon, as I was discussing our mutual patient with her, she noted his strange comment. We both immediately realized that he was talking about us. We shared a laugh over our patient's delusion. Tara would soon go on to Emergency Department nursing, then a management position in Home Care, and finally founding a large information technology company. But Dan was right about us—our thirty-year marriage is still going strong.

"What's wrong," Tara whispered quietly.

"I'm afraid I've got a problem." Everyone pulled in close. "I got stuck with a contaminated needle tonight, and I'm pretty sure the patient has AIDs." The oxygen was sucked out of the room, and you could cut the silence with a knife. "The medical team has started me on AZT. There's not much else to do."

We sat around the fire. No one had much of an appetite. Finally, I broke the silence. "You know, I haven't taken a break for a long time. I'm going to take a leave of absence for a few weeks. I want to go back to St. Barts."

For several years, my wife and I had made this idyllic department of France in the West Indies our winter home. With its mountainous terrain, *sauvage* beaches, and splendid restaurants, it combined the best of primitive island life and Paris sophistication. It was our escape, our haven. We packed minimally, grabbed a Continental flight, took the unique puddle-jumper between the cliffs of the island and presented our passports to the gendarmes. In a few hours, we had escaped the city and were ensconced in the flowery paradise of Iguanas, a small hotel with magnificent ocean views owned by old French friends. The next morning, we headed to the beautiful Gouverneur beach, with a bottle of Sancerre, baguettes, and brie. I had taken my first morning dose of AZT and tried to wipe my mind clear as I listened to the waves crashing against the golden sand.

After a beautiful dinner at a cliffside hotel restaurant—serene and dimly lit, with gorgeous presentations and outstanding wine— we drove our little *Moke* (a sort of open jeep-mini hybrid) over the moonlight-bathed mountains and along the coast to our hotel. The gritty experiences of the past few days began to slip into the gentle fog of the warm French Caribbean.

But it wasn't meant to be. The next morning, I awakened with a pounding headache. I started to stand up but was so dizzy I fell back onto the bed. A wave of nausea hit me, and I felt so weak I could barely move. I held out for a few days, then flew back to New York. I called the Infectious Disease specialist who had taken over my care. "It's the AZT, Tom." I had always prided myself on a pretty strong constitution and an ability to tolerate medicines well. But I couldn't avoid the constant malaise, the nausea, the dizziness that ensued an hour or two after I took this medication. A week later, I was still waiting for the definitive result of the HIV test, but I felt miserably sure that it was going to be positive.

Years had passed since I met the young Haitian man infected with HIV, and I had unfortunately met many patients dying from AIDS. The disease was an incredible curse. It tortured its victims in several sadistic ways. First, a person diagnosed with the disease was immediately stigmatized. With some exceptions, like acquiring the disease from a contaminated blood transfusion, many of the causes of the disease were socially condemned, including IV drug abuse and unprotected sex. It branded its victims as social pariahs, isolating them from loved ones and even normal social interactions. For some time, no one knew exactly what caused the disease or how contagious it really was. So, society kept its distance from those with AIDS.

For me, this isolation was reminiscent of a plague that ravaged the world when I was a small child—polio. Poliomyelitis, generally known at the time as Infantile Paralysis, struck young and healthy children, rendering them with varying degrees of paralysis and often death. The poliovirus attacks the cells of the central nervous system. In 1952, 58,000 Americans were stricken by the virus. Among them was my cousin Marty. Marty was a handsome, dark-haired seven-year-old, smiling and playful. I was five at the time. Parents everywhere were terrified. After Marty developed a flu-like disease, he failed to improve and rapidly deteriorated. My parents, aunts, and uncles spoke in hushed tones, and I assumed that Marty had done something wrong. I was told that Marty was in the hospital, but I couldn't visit him. No one could visit him.

Marty and I and a few other cousins had been playing in a lawn sprinkler that summer, just a few days before he became ill. My parents, like many others that summer, assumed that there might be something in the water that was causing the disease. We weren't allowed to swim for the rest of the summer. My mother told me tearfully that Marty was in an "iron lung." He had been diagnosed with Bulbar polio, meaning that the virus had infected his brainstem and he could no longer breathe on his own. The machine, a negative pressure ventilator, was invented by Philip Drinker at Harvard and was first used for a child with polio at the Boston Children's Hospital in 1928. The idea was to enclose the chest in an airtight chamber that applied negative pressure to the chest, sucking air into the lungs. Reversing the pressure caused the chest to exhale. No one imagined that this was a cure for the disease, but it might buy time for partial or complete recovery.

Thousands of victims survived but were often left with paralysis of the legs or arms or both. The most famous victim of polio was President Franklin Delano Roosevelt. Although he may have been the victim of a different ascending paralysis, Guillain-Barre Syndrome, he developed permanent paralysis of his legs in 1921, at the age of forty, after a brief illness. The fact that his symptoms came on after a vigorous swim at his Campobello Island summer retreat added to the later mythology that polio was waterborne. Roosevelt's illness added impetus to the efforts of the National Foundation for Infantile Paralysis, better known as the March of Dimes. For years, children with slotted cardboard sheets would canvas their neighborhoods, particularly at Halloween. The albums would be filled with Roosevelt dimes and contributed to the foundation.

Unfortunately, no cure or prevention for the disease was discovered until 1948, when Jonas Salk, a physician researcher at the University of Pittsburgh, developed a vaccine from the dead virus that caused the illness. Over the next seven years, 1.8 million volunteers received the injectable vaccine, and, in 1955, it was judged a successful deterrent to polio. I received the vaccine when I was nine. With the introduction of the Salk vaccine, and the later, more effective Sabin oral vaccine based on an attenuated live virus, American medicine conquered this plague decisively. Dropping from 58,000 cases in 1952, there were 5,600 cases in 1957, and 160 cases in 1961. In 2016, less than 200 cases were reported worldwide.

My cousin Marty missed this medical miracle. The vaccine was still in trial when he was infected. Three weeks after becoming ill, he succumbed to the disease. We had not been allowed to visit him, and no children could attend his funeral. My mother later told me that her brother Martin, Marty's father, had to be physically restrained from throwing himself into the grave prepared for the small casket.

My mind had wandered to that time in my childhood, as I faithfully took the AZT that inevitably made me sick but might be my only chance against AIDS. The epidemics were, of course, very different in terms of their victims (although children would also become victims of the HIV virus). Otherwise, there were many similarities—uncertainty about cause, physical and social isolation, suffering, and death. But there were cruel differences— the social stigmatization of the gay community, already subject to discrimination, led to further rejection, even going so far as to blame the victims for their disease and to claim that it may be a verdict of the Almighty against homosexuality. Then there was the physical isolation from loved ones and even caregivers. There was no scientific conviction about the transmission of the HIV; was it by ingestion of contaminated fluid? Close physical contact? Simply breathing the air in the same room as the victim? Early on, the only human contact the sufferer received was from masked and gowned doctors and nurses who generally kept their interactions as brief as possible, not out of cruelty but for fear of carrying this plague into their homes.

The disease itself involved horrific suffering. All the rare infections that had been progressively identified and conquered over hundreds of years emerged from their hidden places and attacked these poor innocents who could not mobilize enough immune power to fight back. Death was a wasting, painful process.

Finally, my friend and Infectious Disease specialist, Gary Wormser, called . . . to tell me that my HIV test was negative. At first, I didn't believe him. Then I felt overwhelming relief. Then a sense of sadness crept in. As I recalled the terror that I felt over the prospect of suffering with AIDS, I thought of all the patients who had to face the reality of the diagnosis and gain the courage to endure it.

Thank God, over the years, the HIV infection rate has dropped substantially with better education to avoid exposure. About 1 million Americans are now living with HIV. New antiretroviral therapies have dramatically improved life expectancy. In 1996, the life expectancy was thirty-nine years old. By 2018, it had increased to seventy years. Soon, we have real hope that it will be an entirely curable illness, not the hopeless epidemic that past generations experienced with bubonic plague, syphilis, tuberculosis, smallpox and polio.

CHAPTER TWENTY-ONE

Decapitated

The mid-90's were a very busy time for me, academically. Our neurosurgery residency was thriving and I was attending national and international cerebrovascular meetings. My research had returned me to an earlier time in my medical career: I was studying the biological behavioral consequences of brain hemorrhage.

And although these studies were fascinating and promising, I continued to have an active clinical practice. Kerry Leshnicki had just dropped her two boys off at school and was driving to work westbound on a very busy Interstate 287. She was driving a Volkswagen beetle. She loved the car. It was comfortable and easy to handle, and she had only had it for five months. She turned up the Doobie Brothers on the radio and relaxed. It was a lovely morning. As she passed Exit 8, she cruised along in the right lane. A large semi was just a couple of car lengths ahead in the center lane. Kerry didn't see the second semi. It entered from the onramp and was picking up speed. By the worst bit of chance, her little car was now in the blind spot of both trucks. The second truck pulled into the right lane. There was the sickening sound of wrenching steel as the VW was crushed between the two trucks. The second truck quickly pulled onto the shoulder. The first truck slammed on its brakes and came to a screeching halt in the center lane. The busy commuter traffic rapidly built up behind the disastrous accident scene. The only tiny fortunate aspect of this disaster was its location, only a couple of miles from our Level One trauma center.

There are five levels of trauma center care, from Level Five, where diagnosis and stabilization are conducted, to Level One tertiary medical centers, where all specialties are available at all times and complete treatment is available. An EMS Advanced Life Support team, returning to the medical center, was only about six cars behind the wreck, and a police cruiser was also nearby. They both quickly worked their way to the shoulder and were at the scene in minutes.

Kerry was not moving and appeared to be unconscious. She was pinned in the wreckage. The jaws of life allowed the paramedics to gently remove her from the car. The EMTs moved her as gingerly as possible, quickly immobilizing her neck in a brace, then assessing her general condition. Amazingly, she seemed to have only a few lacerations; left arm, right leg, and a few bruises on her face and head. However, her respirations were very shallow and she seemed to be going in and out of consciousness. A large intravenous line was started and a sedative given. The EMT introduced an endotracheal tube through her mouth into her windpipe, taped it securely, and began to bag her, applying regular bursts of air mixed with oxygen via an Ambu bag attached to the breathing tube. They lifted the board, immobilizing her into the rear of the ambulance, and sped the short distance to the medical center.

She was thoroughly evaluated by Trauma surgery, the lacerations were sutured, x-rays and CTs were performed to evaluate her chest, abdomen, pelvis, and long bones. No significant findings. But, as Kerry emerged from the sedative, a much more distressing effect of the accident began to become clear.

The young woman was now opening her eyes and regarding the staff, but she was not moving any of her extremities. The emergency team tested her sensation with a safety pin. She appeared to feel nothing. She did not follow instructions to move her arms or legs. She had no reflexes. And when the team paused the ventilator for a few moments, allowing her carbon dioxide to rise, she made no attempt to breathe. I was called and came to the ER as quickly as I could.

Ms. Leshnicki was awake by the time I arrived. The ventilator hummed in the background. I introduced myself and asked her to move any of her limbs. Nothing. I touched a safety pin to her arms and legs, and she did not react. I tapped her knees and arms with a reflex hammer. No response. I asked her if she could feel anything or try to move anything. She only looked at me. I then asked her to blink her eyes twice if she could understand me. For a moment she just stared, then, slowly and deliberately, she blinked twice. I touched her face and asked if she could feel it. She blinked twice. I asked her to swallow and she gulped weakly against the endotracheal tube.

I told Kerry that I would be right back and stepped out to take a look at the cervical spine film. Looking at the junction of the skull and the neck, there should be a few millimeters between the two: the skull is connected to the neck not by bones but by a complex arrangement of ligaments, joints, and muscles. Kerry's cranio-cervical junction was very abnormal. Instead of a close fit, her skull was separated from her spine by about an inch and a half. She had been functionally decapitated in the accident. Kerry Leshnicki, to use a crude bit of medical jargon, was a "head on a pillow."

I sighed hard and walked back into the room. Mercifully, Kerry was asleep. I looked at the ventilator. Its bellows raised and lowered slowly and rhythmically. Her vital signs were displayed on the monitor: BP 117/60, pulse 84. Solid as a rock. My brain was spinning and my soul was in turmoil. I stepped back out into the busy ER hallway and started toward the nursing station in a complete fog. I nearly ran directly into a distraught young man. "I'm John Leshnicki. My wife is Kerry. They told me she's in there. Do you know if she's okay?" Okay? I thought. Your wife couldn't be further from okay.

He read the consternation and depression reflected on my face. "Is she . . . is she dead?" I shook my head, again thinking that in some ways she was worse than dead. I pulled him to the side of the hall and took the liberty of putting my hand on his shoulder. I just felt so very sorry for him, for her, for myself. "John, Kerry is awake but she can't move. She can't breathe on her own. She's had a serious neck injury."

"How long will it take for her to come out of it?"

"I'm not sure that she will ever be able to come out of it."

"You mean she'll stay like this? I need to see her." He swiped a tear quickly from his cheek. I nodded.

About five minutes later, John stepped into the hall, and, when out of view of the door, leaned hard against the wall, his shoulders shaking. I leaned against the opposite wall, arms crossed. A short time later, he noticed me. He raised his hands and shook his head. He walked over and whispered, "what can we do?" I waited for a few minutes, trying to choose my words carefully.

"Has she ever told you what she would want if she was in a . . . hopeless . . . situation?"

"No, we've never talked about anything like that. We're young, we have small children. I don't think the thought has ever occurred to either of us. At least not that we've talked about."

"John, this is a situation where we can go to our ethics committee for advice. But I have to know what you want to do, and, most importantly, what you think Kerry would want us to do. I can't rely on her eye movements for a decision like this."

"I don't know what to do, doctor. You have to decide for us."

I walked back into the quiet room, interrupted only by the steady wheezing of the ventilator and the regular blips of her vital signs. Kerry's eyes were closed. I moved her arms and legs—no resistance. No reflexes, no reaction to the light touch of a safety pin. I waited for a sign from God. Dead silence. I thought of her two years from now, being treated for decubitus ulcers in a nursing home, a tracheostomy and a ventilator, a gastric feeding tube. Still conscious. Her husband divorced and racked with guilt. Never seeing her children because it was too painful for them. My hand was six inches from the power switch on the ventilator. A brief action would turn off the machine, and, in a few moments, Kerry would drift into eternal sleep. No more agony, only pleasant memories for her husband and children. I felt my hand drawn overwhelmingly to the machine.

And then I was struck by a chilling, stunning feeling.

"Who made you God?"

I found myself whispering aloud. My words awakened Kerry, who looked at me with fathomless eyes, unable to express her emotions with her facial muscles. "Kerry, you know we're in a tough spot here." She blinked twice. "It's going to be hard, but I'd like you and I to try to get through this together." A moment passed. She looked at the ceiling, then at me. She blinked twice.

Back in the cold, antiseptic hallway, "John, I think we should try to do everything we can for Kerry. If you come to a different conclusion, we can always revisit the situation." He nodded without expression. But a weight seemed to have been lifted from his shoulders.

The next few days were a flurry of activity. As we could have predicted, her autonomic nervous system tried to adjust to her extraordinary injury and we had to chase her blood pressure and pulse rates all over the chart. We placed cranial tongs on her skull so that we could use a rotating bed to turn her supine and prone. Nursing could then care for her with access to all of her body, including taking pressure off of her back to avoid those dreadful ulcers. Skin cream was applied regularly. On the second day, we accepted the inevitable and asked our general surgery colleagues to perform a tracheostomy and place a gastric feeding tube. This would allow the team to suction the mucus from her breathing tube and upper airway, helping to prevent pneumonia. The feeding tube would let us get started on the hyperalimentation that would keep her in nutritional balance and discourage muscle atrophy and kidney and liver problems.

On day three, I repeated her cervical CAT scan. It still showed the alarming separation between her skull and cervical spine, but the spinal cord swelling was not as horrible as I had expected. I met with the rest of our surgical faculty, and all agreed that, as Kerry had survived the first couple of days after the injury, we had committed ourselves. The next step was to stabilize her spine.

We used the versatile, rotating stretcher to turn her prone after general anesthesia was induced. Adjusting the weights on the cranial traction, we allowed the skull to relax toward the neck and reduced the distance between the two from one and a half inches to just under an inch. Not a perfect distance, but good alignment of the bones. After carefully scrubbing the skin on the back of Kerry's neck and painting it with antiseptic solution, I made a vertical incision from the base of her skull to the middle of her cervical spine. As I gingerly dissected her ligaments and muscles away from the center of her spine and skull, I noticed some old blood clotted around the top of the spine. Suctioning the clot away, I saw the torn ligaments between spine and skull. Using a Kerrison three mm rongeur (one of the long-handled instruments with tiny features at the end, that allow us to operate on small structures with extended instruments without introducing our large human fingers), I bit away pieces of the blood-stained ligament until I could see the dura covering the spinal cord. Although the dura was also bloodstained, there did not seem to be a large amount of clot on its surface. I couldn't see any tears of the dura, nor did spinal fluid bubble up into the wound. It looked like the dura was intact. I irrigated the dura with cool saline to get a better look, as well as to further discourage spinal cord swelling (we had kept her on high doses of intravenous steroids for the same purpose). I could faintly see the spinal cord through the semi-translucent dura. Although the cord seemed a bit widened, confirming the swelling, I could see a very minimal pulsation of the cord. And it didn't appear to be discolored by blood. All of this, plus the view of the spinal cord on the CAT scan, suggested to me that the spinal cord wasn't cut, and that it didn't have a blood clot within it. Rather, it appeared to be contused—badly bruised. This would have been very encouraging if Kerry wasn't so neurologically devastated. I had seen contusions of the brain and spinal cord become lethal on several occasions.

After all of the soft tissue was cleared from the base of the skull and the laminae (the bony arches covering the back of the spinal cord at each of twenty-seven levels) of the first three vertebrae, we contoured a large, U-shaped, titanium plate so that the curve of the U covered the base of the skull flush and the two limbs of the U would lie flat against the cervical laminae. The sturdy plate was perforated all around with holes, and we applied screws through these into the skull and cervical spine until they were rigidly fixed. I then used a small high-speed drill to roughen the bony surfaces all around the plate and placed a thick layer of bone graft over them. Using cautery, we got good control of all bleeding, repeatedly irrigated the wound with antibiotic solution, then closed the wound in three layers—muscle, fascia, and skin (with absorbable sutures). We placed Kerry in a Philadelphia collar, a soft synthetic brace that contoured to her chin, base of skull, neck, and collar bones, for support.

Now the drudgery began. The daily bathing and applications of cream and powder. We had transferred Kerry to a special bed postoperatively. This very expensive device constantly inflated in different small areas all over its surface so that pressure was constantly changed on every skin point, strongly fighting the tendency of the skin to break down under pressure. Every day, physical and occupational therapists massaged and rotated her limbs to maintain their tone and mobility. Special compression devices inflated and deflated regularly to prevent blood clots from forming in the veins of her legs, which could then break off and circulate to her lungs, resulting in a lethal pulmonary embolus. Relying on expert dieticians and intensivists, her tube feedings were progressed, maintaining her electrolytes and proteins. Several times each day, pulmonary treatments were given to dilate her airways and help prevent pneumonia. And on and on.

These were accompanied by another ritual. Every day, John Leshnicki sat at his wife's bedside, cradling her hand in his, gently rubbing her hand or hair. The nurses would bring him food and coffee, inspired by his vigil. After two weeks, he and his family decided to bring eight-year-old Taylor and ten-year-old Michael to visit their mother. They carefully explained to the boys what to expect; that Mommy wouldn't be able to speak to them or hold them. But she would be able to see them and know that they were there and love them. I couldn't tolerate this visit and have always thought that I would have been in the way in any case. But my friend, nurse Beth Collins, told me that no one in the ICU could control their emotions as the two boys stood next to their mother's bed like little soldiers, still and stiff, tears on their cheeks.

I sat in my office that Sunday afternoon, lost in thought. I couldn't read, do my charts, or think about anything other than Kerry Leshnicki. I knew that, morally (and legally), I had made the right decision to keep her ventilator running in the ER that day. But was it really moral uprightness, or was it cowardice? Was I simply afraid of taking the action that would have spared her everything that had happened and was going to happen? But, after all, I would have been committing euthanasia, which is a crime. And I doubt that I could ever have done that.

Days turned into weeks. Kerry was stable. Her vital signs had stopped fluctuating wildly, and her weight, down fifteen lbs. from her already small initial size, had stopped dropping. The nursing staff had done a heroic job of preventing decubitus ulcers, pneumonia, and the myriad trivial problems that could snowball and take her life.

It was October now, and the leaves were turning. The holiday season was about to begin, and Westchester County, New York, the home of Washington Irving and the "Legend of Sleepy Hollow," was getting ready for its huge Halloween celebrations. At 8 a.m., I was in conference with the residents. It was a combination of a clinical conference, examining the cases we had done over the past week, and planning the management of ensuing cases. An intern came over and leaned in whispering, "the nurse in the ICU needs to speak to you about Ms. Leshnicki."

"We're in conference here. Can't it wait?"

"She said it's urgent." Thinking the worst, I picked up the phone.

"Doctor Lansen, it's Barb in ICU. Kerry just moved her left big toe."

I sighed. "Barb, it's reflexic. It's not uncommon for quadriplegics to have reflex movements of their limbs."

"Really? On command?"

"You mean you asked her to move the toe and she did it?"

"You got it."

I managed to finish the conference, but the residents were as disinterested in the presentations as I was. We just wanted to get over to that ICU and see for ourselves if what the nurse told us could possibly be true, or if it was just a cruel accident. Barb was leaning over Kerry when we walked in. "Kerry, wiggle your toe." She moved the toe almost immediately. I let out a very undignified whoop, and the staff laughed and clapped. A tear formed in Kerry's eye.

Over the next several days, Kerry's brain began to take over her body again. First, there were stronger movements of her legs, then her arms. At the same time, she was "breathing over" the ventilator. That is, her ability to breathe was returning, and her respirations were suppressing the machine's triggers. Swallowing tests were weakly positive. Two weeks later, she was transferred to the rehab unit.

I was given reports that she was making progress, but imagine my shock when, about six weeks after her transfer from the acute care hospital, I was seeing patients in my office and I looked up to see John Leshnicki very gingerly guiding Kerry into my office. She still needed a walker, but she was actually walking into my office. The tracheostomy had been closed, she was breathing on her own and speaking, albeit her voice a bit hoarse. She was eating regular food and still getting rehab three times a week. And she was home with her husband and sons. Kerry would make essentially a complete recovery.

I had never seen a case like Kerry's before, and I have never seen one since. But ever since that moment, whenever I have been confronted with a desperate or apparently hopeless situation, I have reminded myself immediately—"And who made you God?"

I have repeated this story and its lesson to my fellows, residents, students, and, yes, even to my colleagues. Kerry turned out to be one of my best teachers.

CHAPTER TWENTY-TWO

You'll Dance at the Wedding

Michael Antonelli was forty-eight years old in 1996. He was a police captain in New York City. He was married with one child, a beautiful ten-year-old daughter, whom he adored. Born in an intensely Italian neighborhood in Staten Island, he was a family guy.

Michael immediately struck me as one of the most positive people I had ever met. He had been in the NYPD for almost thirty years and had no intention of retiring soon. He loved his job. He had worked his way up through the ranks, and he knew every precinct in the city. He knew its upscale neighborhoods and its underbelly. He was a happy guy who had found his perfect niche.

It came as quite a shock to his family and friends when he started to have a little trouble finding his words, and even seemed to be a little confused. Everyone knew that Mike wasn't a drinker. Drugs? Not likely. Then one evening, sitting at dinner with his wife, daughter, parents, and Judy's brother Frank and his wife Irene, Mike's right hand began to tremble. Slightly at first, it started to jerk wildly and rhythmically. He started to speak. "What the hell . . ." Then his body straightened out of his chair like a jackknife, and he fell stiffly to the floor, where his entire body jerked to an unheard beat. Judy and little Mandy screamed. Irene, who was a nurse, ran to Mike and leaned over, turning him on his side so that the secretions in his mouth would drain onto the floor rather than into his lungs.

The seizure lasted about a minute and a half. Then the shaking gradually subsided and Mike slumped into a merciful sleep. Within five minutes, EMS had arrived. They checked his vitals. His blood pressure was a little elevated, but his pulse was steady and he was breathing regularly. They asked the family about the episode, what led up to it. Was Mike taking any medications? Recent illnesses? Frank said that Mike was as healthy as a horse. Had he ever had a seizure before?

He was stabilized that evening in the hospital. He was started on a rather high dose of Dilantin, the anti-seizure medicine that would be tapered to give him a blood level that would help prevent another seizure. By the time I saw him the next morning, Mike was awake, alert, and, of course . . . smiling.

"Captain, nice to meet you. I'm Thomas Lansen from the neurosurgery service."

He raised his eyebrows. "Mike, Doc."

"Then Tom, Mike." I knew I was going to like this guy, which was not necessarily a blessing, given my line of work.

"You gonna operate on my brain, Tom?"

"Let's not get ahead of ourselves, Mike. I'm going to start by examining you."

"That's good, because I didn't want you to be disappointed when you don't find any brains up there." We both laughed. Mike had an endearing space between his front teeth, like Vince Lombardi or Michael Strahan.

I was reminded of the old truism in brain surgery: an unexplained seizure in an adult is a brain tumor until proven otherwise. With that thought in the back of my mind, I set out to find some localizing signs on his examination that might tell me where the cause of the seizure was. I didn't have to wait long. Suddenly, he stopped talking, his right hand trembled gently and rhythmically, and he stared into space, turning his head to the left. This went on for about thirty seconds, then he sighed and regained awareness. He looked at me with arched brow. "Whyalu doozling?" he said. I placed my hand on his shoulder. "Steady, Mike. Let's get you lying down here." I raised the head of the bed electronically and eased him down. In a few moments, he was back to himself.

"What the hell happened? I must have conked out." His speech was still just a bit slurred. I went through the neurological exam that I had done a thousand times. There were two abnormalities—the speech, and a right upper extremity drift. That is, when I asked Mike to hold his arms up in front of him equally, the right arm would drift down consistently. I looked at his retina—no sign of increased brain pressure, although the staff had precautionarily started him on steroids to suppress brain swelling. The tremor of the right hand pointed to the left side of the brain being the cause. The problem with the expression of speech pointed to the left temporal and frontal lobes, the centers of speech comprehension and expression.

"Okay, Mike, I'll be back. I'm going to go have a look at your MRI scan." The nurse assured me that he was on seizure precautions as I left the room. I headed to the neuroradiology reading room, where Mike Tenner was reviewing scans with the residents.

"Whoa, Professor. To what do we owe the honor of this visit?" I smiled and shook Mike's hand warmly.

"Mike, can you pull up Michael Antonelli?"

"Antonelli," Mike repeated. He punched the name into the computer, and, a moment later, we were looking at a series of brain slices that looked like they were picked from an anatomy book. Magnetic Resonance Imaging (MRI) had come a long way in a very short time. As explained earlier, the device used strong magnetic waves on the target organ, polarizing the protons in cells and forcing them to align. A pulse of radiofrequency current is then passed through the cells. This causes the protons to spin out of alignment. When it is turned off, the protons relax back to alignment, but depending on the cell they inhabit, they emit different amounts of energy and take different amounts of time as they do so. These differences can be measured, assigned different values of 'intensity'. These intensity values are then assigned shades on a scale of black to white, and when put together, create an accurate image of the tissue examined. Pretty complicated stuff. But I guess that's what you need to do to win a Nobel Prize. The generations of MRI were allowing finer and finer resolution. The most important advance was the introduction of injectable compounds that could enhance abnormal areas of the brain, such as tumors. Mike had been scanned with and without one such dye, gadolinium.

As Tenner scrolled through slices of Mike's brain, from the base of his skull to the top, he stopped at the level of the temporal lobes. In the front of the left temporal lobe, there was an irregular oval shadow, darker than the surrounding brain, with some swelling near it that pushed the front of the temporal lobe upward and pressed on the frontal lobe, which would account for Mike's speech problem as well as the right-hand tremor. The left frontal lobe controlled the movements of the right side of the body.

The edge of the abnormal area lit up with spots of gadolinium. There were also some islands of gadolinium scattered through the shadowy area. And there was a darker stain around the abnormal area—edema, or swelling, in reaction to the presence of the invader.

I glanced at Tenner. He was impassive. We had seen this picture hundreds of times. "This is a really nice guy," I said, as if that would give him a reprieve. "Maybe it's an oligo (an oligodendroglioma was a brain tumor that, with surgical removal and radiation therapy, could go into remission or even be cured) or a meningioma tethered to the anterior temporal dura (a benign tumor that grew from the lining of the brain and could be removed . . . and cured)."

Tenner's usually smiling eyes squinted into an unwilling frown. "Glioblastoma." My heart sank. I knew he was correct. The "variegated" uptake of the dye, the irregular outline of the tumor, the swelling around it. It was a glioblastoma, the most malignant tumor of the brain, perhaps of the entire human organism.

Glioblastoma has been diagnosed for more than a century. It arises from the glial cells of the brain as opposed to the neurons. For years we have deduced that the neurons are the essential brain cells, carrying information, storing data. The glial cells have been presumed to be conveyer cells, connecting neurons, providing nutrition to them, and disposing of their waste. More recently, it appears that glia are part of the entire functioning system of brain activity, just as essential as neurons to the party.

Tumors of the neurons are relatively rare and usually less ominous. While the glia tend to develop more tumors, they are also prone to developing into the T-Rex of tumors—the glioblastoma. After a century of research, we are still not sure if the glioblastoma, or GBM, develops at one site or several at the same time. And we have tried so many treatments—surgery, radiation, chemotherapy, stereotactic radiation, immune therapy, vaccines—all thus far with very mediocre results. We have watched our stars, from George Gershwin to Senators Ted Kennedy and John McCain, succumb to this monster. All within about one year of diagnosis. Despite thinking outside the box and putting on a full court press . . . one year.

I approached my new friend and perennial optimist patient, Mike Antonelli. His wife had joined him in his hospital room. "Mike, I've got some news about your situation."

"Judy, wait in the family room." I was embarrassed. Shouldn't his wife be in on this? Judy got up and dutifully left the room. Antonelli saw my distress. "Tom, I'm Italian. You have to understand. If I get bad news, I don't want to be emotional around my wife. I'll sit down with her later. Right now, you and I have business." I nodded. He was a straight shooter, so I gave it to him straight.

"Mike, I looked at your MRI. It looks like you have a tumor in your brain. Not only a tumor, but the worst kind. Malignant. And it will shorten your life very cruelly."

"Shorten by how much?"

"The statistics say you probably won't have more than a year."

"Statistics. Shit, statistics. What's the plan?"

"Well, I have to try to get most of that tumor out with an operation."

"Most? What the hell are you talking about? You mean ALL!" In spite of the drama of the situation, we both smiled, then laughed out loud. This guy had more grit than John Wayne.

Three days later, Michael's surgery was over, and he lay quietly in the recovery room, his head swathed in a clean white bandage which covered his entire head from above his eyebrows and the tips of his ears.

"How'd it go?"

"Well, I took out everything that looked abnormal."

"Good." He closed his eyes.

After opening Michael's scalp and skull in the usual fashion (if you've made it to this point, you've got a pretty good idea of what that means), we waited while the brain swelling caused by the tumor was reduced by diuretic agents and hyperventilation to lower his carbon dioxide level (CO_2 raises brain pressure). After a few minutes, the brain was relaxed enough for us to see its normal pulsations. I opened the dura and saw that the gyri of Michael's left temporal lobe were flattened and pale from the pressure the underlying tumor had exerted, pushing the surface of the brain against the inside of the skull. I used the bipolar forceps to cauterize a one-inch-long strip of the front (anterior) middle temporal gyrus. I wanted to stay as anterior as I could, as the center for the understanding of speech was located in this lobe, a bit further back.

Taking a small retractor blade in my left hand, I used my right to dissect down in the direction of the tumor with a fine suction tip. When I got to about a two-centimeter depth, the usual pallor of the brain's white matter began to change to a tallow, yellowish color. I used a cup forceps to take a small biopsy, which I sent off for a frozen section biopsy. The pathologist would stain and freeze the specimen in a waxy medium, then make very fine slices of it, which he would examine under the microscope. This specimen showed only a background of slightly more glial cells (the brain's nutrient and structural cells) than normal. Continuing to dissect with the suction tip in my left hand and to cauterize small blood vessels with my right, I fell into an area of thicker, gray tissue, clearly tumor, with larger cysts, some almost a centimeter in diameter, filled with yellow, clear fluid. These were signs of necrosis, where the tumor had grown faster than its blood supply, leading to the death and destruction of millions of tumor cells, which created a wasteland of dead tissue and these collections of liquid debris. Unfortunately, the tumor grew much faster than it died, and it created this large mass which invaded and killed normal brain tissue. It did further damage by pressing on normal tissue until the adjacent brain couldn't function.

I sent several specimens, each more than a cubic centimeter in volume, to the neuropathologist, who quickly informed me that this was a very aggressive, cancerous, primary brain tumor—the infamous glioblastoma multiforme, named for its parent cell, the glial cell, and the variety of its tissues: areas of necrosis, a proliferation of the blood vessels supplying it, walls of cells lined up in palisades and an extremely dense population of tumor cells.

Knowing the diagnosis, I now moved aggressively to remove as much of the tumor as I could. I used a device that disintegrated the tumor with ultrasound, irrigated the area, then suctioned out the destroyed tissue. Using this tool, along with bipolar cautery, I continued the resection until all of the margins of the tumor bed were back to their natural whitish (white matter) hue. At this point, with several final specimens not showing tumor, I coated the brain where I had removed the tumor with Surgicel anticoagulant net pledgets, placed an intracranial pressure monitor, and closed the dura, the skull, and the scalp.

Glioblastoma multiforme, or GBM, is one of the best known and studied primary brain tumors. George Gershwin, the great American composer and pianist, was operated on for a glioblastoma at Cedars of Lebanon Hospital in Los Angeles in 1937 by Howard Nafziger, who had studied under the great William Halsted at Johns Hopkins and had served in WWI with another mentor, Harvey Cushing, the father of American neurosurgery. Gershwin died within a day of surgery. But decades after the tragedy of Gershwin and having advanced tremendously in the understanding of the genetics and pathology of the disease, with myriad therapeutic trials—surgical, radiotherapeutic, and chemotherapeutic—we don't seem much closer to a cure. At this writing, less than 5% of patients survive for five years, and most are dead within a year.

Michael Antonelli's therapy was no exception. After what I considered a "gross total removal" of the tumor, I knew that the microscopic fingers of the tumor hibernated in his brain, waiting to multiply again. I brought in our radiation and medical neurooncologists. We started with a course of focused external radiation therapy, supplemented by the latest chemotherapy, a platinum-based tumor killer. Mike was compliant and resilient. His optimism continued, and his mind and body remained intact.

I followed Mike's case very carefully. At first, we repeated his MRI every two weeks. When things continued to be stable, with no sign of tumor recurrence, I backed off to one MRI a month.

Unfortunately, this regimen didn't last long. His third monthly MRI showed tumor regrowth on the posterior and medial margins of the tumor bed, the areas most important to his brain function. After a brief discussion, Mike included an exhortation of "What are we waiting for?" I went back in. On opening the brain, there was a clear, liquid cavity where we had operated before, and then, at the base and inner margins of the cavity, we saw what the MRI had warned us of—tuft-like layers of new tumor. It was a recurrence. I used the same technique as before to remove this tumor, skirting the normal brain very carefully, as we were entering some very expensive neurological real estate.

Again, Mike made a quick and full recovery. I had him tested by our neuropsychologists—no deficit. He remained unflappable. "What's next? How do we beat this son-of-a-bitch?" We didn't have long to wait for an answer. Three months later, the MRI detected another recurrence, this time at the front of the tumor bed. Under most circumstances, I wouldn't consider another surgery for tumor at this early stage, with its dismal likelihood of survival. But Mike was absolutely relentless and would take any risk to enhance his chances. For this third surgery, we tried a new technique. We again removed all the tumor we could see, but this time we placed a series of radioactive pellets in the tumor using a technique called interstitial radiation. The idea was that we had given the brain all the external radiation it could stand, but we could boost this with small doses of very localized radiation, which would give any local tumor plenty of radiation but would limit the penetration of tissue-destroying radiation to a very narrow zone.

The amazing Mike Antonelli bounced back from his third brain surgery as he had from the other two. Another curve ball hit him at this time. His wife Judy left him. I tried to determine if his personality had somehow changed due to the tumor or the surgery, causing this mess. No, he said, they'd had trouble for a long time, like so many other spouses of New York's finest. This long run of bad luck had just been the straw that broke the camel's back. "Hey, I still have my baby girl," he said, referring to his beloved daughter. This guy was tougher than sandpaper.

Nine months passed, and Mike was thinking about returning to the job. I was starting to get cautiously optimistic. I had only one other GBM survivor among the hundreds of such patients I had treated. But I had long ago learned that anything was possible. And, as I've said before, God wasn't letting me in on what would happen. So, I was really depressed when I saw on Mike's last pre-employment MRI a bright, enhancing, round spot in the tumor bed. Another recurrence. Damn, after a year. Well, that was about right. He looked great, but it was only a matter of time.

"Hey, doc, what are we going to do? You have to go back in, right?" I couldn't hide my disappointment or my pessimism about the outcome. Mike's famous grin appeared. "Doc, you want to know something? My Mandy's almost eleven. You're going to dance at her wedding." I couldn't help but chuckle along with him.

Three days later, Mike was anesthetized for his fourth brain surgery. As I delicately entered the now-familiar tumor bed, I saw something that astonished me and gave me hope. At the base of what had been the tumor was a large aneurysm, a blood blister emerging from the side of a branch of the middle cerebral artery. This was the lesion we had seen on the MRI. As we traced the course of the artery, it was clear that the artery did not feed any of the brain tissue outside the tumor bed. I carefully dissected the artery, then placed a clip across it just before the aneurysm emerged and another just beyond the aneurysm's origin. I inserted a tiny needle into the dome of the aneurysm, and with a brief jet of blood, it collapsed. I don't know how he developed an aneurysm in the tumor bed, but my conjecture has always been that one of the radiation pellets sat in proximity to the involved blood vessel and eroded its wall.

But this opportunity was not to be wasted. A new kind of local chemotherapy had recently been introduced. Gliadel™ was an agent called carmustine, which was applied as a wafer to the surface of the tumor bed. The agent then leached into the adjacent tissue, hopefully impeding further tumor growth. I applied eight of the wafers to what I judged to be the most vulnerable areas for recurrence. I closed the wound again with a bit of hope and a lot of prayer.

We followed Mike Antonelli with MRI scans for five years. His tumor never recurred. No, he didn't return to the police force. He decided that he had tested his luck once too often. No, I didn't dance at his daughter's wedding. I lost track of Mike after ten years of follow-up. But I know one thing: He was one of the rarest of all GBM patients—a cured survivor.

CHAPTER TWENTY-THREE

A New Dawn

Helen Aspiritis was a surprisingly young-looking sixty-eight. With black, wavy hair, pale skin and ebony eyes, she was a beautiful woman by any standard. Her looks, combined with an outgoing personality, made everyone love Helen. She was a child of the Greek diaspora. Her father had come to Astoria, Queens, New York, just after the war. He made a bee line to Astoria because, like so many other neighborhoods in this nation of immigrants, it had become a perfect replica of the homeland. Astoria (named after John Jacob Astor, who never actually even visited his namesake neighborhood) has become one of the greatest melting pots in America, with a great diversity of ethnic groups. Home to thousands of Greek immigrants, it has a colorful history. A resort town for wealthy mid-18th century Manhattanites, it was home to Heinrich Steinweg, founder of the Steinway Piano Company, and the early headquarters for the motion picture industry. The first talkie Sherlock Holmes film was shot there, and the Marx Brothers made *Animal Crackers* and *The Cocoanuts* in the Astoria studio.

Gloria Swanson made many of her early films there. The location was convenient to Broadway, where stars could dabble in the new motion picture adventure. Paramount Pictures was founded there. Ultimately, as we all know, the movies relocated to Hollywood, where city strictures were avoided and outdoor scenery abounded.

Astoria, Queens has become a savory and exotic blend of Israelis and Balkans, Yemenis and Maltese, Italians and Egyptians, Bangladeshi and Thais. Oh, and yes, Greeks. The neighborhood hosts tavernas, bakeries, restaurants and several Greek Orthodox churches. My first acquaintance with Astoria was through my friend, Dimitrios "Jimmy" Kotsilimbas. I met Jimmy when we both served on the neurosurgery faculty at New York Medical College in the 1980s. I had the privilege of assisting him on several cases. He was a deft and graceful surgeon who had the gifts of self-deprecation and generosity. And his personality was as warm as a gyro fresh off the griddle.

Although twenty years my senior, Jimmy accepted me as a friend, not just a colleague. He invited me to assist him in surgery on a case at Elmhurst Hospital in Queens. I know it's not exactly kosher to say so but operating with Jimmy was fun. He was comfortable enough in the OR to operate meticulously while holding an unrelated, interesting conversation. And so, I learned his story.

Jimmy had been a brilliant medical student and intern in Athens when he was mandated to perform his military service. This is the story he related, and I have no reason to believe otherwise, as he was a man of honor and I had never known him to be anything but truthful. During his on-call weekend, he was informed that there was a man with a ruptured appendix on one of the nearby

Greek islands who required helicopter evacuation. Jimmy was to ride shotgun as the medical officer. He dutifully accepted the patient, who was strapped in a gurney on the helicopter. Jimmy, the patient's wife, the pilot, and copilot began the short return flight to Athens. Twenty minutes into the flight, the engine failed, and they crashed into the Aegean Sea. The helicopter quickly sunk, sucking Jimmy's patient into the depths below. Although he frantically tried to release the belts tethering the gurney to the chopper, it was hopeless.

The copilot was killed on impact. The pilot, the patient's wife, and Jimmy swam away from the vortex as best they could. An island in the distance was their goal. They tried to stay together as best they could, but the currents pulled them apart. Jimmy told me that he had swum for more than two hours before he realized that he was still wearing his uniform, including his shoes. He stripped down and swam for his life. Finally, exhausted and nearly unconscious, Jimmy washed ashore. The patient's wife was not seen again. The pilot, unbeknownst to Jimmy, had swum to the other side of the same island.

He knew that there must be an air rescue underway from Athens after the helicopter disappeared, so he surveyed what he could of the island, sprained and bruised as he was. It was uninhabited as far as he could tell, and he couldn't readily find a source of fresh water. He had no water, and, of course, no food.

The first day passed with agonizing slowness. The second day, he discovered a small peak on the island, and, at the top, a lighthouse. By this time, his mouth was very dry and he was hungry. He deduced that the lighthouse must automatically ignite at about sunset and extinguish at dawn. He made a decision. If by the end of the third day, there was no sign of rescue, he would throw stones until he broke the light. This would certainly be noticed by the air patrols.

His pitching abilities weren't tested. On the third morning, a helicopter landed on the rocky beach in response to Jimmy's frantic waving. The pilot of their sunken craft, already rescued, had seen Jimmy swimming to the cove where they found him. The pilot told him that he had seen the patient's wife swimming to the island when she was caught in the surf on the island's breakwater.

Jimmy returned to his residency to discover that he was a celebrity in the worst sense. The press grabbed onto this amazing story. Why hadn't the doctor saved his patient? If he couldn't, why hadn't he gone down with the ship? And, at the very least, why did he let the man's wife perish? Like vultures, they wouldn't let their victim escape. Finally, beset by the press and his own inappropriate guilt, Jimmy left Greece forever. He would start again in little Athens . . . Astoria, Queens.

Dr. Kotsilimbas left his beloved Greece behind, but he brought his brains and talent, like so many other young immigrants, with him. After coming to the attention of the New York medical establishment, he repeated his general surgical training and his neurosurgery residency. Then he went "home" to Queens, where he quickly became the favorite son of the medical community. Patients with brain tumors, aneurysms, or strokes would be operated on by him, or perhaps transferred to a major medical center in Manhattan—Columbia, Cornell, NYU—but only with Jimmy's permission and recommendation.

One night, over Greek coffee, ouzo, and baklava, listening to a trio of Greek musicians in a lovely old restaurant, Jimmy raised his glass to me. "Tommy, smell the roses." As we were indoors, the point was lost on me. "Life is short. Smell the roses." Ah, I understood. Yes, Jimmy, but we are busy neurosurgeons and we have our obligations. It's hard to balance taking care of our patients, spending a few moments with our families, and keeping up with our continuing medical education, much less . . . taking time to smell the roses. He raised his glass again. "Nonetheless, Tommy, take time to smell the roses."

A few months later, Jimmy's wife called to tell me that he was in the ICU at his beloved hospital dying of a rapid and terminal cancer. I held his hand, trying to tell him what a wonderful mentor he had been and how I would miss him. His funeral was remarkable. At the Archdiocesan Cathedral of the Holy Trinity in Manhattan, hundreds of Jimmy's friends, patients, and colleagues gathered to remember this émigré who had touched so many in his chosen home.

Greeks . . . Astoria. But I digress.

I met Helen Aspiritis in St. Agnes Hospital in White Plains, New York. St. Agnes and its wonderful children's rehabilitation hospital would go the way of so many community hospitals at the turn of the century, either being absorbed into emerging medical center behemoths or closing. In this case, it would close. But at the time, it was a lovely and well-run institution. Helen was sitting quietly in her hospital bed with her two daughters nearby. She looked young enough to be their sister.

"Mrs. Aspiritis. Dr. Tom Lansen. How are you feeling?"

"I don't know. I feel quite fine, really. I'm not sure what happened." She glanced anxiously at her daughters. I had a rough idea from her history that she had had a seizure, with a slight residual deficit afterward. Irene answered.

"Well, the three of us were sitting around the kitchen table having coffee. We were recalling Papa and laughing at some of his antics. You see, he passed away last year (I nodded condolence). Suddenly, Mama's right hand started to shake and the right side of her mouth pulled up in an awful grin. Sorry, Mommy. After half a minute or so, which seemed like an eternity, she just sat there staring. We spoke to her and held her hands, and, after a couple of minutes, she looked at us and asked us what happened. Why were we staring at her? After that, it was just like nothing had happened."

"May I examine you, Mrs. Aspiritis?"

"Only if you call me Helen."

"Okay, Helen, then I'm Tom." She beamed the most gracious smile. I put her through her neurological paces. She passed, with one exception. She had a slight pronator drift of her right arm. That is, when I had her raise her arms equally in front of her then close her eyes, her right arm drifted down a bit and her hand rolled to the left. When she opened her eyes, she was alarmed. "Helen, I think that you had a seizure, and that this is probably the effect of it. And I suspect it's temporary."

She sighed with relief. "What are we going to do?"

"Well, what I'm going to do now is to go and look at your MRI; then, as soon as I'm finished, I'll come back up and report to you."

Once again, the admitting doctor and the neurologist had followed the old adage; if an adult has a seizure, it's a brain tumor until proven otherwise. Well, it was not proven otherwise. The contrast-enhanced MRI showed a bright, round two-and-a-half-centimeter diameter mass in her left hemisphere, just in back of the motor strip and in the area of the homunculus (I'll explain that in a minute) that controlled her right arm and face. There was a modest amount of edema around the tumor. The tumor wasn't attached to any other structure such as the dura covering the brain, so I was pretty sure from the start that this was a foreign invader, not something that grew from brain tissue itself; namely, a metastatic brain tumor from a cancer somewhere else in her body.

I went back to her room with the bad news. "Helen, I've had a good look at your brain scan. I see an abnormal area there. It looks like a brain tumor."

She caught her breath and grabbed her daughter's hand. "Can anything be done?"

"Yes. I need to operate on you and remove the tumor."

"If you can get it out, will I be okay?"

"Well, let me tell you what I think is going on here. I think this tumor can be removed. It's on the surface of your brain, so I won't have to go deep into your brain to get to it. And although there's always the possibility that there may be bleeding or swelling that could really hurt you after the surgery, I have a solid chance of getting it out."

"Okay, that sounds good."

"But we have another problem. The way this tumor looks on the scan suggests to me that it is spread from somewhere else in your body."

"You mean I have cancer? And it's spread to my brain?"

"I think that's true, Helen. We'll only know for sure when we take a piece of the tumor and look at it under a microscope. Then we'll know what it is and where it came from. But the good news is that you're healthy and you don't have any damage from the tumor yet. So perhaps we've caught it in time. Hold out those hands again and close your eyes."

She followed my instruction and, this time, the hands stayed even. As I had suspected, the drift had just been the effect of the seizure. Helen smiled a tentative smile. "Tom, I want you to do what you think gives me the best chance to live. I want to see my grandchildren grow up a little more." She squeezed my hand and transferred all the responsibility to me. Although this had happened many times before, I had never gotten used to the almost physical burden that fell on me in those moments.

Over the next day, we got CAT scans of her chest, abdomen, and pelvis and a bone scan. No obvious source of cancer was seen. I called in Abe Mittelman, the most talented oncologist I knew. He looked at all the labs we had collected, and at the scans. Nothing jumped out at Abe. Abe was an Israeli, smart and intuitive, who was devoted to his profession and his patients. He was a large man but had the personality of a great big teddy bear. His patients worshipped him.

Helen Aspiritis's surgery was uneventful. With her asleep, I made an incision on the left side of her scalp and then created a bone window over the area that I calculated to contain the tumor. After hyperventilation, Mannitol, and steroids, the brain was relaxed. I opened the dura and the tumor, a pinkish, soft marble, sat right in the middle of the operative field. It was about halfway up the brain from base to top, halfway from front to back. Using Penfield dissectors and bipolar forceps to define the margins of the tumor, I first coagulated a small area on the surface of the tumor, then made a small cut through that area and took a sample to send off to the pathologist for a frozen section analysis. Then, using cottonoid pledgets to further separate the tumor from the brain, I worked around it until it was completely free with the exception of a small vascular pedicle, a thin strand of an artery that had been taken hostage and was feeding the invader and allowing it to grow. I coagulated the pedicle and cut it with a microscissor. I passed the tumor to my assistant and inspected the tumor bed—the brain that surrounded the tumor—for bleeding. There was none. I closed the wound, sent Helen to the recovery room, and headed for the pathology lab.

It didn't take long for the pathologist to reach a conclusion. On a simple hematoxylin and eosin stain, he saw a field of large clear cells which he quickly identified as clear cell carcinoma. The source—Helen's kidney. I reassured her daughters that I had removed every bit of tumor that I could see, but because this was metastatic cancer, she would need to have radiation therapy, possibly chemotherapy, and we would have to find the cancer in her kidney and remove it.

Helen met these challenges with the same calm resolve that she had demonstrated since our first meeting. "You're a remarkable woman, Helen," I said after I had explained her situation and she had nodded slowly and acceptingly. "I have a strong faith in God, a belief in the decisions of my doctors, and I am convinced that I have more time on this earth."

Abe and I reviewed the CAT scans with the radiologist. Sure enough, on second look, there was a tiny area of the upper pole of her left kidney that took up just a little too much contrast dye to be normal. Two days later, she had the upper half of her left kidney removed, and, in another three days, she was home. Because all of the kidney tissue around the tumor was normal, the team elected to reserve other therapies but to treat the bed of the brain tumor with a course of radiation. She made an excellent recovery from this as well.

Oh yes, the homunculus. From early history, men have often proposed the existence of tiny humans sometimes controlling their larger human hosts. Whether it's Ireland's "little people" or the monsters of Arnold Schwarzenegger's dystopian movie, *Total Recall*, for eons, we have fantasized about the existence of a race of tiny humanoids capable of controlling their related species—us. Well, there is an anatomical analogy to this concept. Early anatomists suggested that the movement and sensation of humans might be "represented" on the human cortex. It awaited neurosurgeon Wilder Penfield, whom we have mentioned before, to verify and map this phenomenon.

In the 1940s and 1950s, Penfield used conscious sedation to operate on his patients. They were deeply sedated but not under general anesthesia. He could do this because the brain itself has no sensation. After the scalp, skull, and dura were opened under local anesthesia and sedation, Dr. Penfield used a probe with a small electric current to touch areas of the cortex and map the functions that occurred. He confirmed that a homunculus, now usually called Penfield's homunculus, was mapped on the surface of the brain. Specifically, he probed the pre-central gyrus of the frontal lobe, as it wrapped around from the middle of the brain down to the top of the temporal lobe, roughly at ear level. He confirmed on patient after patient the same pattern (between 1928 and 1936 he gathered the data from 126 patients he had operated on under local anesthesia). If he touched the highest part of the brain with his electrical probe, the opposite leg would move; next, moving down, he could elicit movements of the trunk, arm, hand, eyes, nose and, finally, the mouth. He also discovered that the areas responsible for the leg and arm were small, whereas the thumb, fingers and mouth took up much larger areas of the brain. This made for a weird-looking homunculus, with small arms and legs and giant hands and mouth. Of course, it all makes sense when one considers the complexity of the movements of the fingers and of speech.

Penfield also correlated this with the activity of seizures, which were often the manifestation of a brain lesion. So, for example, if observation showed that a seizure began with rhythmic twitching of the right thumb, he would often discover a tumor over the lower mid-portion of the middle of the left frontal lobe. Once again, something that first-year medical students take for granted required the brilliance of brain scientists to prove.

Helen Aspiritis sailed through her convalescence and returned home, increasing her activities until she was back to her energetic, bubbly self. Surrounded by her daughters and grandchildren, she regained her optimism and confidence. Under the scrupulous care of Abe Mittelman, she showed no signs of the cancer that had attacked her.

For a year . . . There's a rather depressing axiom in medicine: a cancer can't be considered cured unless there are no symptoms or signs for at least five years. Helen was feeling very well, but her oncologist was careful to follow up on a regular basis. Thirteen months after her initial diagnosis, a blood test for her cancer turned up slightly positive. On repeat, it again was slightly positive. She underwent an urgent abdominal CAT scan, which showed a small area of enhancement, just outside the border of her previous partial kidney removal. Her chest and bone scans were normal, but the brain MRI showed a 1 cm tumor in the left frontal lobe, well in front of the tumor we had previously removed. A few days later, her left kidney was removed. If the kidney had harbored tumor cells where it recurred, then it could hide anywhere in the kidney.

This left the brain tumor for us to deal with. Fortunately, an amazing new arrow had been added to our quiver in 2005. Stereotactic radiosurgery. In 1949, another neurosurgical pioneer, Lars Leksell, who would lead the Karolinska Institute in Stockholm, developed his stereotactic frame. By using several x-ray-determined coordinates, he could introduce a probe into a specific area anywhere in the brain. He applied this principle to another idea. If he could direct slender beams of radiation, each harmless to the brain, through multiple holes in a "sieve" that covered the brain and blocked other beams, they would focus at a target point or points with substantial destructive force. This could be an option for treatment of deep-seated brain tumors that would be very dangerous to approach surgically. The mathematics of this concept was so challenging that the procedure remained largely experimental for years. In 1968, with the incredible ability of computers to cut through data, Leksell introduced the Gamma Knife. It gradually gained enough data to be more widely accepted and used. Ultimately, it has come to be used not only for tumors but vascular malformations and even disorders of individual nerves, such as trigeminal neuralgia. Another type of radiosurgery allows a single rotating radiation source to apply small single beams, which again gather together to deliver a lethal blow to the target. Bill Friedman would help perfect the application of this technology to the brain.

Bill Friedman was a *wunderkind*. Finishing Oberlin College, he completed his doctorate at Ohio State University School of Medicine by the time he was twenty-one (most of us are at this level at age twenty-five). Joining the University of Florida neurosurgical team as an intern a couple of years after Bruce Woodham and I, Bill became a fast friend. The three of us worked hard and played hard together. But Bill was a neurosurgery resident on steroids: he learned the answers to Dr. Rhoton's questions quickly; he wrote an NIH research grant and did important work on spinal cord regeneration; he did all of his clinical work, and still found time to read a biography or a novel once a week. Ultimately, Bill would be Dr. Rhoton's choice to succeed him as chairman of the department. Under his guidance, the McKnight Brain Institute at the University of Florida would become internationally renowned. He was also an early innovator of the technology that emerged with the potential to treat brain lesions without an incision, and to re-introduce the possibility of addressing the Holy Grail of behavioral and functional neurosurgery—stereotactic radiosurgery.

My introduction to radiosurgery was at the University of Pittsburgh, under the tutelage of two outstanding neurosurgeons— Dade Lunsford and Doug Kondziolka. I became fascinated with its potential to treat tumors, vascular malformations, even functional and psychiatric problems by 'operating' on the brain without surgical invasion. This was the marriage of neuroanatomy and psychology that I had dreamed of as a medical student.

As mentioned earlier, after years of practice, initially completely in community and later totally in academic neurosurgery, several of my colleagues and I started a practice that combined academic and private practice neurosurgery. Our practice included the

Westchester Medical Center, our academic focus. WMC is a nationally prominent trauma center as well as the headquarters of New York Medical College. Collectively, we were also on the faculties of New York Med, Weill Cornell University, and Yale University medical schools. Now a large multispecialty practice, it is run by John Abrahams, who had been a medical student under my tutelage at New York Med. John succeeded my old friend, colleague, and founding partner of our group, Jack Stern. With master surgeon Kent Duffy, spinal orthopedist Seth Neubardt, and Ed Kornel, we would dominate regional neurosurgery. In addition to the medical centers, we operated at several community hospitals.

My personal favorite was Northern Westchester Hospital. It was located near my home and was very well run. It had a strong charitable foundation in the regional communities. Ultimately, I would serve as chief of neurosurgery there for ten years and as a hospital trustee for six years. One of my partners, Ed Kornel, a very skilled surgeon and a perennial optimist, and I worked hard to develop the hospital as a neurosurgical center. Ed started a spine and neuroscience center there, and I convinced the very informed board of trustees to acquire the latest model of the Gamma Knife to enable brain radiosurgery in our region.

This was, at the time, the gold standard for accuracy in the field. To complete our program, I invited Dr. Alain DeLotbiniere, the director of radiosurgery at Yale University and a seventeen year veteran of Yale's neurosurgery faculty, to join our practice. His surgical expertise and experience with the Gamma Knife added depth to our armamentarium.

So, after careful planning, Ms. Aspiritis' head was placed in a rigid frame under local anesthesia and sedation. Then she was transferred to a moving table where the head frame was secured. The table was moved into the opening of the device, physically much like a CAT scan, and the head frame was locked into the "sieve" with some of its openings open and some blocked to achieve the perfect distribution and shape of radiation to match the exact size and shape of the tumor. The chamber holding the machine was closed and secured. We (the radiation oncologist, the radiation physicist and myself) then sat at the control panel and fed the data about the tumor into the computer, which then moved the table into multiple positions where brief bursts of gamma radiation were blasted at the entire tumor and its outline. She went home the same day, and an MRI done four weeks later showed a hollow "ghost" where the tumor had been. She had no neurological deficits. A year later, she returned with a similar tumor on the right side of her brain and underwent another Gamma Knife treatment. Two brain tumors had been successfully treated without an incision. Five years later, Helen returned with a recurrence of the renal tumor, this time a "mirror-image" lesion in her right kidney. She had metastases to her lungs and liver, but not to her brain. This recurrence took her life. But a new and remarkable space-age technology had given her six more years of good health.

CHAPTER TWENTY-FOUR

How Much is Too Much?

Jonathan Miller was born in the thirtieth week of his gestation. He weighed three- and one-half pounds, and he had a low Apgar score (a test devised by Dr. Virginia Apgar, an anesthesiologist at New York Presbyterian Hospital in 1952). The score gives a weight of 0-2 to five behaviors—Appearance, Pulse, Grimace, Activity, and Respiration. A "perfect" baby would score 10. Jonathan had an Apgar 4. His breathing was slow and intermittent, and the pulse oximeter on his tiny finger showed that he was not getting enough oxygen. The anesthesiologist intubated the baby and placed him on a ventilator.

But Jonathan was faced with an even larger challenge. He had been born with hydrocephalus, with his head circumference nearly twice that of a normal child. He also had spina bifida. The coverings and layers over his spinal cord, near the bottom of his back, had failed to develop and close properly. A large plaque of incompletely formed tissue at the bottom of his spinal cord was visible on the surface of his back, leaking spinal fluid. It was clear from simple observation and mild stimulation that the baby was paralyzed below the waist. He would likely require a wheelchair and a urinary catheter for his entire life. A gauze moistened with saline was placed over this defect, and little Jonathan was taken to the Neonatal Intensive Care Unit.

Samuel Kasoff had been one of my neurosurgical partners for years. Educated at New York's elite public high school—Stuyvesant, and the City College of New York, he completed medical school at the University of Pittsburgh, and his residency at Montefiore in New York. He was the founding chairman of the Department of Neurosurgery and its Neurosurgery Residency Program. I served as vice-chairman and director of cerebrovascular surgery. Sam was an excellent surgeon who did many types of procedures, but he had trained as a pediatric neurosurgeon. He was a tough street guy, New York born and raised, but had a very soft spot for his little patients and their parents. I also had a soft spot for ill and injured children—too soft.

I had always included pediatric neurosurgery in my surgical repertoire and had received excellent instruction at the University of Florida under the tutelage of John Vries and J. Parker Mickle. I had operated on injured children, as I've outlined above. I had performed many shunts to divert blocked brain spinal fluid in hydrocephalic children to their abdomen, chest, bladder, heart and even, on one or two occasions, gallbladder.

However, one Saturday evening about five years before Jonathan Miller was born, I had been called to see a toddler with a skull fracture. The child was in distress, in and out of consciousness, with multiple injuries. As I assessed him and directed the residents to perform testing, his face suddenly transformed, and I was looking at the face of my own son Dan. I turned and walked out of the room, took a few deep breaths, and walked back in. The child's face was no longer that of my son. But I quickly realized that this particular work was taking a real toll on me and could interfere with my ability to take objective, calm care of children.

Next morning, Sam and I talked about this over coffee. I explained my experience to him and told him that I no longer felt that I could take care of kids, except to assist him at surgery or to do surgery that my colleagues were not comfortable with or that I had special expertise in (e.g., aneurysms). Sam was understanding and said that he would take my share of these cases.

Later in the morning of Jonathan's birth, Sam placed a ventriculostomy. This was a small plastic tube into the lateral ventricle of the brain. Since his skull was thin, the ventricle massive, and the anterior fontanelle ("soft spot") still soft, all that was necessary was to make a small nick at the right side of the fontanelle, pass a thin soft plastic tube into the ventricle, make a small tunnel under the skin to bring the tube to the surface without contamination, and secure it to a drainage bag attached to a manometer so that the brain pressure could be measured. Why did this procedure have to be done? Well, in addition to the blockage of the circuit of spinal fluid flow caused by the spina bifida, we would also find out on a CAT scan that Jonathan had aqueductal stenosis.

Spinal fluid is created in the two lateral ventricles and the third ventricle, in the depths of the cerebral hemispheres. They then drain through a very narrow tunnel in the brainstem, the cerebral aqueduct, into the fourth ventricle in front of the cerebellum, then out over the surface of brainstem, down over the spinal cord, then back up over the surface of the brain to large tufts of tissue, the

Pacchionian granulations. The spinal fluid is finally absorbed and routed into the large veins within the dura mater.

As mentioned earlier in this volume, the cerebral aqueduct is by far the narrowest point in the system of spinal fluid circulation, and, therefore, it tends to be the site where abnormalities can make it narrow or even closed. The spinal fluid is backed up, and the lateral and third ventricles gradually enlarge and put pressure on the brain enclosing them. More recently, procedures have been developed that allow the opening of a membrane at the base of the brain to restore the spinal fluid circulation directly, even in utero. But the gold standard of treatment for years has been the ventriculoperitoneal (VP) shunt, which bypasses the blockage by running a tube from the lateral ventricle out through the brain and skull, under the skin of the scalp, neck, and chest, and to the abdomen, where the fluid is emptied into the abdominal cavity and absorbed by the omentum, a kind of fatty apron that keeps the intestinal area clear of debris and inflammation.

Sam placed the ventricular catheter and the fluid emerged, slightly cloudy and under pressure. A quick laboratory analysis told us that the fluid was infected; not surprising since the fluid was leaking through the skin of his back. Intravenous and intraventricular (through the tube) antibiotics were begun. But, of course, placing the other end of the tube into the abdomen, with its active infection, had to be deferred.

That afternoon, Sam and I closed the meningomyelocele, the open spine, with the help of our pediatric plastic surgeon. Jane Petro undermined the normal skin around the plaque of abnormal tissue while we removed the neural placode, the functionless clump of spinal cord that sat on the surface. We then developed the remnants of dura around the placode and closed it using a patch of soft graft. Finally, we helped Jane develop a layer of muscle and skin to close over the abnormal area. Over the next few days, we watched closely to make sure that the wound didn't become infected or develop breakdown because the skin didn't have enough blood supply. It healed well.

But the hydrocephalus was another story. A week passed, and there was still evidence of infection in the spinal fluid. The antibiotic treatment continued, but we had to replace the ventriculostomy to make sure that the infection wouldn't find a home in the plastic tubing. Another week, another tube. The third week, the original bacterium had disappeared, but a new, more virulent infection had taken over. A new, stronger antibiotic was used. Little Jonathan had not developed a strong enough immune system to help us fight the infection.

Finally, after six weeks, the fluid was clear, the protein level normal. There were no inflammatory cells in the fluid, and no bacteria grew out of the sample. An entirely new shunt system was placed, with the ventricular tube integrated with a valve to give us access (by a needle through the skin) to a sample of fluid and to control the flow (if not enough fluid drained, the symptoms of brain pressure would continue; if too much drained, the surrounding brain could collapse, leaving an empty space between the brain and the skull that could be filled with blood—a dangerous subdural hematoma). The end of the valve was attached to the distal catheter, which was drawn through a tunnel under the skin and placed in the abdomen. We were careful to place the tube outside of the intestines but within the peritoneal cavity, which would allow it to be enfolded by the omentum. Finally, the valve could be accessed by a needle through the skin to measure the spinal fluid pressure in the event that a malfunction of the shunt was suspected.

For two weeks, little Jonathan improved, gaining weight (he was back up to almost four pounds after losing weight in the first week) and becoming more active. His CAT scan showed a reduction in the size of the ventricles. Then, during the third week, his white blood cell count started to rise. A fever followed. We tapped the shunt—bacteria, white cells, and elevated protein. We took out the abdominal end of the shunt so it would act as a ventriculostomy and gave him another course of IV antibiotics. He didn't improve, and the spinal fluid gained the consistency of motor oil. We had to take the entire shunt out and place a fresh ventriculostomy, this time on the left side, to improve the chance of sterilization of the fluid. Another week, another tube. Each day, Jonathan's mother sat by the side of his incubator watching his ventilator and tending to his feeding tube. Mrs. Miller was in her early forties, and Jonathan was her first child. She arrived early each morning and left after dark. Her husband was there every day for the first month, then less and less.

Sam Kasoff became the advocate for Jonathan and for Judy Miller. He was their medical and emotional pillar. While we began to lose hope, as Jonathan failed every treatment and started to lose weight again, Sam never wavered. Finally, the fluid became clean again, and another VP shunt was placed. This one lasted for three weeks until it too became infected. Back to square one.

After multiple surgeries on this little being, whom I suspected would always have severe cognitive, as well as physical, problems, I needed to have a candid conversation with my partner. "Sam, I'm concerned that you may have lost perspective on the Miller case.

He doesn't seem to be making progress. He's had to endure so much. His mom must be at the end of her tether. When is enough too much?"

"I know just what you mean, Tom. It kills me to see that little guy there, with all he's gone through, all he has to still go through. I'm not sure how he will finish. I've spoken to his mother for hours. She doesn't know what the right answer is, nor do I. But this is her baby; she loves him more than she loves herself. And while there is any chance of meaningful survival, I'm going to be there for them, as a surgeon and as an advocate."

"Then count me in. I'm on the Miller team." I knew that Sam, who was often gruff and combative, had a big soul. But I gained real admiration for him after this one.

Gradually, almost imperceptibly, Jonathan improved and gained weight. His ventricles came down to normal size, and his cortical mantle—the thickness of the brain outside the ventricles—enlarged. Another shunt was placed.

The infection finally resolved as Jonathan's immune system matured and his strength increased. But further revisions would be required. On two occasions, the spinal fluid protein and debris would clog the ventricular catheter, and it alone would have to be replaced. Once, the same thing happened to the peritoneal catheter, and it was replaced. Later revisions would also be required to lengthen the tubing as he grew.

Over the next several years, Jonathan Miller would have over twenty surgeries, including those to relax the spasticity in his legs, to lengthen his tendons, and to further revise his shunt. Like many families of children with such enormous challenges, his parents' marriage collapsed. His mother soldiered on. After nearly a year in the hospital, the little boy was discharged to a special children's rehabilitation hospital, where he would spend two more years. He would then live at home with his mother but would attend special schools and ongoing outpatient physical therapy. I would see Jonathan and his mother from time to time at Sam's outpatient pediatric neurosurgery clinic.

As time passed, a remarkable thing happened. Jonathan was not mentally challenged. In fact, he was very bright. He also developed a sweetness and kindness that was disarming. He never failed to ask after the doctors and nurses who had taken care of him for so long. How was I? And my family? How old were my children now, and what were they doing? You couldn't help but be uplifted and happy as you had a conversation with this smiling, optimistic boy.

Ten years or so later, I was walking through the aisles of my local drug store when I saw a handsome young man in a wheelchair stocking shelves. He looked up and smiled. I recognized the smile.

"Jonathan?" I was tentative and almost couldn't believe my eyes.

"Dr. Lansen! Wow, this is great. How are you?" He pumped my hand vigorously and laughed out loud. The strength in his hands and muscular arms had compensated for the paralysis of his legs.

"Jonathan, how are you? And how's your mom? You're working here?" He laughed again and his eyes sparkled. "She's fine. Yes, I'm well and working here . . . part time." This gave me pause. He must still be having a tough uphill fight. But then, nothing had ever been easy for this guy. "It helps make up what my scholarship doesn't cover. See, I graduated from Fordham University two years ago, and I'm finishing my Masters in medical social work. I've got a job lined up at the children's hospital to work with kids who have challenges. It's very exciting." I had to glance away for a couple of seconds, until my teary eyes cleared.

"That's just wonderful, Jonathan. Hope I see you at the hospital, and regards to your mother."

"Terrific to see you, Dr. Lansen. Be well."

Sam Kasoff died a few years later. A non-smoker, he died of a very aggressive lung cancer. Seems like life is never quite fair. But once in a while you bump into a Jonathan Miller, and all of the effort seems worthwhile.

CONCLUSION

Twenty cases, out of the thousands of surgeries that I was involved in for almost four decades. This slice of the career of one neurosurgeon isn't necessarily scientifically important. There weren't any real breakthroughs that would change medicine, just a series of memories: of patients and families whom I came to know and care about; of doctor and nurse colleagues who shine like bright stars in the fabric of my life; of a career based on science and art that gave me a satisfaction that I'm not sure I could have gained doing anything else.

I've constructed this memoir from experiences that happened several to many years ago, although they seem quite fresh in my mind. But a glance at the calendar tells me that a lot of time has passed. Several years ago, I stopped performing surgery. My daughter, the little girl who loved Disney World so much, is a physician executive in Manhattan. And her brothers, Tom and Dan, are grown and successful, a lawyer and a corporate CEO. Five grandchildren add to our many blessings.

I last operated in 2012. My partner, Jack Stern, sat down in my office after I announced my retirement and told me that I wouldn't be able to quit neurosurgery. I would "be back in six months." Jack is still going strong, but I have never looked back. My wonderful wife, Tara, and I have traveled the world, made new friends, and watched the children mature and the grandchildren grow. I still see my old buddy from medical school, Al Krug. He and his wife Kathy, like my wife and I, spend much of our time in Naples, Florida. I'm also fortunate to be able to have frequent reunions with my dear friend Bruce Woodham, a busy and successful neurosurgeon in Dothan, Alabama. Still tireless, and with the best sense of humor in the world, Bruce plays full court basketball four days a week. We have traveled together, visited each other's homes, and laugh regularly on the phone.

And, speaking of reunions. We had an extraordinary one a couple of years ago. I had known for some time that my mentor, Albert Rhoton, was very ill. He had advanced metastatic prostate cancer. Two of my dear friends from residency, Bill Friedman and Dick Lister, were now chairman and vice-chairman of the Department of Neurosurgery at the University of Florida, now one of the world's most prestigious neuroscience centers. Dick had contacted us regarding a party the faculty were going to hold at Bill's home in Gainesville for Dr. Rhoton's eightieth birthday. Dick made the point that it made a lot more sense for us to be with him and celebrate his life rather than attend a memorial service for him in a few months.

The afternoon was moist and hot, like so many afternoons I remembered from the Gainesville of my youth. Spanish moss and flowers were everywhere. Bill had set up two large tents with tables, beer, wine, and great Southern food. About forty neurosurgeons from all over the country also thought Dick's idea was a good one. Most attended with their spouses. It made us all so happy to see each other and reminisce after so many years had passed. And in the center of it all, Albert Loren Rhoton, Jr.

Slightly gaunt and perhaps a bit frail, but still tall and straight, with a smile that beamed so wide it outshone the sunny Florida day. The boss spent time with each of us, and everyone had a chance to stand up, take the microphone, and express our experiences and our gratitude to him. Then it was his turn. As usual, his speech was brief, self-deprecating (he was so proud of the "team," as if he hadn't created it from whole cloth), and profound. I will never forget those last words: "We are a very fortunate group. We have been given the sacred privilege of exploring the human brain—the crown jewel of creation, and our greatest unexplored scientific frontier." A few weeks later, he was gone. But rarely a day goes by without my referencing one lesson or another that he taught me—not just about neurosurgery, but about life.